Owain Glyndŵr

About the Author

Terry Breverton is the author of fifteen books of Welsh interest, five of which have been awarded 'Welsh Book of the Month' by the Welsh Books Council (more than any other author). He lives in Cowbridge in the Vale of Glamorgan.

Praise for Terry Breverton:

100 Great Welshmen
Welsh Book Council Book of the Month June 2001
'A celebration of the remarkable achievements of his countrymen' *The Guardian*

A-Z of Wales & the Welsh
'A comprehensive overview of Wales & its people' *The Western Mail*
'A massive treasure chest of facts & figures' *Cambria*

The Welsh Almanac
Welsh Book Council Book of the Month August 2002
'A must for anyone with a drop of Welsh blood in them' *The Western Mail*

100 Great Welsh Women
'A fascinating read' *The Daily Mail*
'Breverton's breadth, generosity and sheer enthusiasm about Wales are compelling' *The Sunday Express*

Owain Glyndŵr

THE STORY OF THE
LAST PRINCE OF WALES

TERRY BREVERTON

AMBERLEY

Front cover: *Owain Glyndŵr*, Corwen, Denbighshire cast bronze sculpture
by Colin Spofforth.
Back cover: *Owain Glyndŵr*, watercolour by A.C. Michael. Author's Collection.

First published 2009

Amberley Publishing
Cirencester Road, Chalford,
Stroud, Gloucestershire, GL6 8PE

www.amberley-books.com

British Library Cataloguing in Publication Data.
A catalogue record for this book is available from the British Library.

ISBN 978 1 84868 328 0

Typesetting and Origination by Diagraf (www.diagraf.net)
Printed in Great Britain

CONTENTS

Map of Wales and Marches, showing the historic thirteen counties of Wales dating from the Laws in Wales Act of 1535, the counties based upon far older divisions. Courtesy of Dr Ed Conley.

Preface

This book chronicles the development of the war between the Welsh nation and the Norman-English invaders, a war that was crucial in reviving Welsh independence. Even today, English historians and critics declaim that Wales was 'never a nation', which betrays not just intellectual ignorance but the arrogance of indifference. Owain Glyndŵr's War of Independence has variously been called a rebellion, insurrection, revolt or uprising. It was none of these, being a full-scale war which united the whole nation for the first time since its conquest in 1283. Wales had been a collection of princedoms since recorded history began, and had survived for more than 200 years after the Normans had conquered England. Under Owain Glyndŵr, unpaid Welsh volunteers fought off no less six large-scale royal invasions of paid soldiers and foreign mercenaries. However, even today the nationalism aroused by the word Glyndŵr strikes fear into the heart of every mainstream politician, whether Plaid Cymru, Conservative, Liberal-Democrat or Labour. Equally the Welsh media, especially BBC Wales, is wary of being associated with the word 'nationalism'. Fidel Castro, a successful and noted revolutionary of our era, has described Glyndŵr as one of the greatest freedom fighters of all time. Owain has been called 'a genius at guerrilla warfare' (Philip Warner, *British Battlefields*). The romance and fascination of Glyndŵr is that from 1400 for over a decade, he led a war of independence for an impoverished country with few resources against the most powerful military force in Europe. Most Welsh uprisings since 1282 had been brief and suppressed with violence, land grabs and torture. This war was different – it lasted fifteen years from 1400. Only years later, in 1421, did his heir Maredudd ab Owain, accept a pardon from the English crown. In this unjust war, not sought by Glyndŵr, many family members and friends were killed or captured, but he was never taken nor betrayed.

Glyndŵr's 600-year celebrations and commemorations from 2000 to 2009 were boycotted by all senior Welsh politicians and the Welsh media. However, modern Welsh nationalism has nearly always been that of the pacifist variety. It seems that these people do not realise cultural nationalism is an awareness of, and pride in, one's heritage, not a desire to invade Poland or kick off another world war in the Balkans. These same politicians are covering Wales with wind turbines and pylons, some planned for the site of the Battle of

Hyddgen – the battle that, more than any other, meant that the war became serious and solidified Welsh nationhood.

The Sunday Times ran a poll of 100 world leaders, artists and scientists, published on 28 November 1999, asking for the names of the most significant figures in the last 1000 years. Remarkably, in seventh place was Owain Glyndŵr. (The list started with Gutenberg, Shakespeare, Caxton, da Vinci, Elizabeth I and Faraday in the first six places. Newton, Lincoln and Galileo followed Glyndŵr in the Top 10). Thus even today Owain is regarded above Churchill, Mandela, Darwin, Bill Gates and Einstein. Among the voters were President Clinton and Boris Yeltsin. Elizabeth I was in fourth place. We can understand that the flowering of the Elizabethan era should be recognized through its queen of Welsh descent, but for Owain Glyndŵr to feature in this poll of *Makers of the Millennium* is unexpected. His name barely figures as a footnote in British history books or syllabi. Even those aware of his name may know little of his life, his achievements and what he represented to his countrymen in the fifteenth century. However, on a global scale, Glyndŵr is both hugely admired and respected. He has been described variously as 'this wonderful man, an attractive unique figure in a period of debased and selfish politics' (G.M. Trevelyan); 'a man of genius and courage' (H. Martin) and 'the symbol for the vigorous resistance of the Welsh spirit to tyranny' (J.E. Lloyd).

Owain was the bards' 'mab darogan', the son of prophecy, who would reclaim Welsh independence lost in 1283 with the murder of Llywelyn ap Gruffydd and his brother Dafydd. An earlier 'mab darogan' and sole descendant of Llywelyn II, Owain Llawgoch was assassinated in France in 1378, on the orders of the English crown. Twenty-two years later, some of his surviving battle-hardened captains returned to Wales to support Glyndŵr in his fight to free a suppressed nation. Owain received spontaneous and passionate loyalty from every corner of Wales. Not for him the brutal public death of Braveheart, William Wallace (a Scot of Welsh descent), nor a known grave to desecrate. Glyndŵr, the essence of Welshness, is one of the greatest heroes in two millennia of British history: a cultured and learned linguist, a lawyer and not least a warrior. He had fought valiantly for the Crown before his betrayal by Earl Grey and the King of England. Glyndŵr had no secret agenda; he wanted only justice for Wales and to defend it against invaders. Because of Glyndŵr, more than anyone, our sense of nationhood survived. It lives, as does Glyndŵr. Owen Rhoscomyl, in *Flamebearers of Welsh History* (1905) summarised the feelings of all true Welshmen:

> It is not known where he died, though it is inferred that he died in 1416. In Gwent they say that he did not die. They say that he and his men sit sleeping in Ogov y Dinas, buckled in their armour, their spears leaning against their shoulders, their swords across their knees. They are waiting till the day comes for them to sally forth and fight for the land again.
>
> But other and learned men have vexed themselves looking for his real grave. They say they cannot be sure where it is. But that is because their eyes have wandered from the right way – looking to Kentchurch or to Monnington, in the green shire of Hereford, where his loving daughters lived.
>
> They are all wrong. His grave is known – well known. It is beside no church, neither under the shadow of any ancient yew. It is in a spot safer and more sacred still. Rain does not fall on it, hail

nor sleet chill no sere sod above it. It is forever green with the green of eternal spring. Sunny the light on it: close and warm and dear it lies, sheltered from all storm, from all cold or grey oblivion. Time shall not touch it; decay shall not dishonour it; for that grave is in the heart of every true Cymro. There, for ever, from generation unto generation, grey Owen's heart lies dreaming on, dreaming on, safe for ever and for ever.

Note: In the text I have standardised the spellings of Tudor to Tudur, Gruffudd to Gruffydd, Maredydd and Meredudd to Maredudd, Llewelyn to Llywelyn etc. For some places the English place-name is in brackets following the Welsh original, but sometimes the English place-name is left alone, in the interests of sequence. In the interests of convenience, place-names have been standardised to suit the general reader. For instance, the Welsh for St Asaph is Llanelwy, which is little-known, so it has been standardised in the text as St Asaf. Equally, Abergavenni was originally Y Fenni, and is standardised for understanding as Abergafenni. Some towns have been left in their Anglicised state as their Welsh names are less used, e.g. Presteigne instead of Llanandras, Hay-on-Wye (Y Gelli Gandryll), Usk (Brynbuga), Welshpool (Y Trallwng) and Cardiff (Caerdydd).

CHAPTER 1

Introduction:
The Battle for Wales 1066-1378

THE NATION OF WALES

With the invasions of the Germanic Angles, Saxons and Jutes from the fifth century onwards, the British were pushed back westwards over the centuries, stabilising in the western regions of Strathclyde in south-west Scotland, Cumbria in north-west England, Wales and the West Country of England. By the seventh century, the British in Wales had been cut off from their cymbrogi (fellow-countrymen) in the rest of western Britain. Consisting of several princedoms and kingdoms, the remaining Britons in Wales (Cymru) were united by their Christian faith, and constantly fought off attacks from the barbarian Saxons, Picts, Vikings and Irish. Some of the British had escaped the constant aggression from the east by moving to Brittany with their language, which is why Breton is similar to Welsh. It must be noted that the fifth to eighth centuries in Christian Wales were known as the Age of the Saints, while the rest of pagan Europe endured the Dark Ages. Several great leaders emerged, and at the time of the Battle of Hastings, Wales had an uneasy truce with King Harold's realm of Saxon England. Gruffydd ap Llywelyn, who had ruled Wales since 1055 and was styled King of the Britons, was killed after fighting Harold Godwinsson in 1063. Harold married Gruffydd's widow, and did not attempt to take over the Welsh, then still known as the British. The other British remnants in the west of Britain had been absorbed into England and Scotland.

THE NORMAN INVASION

Wales was to some extent left alone as events unfolded elsewhere. Robert, Duke of Normandy, was known as Robert the Devil, as it was thought he had killed his elder brother Richard to gain the dukedom. Robert made his illegitimate son William his heir, and he was known as William the Bastard throughout his lifetime. On the death of Edward the Confessor, the witan (Saxon council of elders) voted for Harold Godwinsson to become King of England. However, King Harold and his troops fought the Battle of Stamford Bridge in Yorkshire, against his brother Tostig and King Harald of Norway in 1066. A fortnight later, his exhausted and depleted army unluckily lost at the Battle of Hastings in 1066. William the Bastard, whom later historians would rename William the Conqueror, began the Norman Invasion of England. Thus began an unbroken line of French-speaking French kings until the succession was broken with Henry Bolingbroke, Henry IV in 1399. He was the first English King since the Saxons to address his parliament in the English language. (These Norman French-speaking kings constantly attacked Wales, burning its monasteries and building castles to consolidate land-grabs.) Henry IV usurped the Plantagenet Richard II, the last King whose claim to the throne was hereditary and unchallenged. This change was accompanied by the War of Independence of Owain Glyndŵr, 1400-1415.

William the Bastard had quickly subdued England, but never attempted to invade Wales. Instead Marcher Lordships were established to guard his western border. These lords of the marche were given territories equating to the border counties of Gloucester, Worcester, Hereford, Shropshire and Cheshire today. They were told that they could expand their territories by attacking Wales, and effectively acted as a buffer between England and Wales. The fluctuating border is shown in the Welsh place-names that still exist in these English counties, and many of their inhabitants were Welsh-speaking for centuries after the Norman Conquest of England. The Norman-French battle for Wales raged for centuries, with scores of invasions beaten off, and is seen in today's landscape, where Wales has by far the greatest density of castles of any nation in the world. The most powerful Marcher Lords eventually pushed into Radnor and part of Powys Fadog (the Mortimers of Wigmore); Usk and Newport (de Breos and Fitzmartin); Glamorgan (de Clare) and Brecon (de Bohun).

Minor Welsh princes held onto Radnor, Flint and Denbigh, while the great House of Gwynedd in North Wales and Anglesey ruled from Aberffraw and Garth Celyn. The House of Powys in Central Wales was always bearing the brunt of warfare, as its soft rolling landscape was easily invaded along the valley of the Severn. The House of Deheubarth generally held firm in the south-west and west Wales, ruling from Dinefwr and Cardigan. Wales' south-eastern princedoms of Gwent and Glamorgan were subjected to Norman sovereignty fairly quickly, as they were less easily defended and more prosperous than most of the rest of Wales. The far south-west of Pembroke in general was held in the south by the English and Flemish settlers, but north Pembroke and Carmarthen remained firmly within the lands of the princes of Deheubarth. In times of continuous warfare, the Normans were sometimes pushed back past Offa's Dyke, which became the traditional border. Wales still retained its nationhood through 200 years of war with the Norman and French kings of England.

CAER DREWYN 1165

The hill fort of Caer Drewyn, overlooking Corwen, marked two seminal and defining moments in Welsh history. The latter was the raising of Owain Glyndŵr's standard in 1400, but over 200 years earlier a united Welsh army routed Henry II. Henry ruled from 1154-1189, and intended to finally complete the Norman Conquest by taking Wales. At the battle of Crug Mawr, Owain Gwynedd had thrown the Norman lords out of Ceredigion, to add to his princedom of Gwynedd. Henry commandeered forces from Gascony, Anjou, Normandy, Flanders, England and Scotland, and a fleet was summoned from Dublin, proposing to destroy the whole of the Britons (note that the Welsh were known as the Britons until the time of Elizabeth I). A great army of 30,000 men was assembled at Oswestry and Weston Rhyn in Shropshire, and began to march across Wales, heading to Corwen. Owain Gwynedd was the son of the great Gruffydd ap Cynan, and, with his brother Cadwaladr, ambushed the English army. Henry had made the serious tactical blunder of trying to march from Oswestry up the Ceiriog Valley and across the Berwyn range, rather than follow the traditional coastal routes.

The Battle of Crogen was at Bron-y-Garth in the Upper Ceiriog Valley, and Henry narrowly escaped with his life. Owain Gwynedd's outnumbered force fought with such valour that for some years after the word Crogen was used as a synonym for a warrior of desperate courage. The place where this clash occurred is called Adwy'r Beddau, 'the Pass of the Graves'. The fight gave time for the forces of The Lord Rhys, Owain Cyfeiliog, and the other lords to gather at Caer Drewyn, overlooking Corwen. (The Chronicle of Ystrad Fflur places the battle after Caer Drewyn, not before it, however). Henry marched on and drew up his forces across the valley from Caer Drewyn, amazed at the size of the Welsh army. With Owain ap Gruffydd (Owain Cyfeiliog) of Powys, Owain Gwynedd had united with The Lord Rhys of Deheubarth in their defiance, assembling forces including those of Cadwallon ap Madog and his brother Einion Clud. Gruffydd ap Rhys of Deheubarth, the husband of the murdered Gwenllian, was also with his followers in the Welsh army. Princess Gwenllian was the sister of Owain Gwynedd, beheaded by the Normans at Cydweli, before her husband and Owain avenged her at Crug Mawr. With the forces of the three ancient kingdoms of Wales - Gwynedd, Deheubarth and Powys - this may have been the largest Welsh army ever assembled.

There was a standoff, with both sides occupying high ground and unwilling to move first and lose the advantage. Henry retreated back across the Berwyn Mountains to England, being constantly attacked, thus ending the invasion.

> And after remaining there a few days, he was overtaken by a dreadful tempest of the sky, and extraordinary torrents of rain. And when provisions failed him, he removed his tents and his army to the open plains of England; and full of extreme rage, he ordered the hostages, who had previously been long imprisoned by him, to be blinded; to wit the two sons of Owain Gwynedd ... and the sons of the Lord Rhys.

This defeat of Henry enabled the Welsh princes to concentrate their efforts on building a sustained peace, though with some of the usual disputes amongst themselves. This also allowed the Welsh to take the initiative once more, making some headway on the Welsh borders. The Chronicle of Ystrad Fflur records 1165 thus:

> In this year Henry the king came to Oswestry, thinking to annihilate all Welshmen. And against him came Owain and Cadwaladr, the sons of Gruffydd ap Cynan, and all the host of Gwynedd

with them, and Rhys ap Gruffydd and with him all the host of Deheubarth, and Owain Cyfeiliog and the sons of Madog ap Maredudd and the host of all Powys with them, and the two sons of Madog ab Idnerth and their host. And both sides stayed in their tents until the king moved his host into Dyffryn Ceiriog and there he was defeated at Crogen. And then the tempest drove him back to England. And in rage he had the eyes of 22 hostages gouged out; and these included two sons of Owain and two sons of Rhys. And Rhys took the castles of Cardigan and Cilgerran. And through the will of God and at the instigation of the Holy Spirit, and with the help of Rhys ap Gruffydd, a community of monks came to Ystrad Fflur. And died Llywelyn ab Owain Gwynedd, the flower and splendour of the whole land.

The king personally oversaw the torture of the hostages, which led to further distrust of the Normans. According to Giraldus Cambrensis, the hostages were dismembered before Henry's retreat to England, which would mean that the bodies had been discovered.

> King Henry II entered the country of Powys, near Oswaldestree, in our days, upon an expensive, though fruitless, expedition. Having dismembered the hostages whom he had previously received, he was compelled, by a sudden and violent fall of rain, to retreat with his army. On the preceding day the chiefs of the English army had burned some of the Welsh churches, with the villages and churchyards; upon which the sons of Owen the Great, with their light-armed troops, stirred up the resentment of their father and the other princes of the country, declaring that they would never in future spare any churches of the English. When nearly the whole army was on the point of assenting to this determination, Owen, a man of distinguished wisdom and moderation – the tumult being in some degree subsided – thus spake: 'My opinion, indeed, by no means agrees with yours, for we ought to rejoice at this conduct of our adversary; for, unless supported by divine assistance, we are far inferior to the English; and they, by their behaviour, have made God their enemy, who is able most powerfully to avenge both himself and us. We therefore most devoutly promise God that we will henceforth pay greater reverence than ever to churches and holy places.' After which, the English army, on the following night, experienced (as has before been related) the divine vengeance.

Giraldus attributed the failure of Henry's three royal expeditions to lack of local information. 'In all these expeditions, the King was unsuccessful because he placed no confidence in the prudent and well-informed chieftains of the country, but was principally advised by people remote from the Marches, and ignorant of the manners and of the customs of the natives.'

Questioned by Emanuel, Emperor of Constantinople, as to the peculiarities of the British Islands Henry told him that: 'In a certain part of the island there was a people, called Welsh, so bold and ferocious that, when unarmed, they did not fear to encounter an armed force, being ready to shed their blood in defence of their country, and to sacrifice their lives for renown, which is the more surprising, as the beasts of the field over the whole face of the island became gentle, but these desperate men could not be tamed.'

Giraldus also paid tribute to the courage of the Welsh: 'Not only the nobles but all the people are trained to war, and when the trumpet sounds the alarm, the husbandman rushes as eagerly from his plough as the courtier from his court. They anxiously study the defence of their country and their liberty; for these they fight, for these they undergo hardships, and for these they willingly sacrifice their lives; they deem it a disgrace to die in their bed, an honour to die in the field of battle.'

LLYWELYN THE GREAT, 1173-1240

In 1194, Llywelyn ab Iorwerth, the grandson of the great Owain Gwynedd, was ruler of North Wales and decided to push back the increasingly aggressive intrusions of the Marcher Lords. After an invasion in 1210 by King John, whose illegitimate daughter Joan had married Llywelyn, Llywelyn gathered together a league of Welsh princes. Powys, Ceredigion, Carmarthen and South Wales were reunited under Llywelyn the Great. Only the settlements in the south of Pembrokeshire held out under the Normans, and in 1215 Llywelyn retook the old Welsh capital of Powys, Shrewsbury. He allied with the rebel English barons in forcing King John to sign the Magna Carta in 1215. The Welsh princes now formally paid homage to Llywelyn as ruler of all Wales at Aberdyfi, in 1216. By the Peace of Worcester in 1218, Llywelyn was acknowledged by John's young son Henry III, as ruler of Wales. However, Llywelyn would not style himself Prince of Wales for fear of creating jealousy among the other Welsh princes, who ruled their territories under his suzerainty. He was content to be known as Lord of Snowdon, Prince of Aberffraw. Llywelyn defeated royal forces under Hubert de Burgh, Justiciar of England, at Ceri in 1228, and in 1231 cleared Norman forces from Glamorgan. Henry III formally recognised the right of Llywelyn's son Dafydd ap Llywelyn as his successor as ruler of Wales.

Llywelyn died in 1240, and was buried at Aberconwy Abbey. In August 1241, however, Henry III treacherously and unexpectedly invaded Gwynedd, and Prince Dafydd was forced to give up all his lands outside Gwynedd. Dafydd now entered into an alliance with other Welsh princes to attack English possessions. By 1245, Dafydd had recovered Mold and Flintshire, and in that year Henry again invaded Gwynedd, but his army suffered a defeat in a narrow pass. Henry led the rest of his army to Deganwy, where he tried to build a castle under constant attacks from the Welsh. A truce was agreed and Henry's army withdrew in the autumn. The truce remained throughout the winter. The war was effectively ended by the suspicious death of Dafydd (probably by poison) in the royal palace of Garth Celyn in February 1246, aged only thirty.

THE MURDER OF LLYWELYN THE LAST 1282

Dafydd had died childless and the leadership of Wales eventually passed to a grandson of Llywelyn the Great, Llywelyn ap Gruffydd, whose father had died in 1244 trying to escape from the Tower of London. By 1258 Llywelyn ap Gruffydd effectively controlled all of Wales, and by the 1267 Treaty of Montgomery, Henry III formally recognised him as the ruler of Wales. Edward I became King in 1272, and Llywelyn refused to pay homage to him in Chester in 1275. Llywelyn feared being taken prisoner, as King Edward had earlier that year captured and imprisoned Llywelyn's wife-to-be, Eleanor de Montfort. She was the daughter of Simon de Montfort, sixth Earl of Leicester and the granddaughter of King John. After her father's death at Evesham in 1265, her family was forced to live in exile in France, but she had been betrothed to Llywelyn. They married by proxy under canon law in 1275, before Eleanor attempted to join him in North Wales, but she and her brother were captured off the Isles of Scilly. Her cousin Edward I paid 220 marks to six sailors, and £20 to an archdeacon, for arranging her capture. Llywelyn offered a ransom for her release but Edward refused, making extra demands upon Llywelyn.

Without warning, Edward I invaded Wales in 1276. Unprepared, Llywelyn was cut off in Gwynedd and forced to surrender. Princess Eleanor was held at Windsor until the Treaty of Aberconwy was signed in 1278. Llywelyn was left with just part of Gwynedd, the other being taken by his younger brother Dafydd. Eleanor and Llywelyn were formally married at Worcester Cathedral in 1278, but before the wedding mass was celebrated Edward forced Llywelyn to sign an unfavourable change in the treaty. The Archbishop of Canterbury confirmed this action. Eleanor was now known as Princess of Wales and Lady of Snowdon, but died in childbirth in 1282 giving birth to Gwenllian. Edward began to build huge castles at Rhuddlan, Flint, Builth and Aberystwyth – the beginning of his 'Iron Ring' of castles – to cut off the princedom of Gwynedd.

Seeing this threat to their remaining lands in Gwynedd, in 1282 Prince Dafydd attacked Hawarden Castle and laid siege to Rhuddlan Castle. His brother Llywelyn had little choice but to now lead the revolt. War quickly spread across Wales, and Aberystwyth and Carreg Cennen castles were soon captured. An English force in Anglesey was defeated while trying to cross to Gwynedd. Llywelyn was offered estates in England if he surrendered Wales, but refused to abandon his people. Llywelyn left Dafydd in Gwynedd as he was lured into a meeting with the Mortimers, Gwenwynwyn of Powys and other nobles near Builth. Llywelyn had been promised an alliance against King Edward I in his war of independence for Wales. With only an eighteen-man bodyguard, the Welsh contingent for the meeting were killed by arrows and spears. The badly wounded Prince of Wales was executed on the spot, and his head taken to London to be spiked for display on the Tower of London. His nearby leaderless army of 3,000 men surrendered and was massacred, unarmed, to a man by the King's troops and foreign mercenaries. There was not one English casualty. Letters from the Archbishop of Canterbury confirm 'the treachery at Builth' and its subsequent cover-up in English history. Bards were arrested across Wales to prevent the news spreading, and repressive laws were passed.

In 1282, Gruffydd ab yr Ynad Coch's magnificent elegy to Llywelyn tells us:

> Great torrents of wind and rain shake the whole land,
> The oak trees crash together in a wild fury,
> The sun is dark in the sky,
> And the stars are fallen from their courses.

The poem ends with:

> Do you not see the stars fallen?
> Do you not believe in God, simple men?
> Do you not see that the world has ended?
> A sigh to you, God, for the sea to come over the land!
> What is left to us that we should stay?

Because of the loss of independence of Gwynedd and Powys after a thousand years, Gruffydd wrote:

> Oh God! That the sea might surge up to You, covering the land!
> Why are we left to long-drawn weariness?
> There is no refuge from the terrible Prison.

Llywelyn's brother Dafydd now assumed the princedom of Wales, but was hunted down and captured in 1283. On 30 September, Dafydd ap Gruffydd, Prince of Wales, was condemned to death. King Edward I invented the punishment for high treason of hanging, drawing and quartering for Prince Dafydd, later to be inflicted on William Wallace in Scotland and used for centuries by the English as the punishment for high treason. (Even the ringleaders of the Chartist march at Newport in 1839 were sentenced to hanging, drawing and quartering, before their reprieve after massive protests.) Dafydd was dragged through the streets of Shrewsbury attached to a horse's tail then hanged alive, revived, then disemboweled and his entrails burned before him for 'his sacrilege in committing his crimes in the week of Christ's passion'. Geoffrey of Shrewsbury was paid 20 shillings for disemboweling Dafydd on 2 or 3 October 1283. Owen Rhoscomyl wrote in his *Flamebearers of Welsh History* 1905:

> The death of Llywelyn left his brother Davydd to carry on the war. But Davydd was no such leader of men as Llywelyn had been. Edward brought over an army of Gascon cross-bow men to the help of his other armies, and in 1283 Davydd was captured. More fortunate by far would he have been if he had died in battle, for the savage Edward invented a manner of death for the helpless captive which is too shocking to be described here. It is so full of horror upon horror that to read it would only sicken the reader. Llywelyn had indeed been right in his judgment of Edward's character. Let us pass on.

Legend recounts that Dafydd's heart leapt out of the flames and blinded his executioner, and the story was used to save Owain Glyndŵr's life over a century later. Dafydd's body was cut into four quarters 'for plotting the King's death', then salted and sent for display to York, Winchester, Bristol and Northampton. The representatives of York and Winchester disputed over which city should have the honour of receiving the right shoulder. It went to Winchester. Dafydd's head was led on a pole through the streets of London, crowned with ivy, to the sound of horns and trumpets. It was spiked on the White Tower in London, next to his brother Llywelyn's. Conwy Castle was symbolically built on the tomb of Llywelyn the Great at Aberconwy Abbey. By The Statute of Rhuddlan, in 1284, Edward finally and formally took control of Wales, 218 years after his forebears had conquered England.

Without the bards' Celtic oral tradition, much of Welsh history and heritage would have been lost forever. There has been a strong oral tradition that 500 Welsh bards were slaughtered after the death of Llywelyn II, because they may have inflamed the Welsh to rebel against their new conquerors, the French kings of England. The event is better known in the rest of Europe than in Britain, as any country's history is uniformly biased in favour of the succeeding rulers. One of the most famous and popular Hungarian poems, written by the renowned poet Janos Arany (1817-1882), celebrates the story of the bards after Llywelyn II's murder. The Austrian Emperor Franz-Josef defeated Hungary in its War of Independence (1848-49), then made his first visit there. He asked Janos Arany to write a poem to praise him, and this was the poet's nationalistic response. The last verse is:

> But high above all drum and fife
> And trumpets' shrill debate,
> Five hundred martyred voices chant
> Their hymn of deathless hate ...

Thomas Gray (1716-1771), who wrote *Elegy Written in a Country Churchyard*, considered his two Pindaric odes, *The Progress of Poesy* and *The Bard*, to be his best works. *The Bard* tells us of a Welsh poet cursing Edward I after the conquest of Wales, and prophesying in detail the downfall of the House of Plantagenet. He then hurls himself from a cliff, rather than face a more horrific form of death. As well as the rounding up of bards and the imprisonment and execution of their employers, Henry IV, in 1403's Ordinance de Gales, forbade their existence. Thus truth becomes hidden forever.

WHAT HAPPENED TO PRINCE LLEWELYN'S FAMILY

The records of what happened to Llywelyn's family have resonances of what happened to Glyndŵr's family 130 years later, and in that context must be mentioned. Edward I referred to the House of Gwynedd as the 'treacherous lineage' of a 'turbulent nation', although the Norman/English Crown had never fully controlled Gwynedd or its ruling dynasty. He decided upon a policy of imprisonment and extermination to kill off the entire line of the Princes of Gwynedd.

Prince Dafydd had married Lady Elizabeth Ferrers, daughter of the Earl of Derby, sometime after 1265, and their two sons were Owain and Llywelyn. On 22 June 1283, Prince Dafydd and Owain ap Dafydd had been captured in a hiding place on Bera Mountain, near their palace at Garth Celyn. Dafydd was gravely injured, but dragged to Edward's camp at Rhuddlan that night, then taken to Shrewsbury and then Chester. His wife Elizabeth, their children, and the dead Llywelyn's daughter Gwenllian were also taken prisoner at the same time. (Gwenllian's mother had died of childbirth complications soon after giving birth to her). A week later, on 28 or 29 June, Dafydd's eldest son, Llywelyn ap

Dafydd, was taken, and Welsh resistance to the invasion came to an end. Young Llywelyn was taken to Rhuddlan to be imprisoned alongside his brother Owain. On that day, Edward summoned a parliament to meet at Shrewsbury. Upon Dafydd's execution, the only child of his brother Llywelyn was taken away to be locked up in a nunnery for the rest of her life in England. Gwenllian, Princess of Wales, was incarcerated in the convent of the Gilbertine priory at Sempringham, Lincolnshire from the age of eighteen months, until her death fifty-four years later. Llywelyn had no other issue according to most genealogies. However, some genealogies tell us that Gwenllian had an older sister, Catherine (or Catrin) born in 1279 or 1280, and thus two-three years older. This Catherine supposedly gave birth to Elinor Goch, the mother of Owain Glyndŵr's mother Elen, giving Glyndŵr ancestry in the House of Gwynedd. Catherine was either an illegitimate child, or had been hidden. Gwenllian had been taken as Prince Dafydd's wife was sheltering her.

Of Dafydd's own children, his sons were imprisoned for life and his daughter also sent to a nunnery in England for the rest of her life. Gwladys ferch Dafydd was thirteen when she was taken to the convent of the Gilbertine priory at Six Hills in Lincolnshire and died there fifty-three years later, a year before Gwenllian. The two Princesses, Gwladys and Gwenllian, never met in more than fifty years of imprisonment. Dafydd's only two legitimate sons, Llywelyn and Owain, were taken to Acton Burnell in Shropshire and then imprisoned in cages at Bristol Castle. Llywelyn ap Dafydd had been born in 1260, and was de jure Prince of Gwynedd from his father's death in 1283. Prince Llywelyn was probably murdered or starved to death in 1287. Owain was born around 1265, and caged like his brother until he died in 1325. An order from Edward I to the Constable of Bristol Castle, October 1305 reads:

> As the King wills that Owain son of Dafydd ap Gruffydd, who is in the Constable's custody in the castle, should be kept more securely than he has been previously, he orders the Constable to cause a strong house within the castle to be repaired as soon as possible, and to make a wooden cage bound with iron in that house in which Owain might be enclosed at night.

There is a pathetic letter from the adult Owain asking to be allowed to leave his cage to 'play on the grass' inside the castle.

The House of the Princes of Gwynedd had been systematically wiped out. Llywelyn ap Gruffydd's other brother Owain Goch ap Gruffydd had died around 1282, with no issue. Llywelyn's sister Gwladys was already dead, childless. Llywelyn's sister Margaret (Marged) had married Madog ap Gruffydd of Powys Fadog in 1277. Their infant boys Gruffydd ap Madog and Llywelyn ap Madog were killed in mysterious circumstances during the war of 1282. Thomas Pennant states that the boys were 'drowned in the River Dee' at Holt by their guardians Roger Mortimer the Younger and the Earl of Surrey, to gain their lands. David Powel mentions the 'destruction' of these two Princes, whose guardians, Warenne and Mortimer, 'did obtain the same lands (known as Maelor or Bromfield) to themselves by charters of the King.'

However, Llywelyn II's only other brother, with Owain Goch and Prince Dafydd dead, was Prince Rhodri ap Gruffydd, known on his English estates as Roderick Fitz Griffin (c.1230 - c.1315). He had sold his inheritance rights to his brother Llywelyn and bought an estate in Gloucestershire. He then gained property in Cheshire and the manor of Tatsfield in Surrey. On Prince Owain ap Dafydd's death in prison, the only surviving senior member of the House of Gwynedd was his cousin Thomas ap Rhodri ap Gruffydd, who was living in England, at Tatsfield. His son, Owain Lawgoch ap Thomas ap Rhodri was the single descendant left, of whom more later.

In August 1284, Edward set up his court at Llywelyn's palace of Garth Celyn. He extended his great castle-building programme across Wales. The Iron Ring of massive castles, now a World Heritage Site, at Caernarfon, Conway, Harlech, Ruthin, and Beaumaris, was completed by 1295. Adjacent to each castle was a fortified bastide, as foreign settlement, an idea copied by the English kings from their native France. Conwy was deliberately built upon Aberconwy Abbey, which held the tomb of Llywelyn the Great. Edward took the crown jewels of Gwynedd – Llywelyn's crown was given to the shrine of St. Edward at Westminster Abbey; the relic known as Coron Arthur (Crown of Arthur) was taken; the matrices of the seals of Llywelyn, of his wife Eleanor, and his brother Dafydd were melted down to make a chalice; the fragment of the True Cross, known as the 'Croes Naid', was paraded through London in May of 1285 in a solemn procession on foot, led by the King, the Queen, the Archbishop of Canterbury, fourteen bishops and the magnates of the realm. Welsh monasteries and abbeys were ransacked. Documents confirming land possessions were destroyed, and estates granted to Franco-English lords. With the following wars, culminating in the Second Civil War and the burning of Raglan Castle's great library, nearly all of Welsh recorded history was lost.

THE REVOLT OF RHYS AP MAREDUDD, LORD OF DRYSLWYN 1287-1288

Rhys ap Maredudd, Lord of Dryslwyn in Ystrad Tywi, had surrendered Dinefwr Castle to Edward I in 1277, but was allowed to keep Dryslwyn Castle. In 1282, before his war began, Prince Llywelyn II had put forward the grievances of Maredudd against royal officers on his lands. However, Maredudd sided with Edward when war came, attacking Llanbadarn (Aberystwyth) Castle and keeping order in Ceredigion. When the war ended, he was recognised as ruler of much of Carmarthenshire, but was in a terrible feud with the Norman Giffards of Llandovery. He rebelled on 27 June 1287, taking over Iscennen, expelling the Giffards and fighting throughout west Wales. The Earl of Cornwall led a royal army to take Dryslwyn in September, and Newcastle Emlyn in January of 1288. Rhys kept fighting and tried to escape to Ireland but was caught and executed at York in 1291.

THE REVOLT OF PRINCE MADOG AP LLYWELYN 1294-1295

An even more serious revolt broke out in 1294. Prince Madog ap Llywelyn ap Maredudd was of a cadet branch of the House of Gwynedd, and the son of the last vassal Lord of

Meirionydd (Merioneth). Madog lived in England where his father was a royal pensioner, but returned to Wales in 1282, receiving lands in Anglesey. A fifth cousin of Prince Llywelyn ap Gruffydd, he was asked to lead a rebellion in North Wales, and called himself Prince of Wales in the Penmachno Document. The revolt was caused by oppressive new royal officials and punitive taxation. In South Wales, Cynan ap Maredudd, Maelgwn ap Rhys, and Morgan ap Maredudd of Glamorgan joined the revolt. Caernarfon and its great castle were taken, along with Hawarden, Ruthin and Denbigh castles. Cricieth and Harlech castles were besieged for months. In the south, Builth was besieged, and in Glamorgan Morlais and Cynffig (Kenfig) castles taken and Caerffili burnt, although that powerful castle did not fall. Harlech's defenders fell to just thirty-seven men during its siege. Edward I was besieged at Conwy for all the winter of 1294, until relieved by his navy in 1295.

In March, however, Madog led a force into Powys, where, being taken unawares by the Earl of Warwick, he was defeated with heavy losses on the field of Maes Meidog (or Moydog, Madog) in Caereinion. It seems that the Welsh army was sleeping, and Madog hastily formed schiltrons (formations of pikemen resembling porcupines) to fend off the English cavalry, but they were massacred by English archers. Madog barely escaped with his life into the hills of Snowdonia, where he remained a fugitive until his unconditional surrender to John de Havering late in July or August 1295. Even more punitive laws, further restricting the civil rights of the Welsh were passed, with the few privileges left to the Welsh in The Statute of Rhuddlan being abolished. However, the bards still longed for, and prophesied a 'Mab Darogan' - a son of prophecy to free Wales again.

THE REVOLT OF LLEWELYN BREN, LORD OF SENGHENYDD 1316

Llywelyn ap Gruffydd ap Rhys, 'Llywelyn Bren', Lord of Senghenydd and Meisgyn, led the last serious challenge to English rule in Wales until the attempts of Owain Lawgoch to invade Wales in the 1370s. Llywelyn's father Gruffydd had lost the lordship of Senghenydd to Gilbert de Clare in 1267, and had been imprisoned in Ireland. Edward II appointed a new administrator for Glamorgan, Payn de Turbeville, who severely persecuted the Welsh and confiscated lands from men loyal to the crown, so Llywelyn Bren appealed to Edward II. The King responded by charging Llywelyn Bren with treason and summoned him to face Parliament. He also threatened Llywelyn with hanging, so in 1316 the desperate Llywelyn led his men to attack Caerffili Castle, taking some of the outer defences and burning a gatehouse. The town was burnt and rebellion spread across Glamorgan and Gwent. Many castles were taken and attacked, but a battle at Castell Morgraig forced Llywelyn to halt his siege of Caerffili. Separate English armies followed Llywelyn's army to Ystradfellte, and he surrendered himself to ensure that his army was not annihilated. His seven sons also participated in the revolt. The Earl of Hereford and Roger Mortimer pleaded with the King on Llywelyn's behalf for his noble behaviour in sacrificing himself for his troops.

In 1318, Llywelyn became the prisoner of Hugh Despenser the Younger, Lord of Glamorgan, who took Llywelyn to Cardiff Castle and had him hanged, drawn and quartered without any proper trial. Despenser then illegally seized Llywelyn's lands, and imprisoned Llywelyn's wife and some of his sons. In 1326 Roger Mortimer caught Edward II and Hugh Despenser (possibly a lover of Edward II) in Glamorgan. Roger Mortimer was the lover of Edward II's wife Queen Isabella. Edward II was despatched in Berkeley Castle. (Although Ian Mortimer's book, *The Greatest Traitor*, a biography of Roger Mortimer, makes a persuasive case that Edward II did not die and lived on the continent.) After Despenser's peremptory trial in Hereford, he was to suffer the same fate as he had illegally inflicted on Llywelyn Bren.

Despenser was dragged behind four horses, stripped naked and hung from a 50-foot-high gallows, so that everyone could see the great man's demise. He was cut down before he choked to death and tied to a tall ladder, and the executioner climbed up to slice off his penis and testicles, which were then burnt before his eyes. Next, the executioner cut him open to pull out his heart and entrails, which were also then burnt before him. The mark of a good execution was to draw out the process as long as possible for the benefit of the queen, Mortimer and the huge crowd. There was a 'ghastly, inhuman howl' just before Despenser died, which greatly entertained the huge crowd. His head was taken to be displayed at London, and his body quartered for display across the kingdom. To some extent, Llywelyn Bren's unlawful death helped lead to the eventual overthrow of both Edward II and the Despensers. It is necessary to relate this barbarous punishment for treason, as the followers of Glyndŵr knew what their punishment would be. It makes their following him all the more remarkable:

> The Welsh habit of revolt against the English is a long-standing madness ... and this is the reason. The Welsh, formerly called the Britons, were once noble, crowned with the whole realm of England; but they were expelled by the Saxons and lost both name and a kingdom ... But from the sayings of the prophet Merlin they still hope to recover England. Hence it is they frequently rebel.
> (Vita Edward Secundi c. 1330.)

THE ASSASSINATION OF OWAIN LAWGOCH, PRINCE OF WALES 1378

In 1361-62, the Black Death swept across Europe, and with the consequent lack of manpower the villeinage system began to crumble. Some men ran away from their bondage, but many were granted freeman status by their lords. Virtual anarchy reigned across Europe in these turbulent times, and one of its greatest warriors was 'Yvain de Galles, Owen of Wales', Owain ap Thomas ap Rhodri, the only direct survivor of the House of Gwynedd. Born around 1330, he became one of France's leading mercenary captains, leading a 'Free Company'. He fought against the English during the 1360's and 1370's, and became known as Owain Lawgoch (Red Hand) because of his skill in battle. Owain constantly proclaimed himself the true heir of Aberffraw (the court on Anglesey of the Princes of Gwynedd), and only de Guesclin features more highly in French literature as an enemy of the English at this time. Described by Edward Owen as 'possibly the greatest military genius that Wales has produced', he crossed to England in 1365 to claim his inheritance, but was forced to return to France as he feared capture and death. 'Owen of Wales' had been brought up at the court of King Philip VI of France, and had fought heroically against the English at Poitiers in 1356 (one of the few knights surviving against all the odds). Owain next campaigned in the Lombard Wars of the 1360's, and for and against the Dukes of Bar in Lorraine, and fought alongside Bertrand du Guesclin in the campaigns of the 1370's. In 1366, he had led the Compagnons de Galles (Company of Welshmen) to fight Pedro the Cruel in Spain.

Many Welshmen followed him, including Ieuan Wyn, who took over Owain's company of soldiers after his death. Owain still features in the folk literature of Brittany, France, Switzerland, Lombardy and the Channel Islands. An Anglesey man, Gruffydd Sais was executed, and his lands confiscated by the crown in 1369 for contacting 'Owain Lawgoch, enemy and traitor', and in the same year Charles V gave Owain a fleet to sail to Wales from Harfleur. It was sadly repulsed by storms. The French King Charles now gave Owain 300,000 francs, another fleet and 4000 men to win back his land. Owain proclaimed that he owned Wales 'through the power of my succession, through my lineage, and through my rights as the descendant of my forefathers, the kings of that country'. Taking Guernsey from the English, Owain captured the legendary Captal de Buch, the Black Prince's comrade, hero of Poitiers and one of England's greatest soldiers.

Owain prepared to invade Wales after his seizure of Guernsey, and towns and castles across the south of England and in Wales were placed on high alert, with castles being re-garrisoned and repaired. The English Parliament warned of this coming invasion from France, led by one of the most famous warriors of the 100 Years War. However, instead a message now came from the French King telling him to help the Spanish attack the English-occupied La Rochelle in 1372. Owain responded and fought again against the English. Owain never had another chance to return to Wales. The signed Treaty of Paris between Owain Llawgoch and King Charles V of France, of 10 May 1372, still survives. It begins:

> OWAIN OF WALES, to all those to whom these letters shall come, greetings. The kings of England in past times having treacherously and covetously, tortuously and without cause and by deliberate treasons, slain or caused to be slain my ancestors, kings of Wales, and others of them have put out of their country, and that country have by force and power appropriated and have submitted its people to divers servitude, the which country should be mine by right of succession, by kindred, by heritage, and by right of descent from my ancestors the kings of that country, and in order to obtain help and succour that country which is my heritage, I have visited several Christian kings ...

In 1375, Owain took part in the successful siege of Saveur-le-Comte in Normandy, where for the first time cannon were used really successfully to break the English defences. He then took a contract from the great Baron Enguerrand de Coucy, Count of Soissons and Bedford, to lead 400 men at a fee of 400 francs per month (with 100 francs per month going to his assistant, Owain ap Rhys). Any town or fortress taken was to be yielded to De Coucy. Again, the treaty contract survives, dated 14 October 1375. The capture of Duke Leopold of Austria was to be worth 10,000 francs to Owain, who even attracted 100 Teutonic knights from Prussia to his banner. With The Treaty of Bruges, English knights also came to offer their services under the leadership of the great Owain. Probably around 10,000 soldiers eventually formed an army for De Coucy and Owain. The knights wore pointed helmets and cowl-like hoods on heavy cloaks, and their hoods, called 'gugler' (from the Swiss-German for cowl or point), gave their names to the The Gugler War.

The companies making up the army plundered Alsace, and took ransom of 3000 florins not to attack Strasbourg as the Habsburg Duke Leopold retreated, ordering the destruction of all resources in his wake. He withdrew across the Rhine, relying on the Swiss to stave off the attack, although the Swiss hated the Hapsburgs almost as much as they hated the Guglers. De Coucy's invaders were allowed entrance to Basle, but their forces became increasingly scattered as they sought loot in the wake of Leopold's depredations. Near Lucerne, a company of Guglers was surrounded by the Swiss and routed. On Christmas night a company of Bretons was ambushed by citizens of Berne, city of the emblem of the bear. On the next night, the Swiss attacked the Abbey of Fraubrunnen, where Owain was quartered, setting fire to the Abbey and slaughtering the sleeping 'English'. Owain swung his sword 'with savage rage' but was forced to flee, leaving 800 Guglers dead at the Abbey. Ballads tell of how the Bernese fought '40,000 lances with their pointed hats', how 'Duke Yfo (Owain) of Wales came with his golden helm' and how when Duke Yfo came to Fraubrunnen, 'The Bear roared 'You shall not escape me ! I will slay, stab and burn you!' In England and France the widows all cried 'Alas and woe!' Against Berne no-one shall march evermore!'

The following details are next recounted in *Froissart's Chronicles*. In 1378, Owain was conducting the siege of Mortagne-sur-Gironde in the Gironde on the Atlantic coast. As usual, early in the morning, he sat on a tree stump, having his hair combed by a new squire, while he surveyed the scene of siege. His new Scots manservant, James Lambe, had been taken into service as he had brought news of 'how all the country of Wales would gladly have him to be their lord'. But, with no-one around, Lambe stabbed Owain in the back with a short spear and escaped to Mortagne – the English King had paid £20 for the assassination of the person with the greatest claim to the Principality of Wales, the last of the line of Gwynedd and Rhodri Fawr. It seems that Owain was buried at the chapel of St Leger, his possible headquarters during the siege. Owain's men swore to continue the siege and avenge their lord, but were surrounded by an English relieving army under Neville. In respect to their valour, the survivors of Owain's company were given a safe-conduct to leave Mortagne, and rejoined the main French forces.

Owain's importance to King Edward III of England is shown in a payment of 100 francs, and in the Issue Roll of the Exchequer dated 4 December 1378: 'To John Lamb, an esquire from Scotland, because he lately killed Owynn de Gales, a rebel and enemy of the King in France ... By writ of privy seal, &co £20.' As well as the £20 blood money, there were expenses to be paid. A letter from Sir John Neville, Governor of Aquitaine, to Richard Rotour, Constable of Bordeaux noted the payments made to Lambe's assassination squad, three of whom were killed by Owain's men while Lambe effected his escape. Part of the letter is translated as:

... they, in the country of the French, and, especially for the great and perilous adventure in which they risked life and limb to bring about the death of Owain of Wales, traitor and enemy to the King our said Lord.by which deed they diminished the evils and destruction wrought on the lands of the subjects of the King our Lord ... owing to the great profit and service they have rendered in this recent foray to Mortagne ... the said John Lamb and his companions have as outgoings the sum of 522 livres and 10 sous of current money, in payment for coats, helmets, hauberks, arm harness, gauntlets and many different harnesses and clothes purchased in the town of Bordeaux, to arm and array themselves.

There is also the receipt and letter signed by John Lamb(e). The Owain Lawgoch Society initiated a memorial in Mortagne on the 625th anniversary of Lawgoch's assassination, in 2003.

THE NEXT MAB DAROGAN (SON OF PROPHECY)

With Owain Lawgoch's death, the prime claim to the heritage of Llywelyn the Great, Llewelyn the Last, Rhodri Mawr and the leadership of Wales passed on eventually to another Owain. Owain Glyndŵr became the next Mab Darogan (Son of Prophecy) of the Welsh bards. When Glyndŵr, in 1404, requested French help against England, he reinforced his case by referring to Owain Lawgoch's great service to the French crown. After Glyndŵr's time, there was an abeyance of seventy years until the last Mab Darogan, Henry Tudur, marched through Wales and gathered forces to at last defeat England and claim the throne of Britain.

We can see a constant battle to keep Wales independent from foreign invaders from the first century with the Romans, through the Vikings, Picts, Irish, Saxons and Normans. Coming to the last year of the fifteenth century, events on the throne of England had huge repercussions for Wales. Edward III's heir had been the Black Prince (died 1376) but his predecease meant that the Black Prince's son Richard II (Edward III's grandson) took the throne in 1377. In 1381 Wat Tyler led a revolt against Poll Tax, burning John of Gaunt's Savoy Palace in the Strand and killing some of Richard II's ministers. The revolt failed after Richard promised to give them what they asked – of course he did not, but Richard II's weakness had been noted by his nobles.

Owen M. Edwards, in *A Short History of Wales* gives us the background to these times, and tells us that the next rising was not to come in Gwynedd or Glamorgan, but most unexpectedly in another part of Wales:

The Scotch and French wars of the English kings gave employment to hosts of bowmen and of men-at-arms, and to the numerous attendants required to look after the horses by means of which the army moved. The greater use of infantry after the reign of Edward I caused a greater demand for the peasant; and the use of the cheap longbow gave him a value in war. There were five thousand Welsh archers and spearmen on the field of Cressy (Crecy). In these and other ways the serf was becoming free. You would expect a gradual, almost unconscious, struggle between the serf and his lord for political power. The struggle came, but it was conscious and very fierce. It was brought about by a terrible pestilence, known as the Black Death. This plague came slowly and steadily from the East; in 1348 it reached Bristol, and it probably swept away one half of the people of the towns of Wales. It was not the towns alone that it visited; it came to the mountain glens as well. It was a most deadly disease. It killed, for one thing, because people believed that they would die. They saw the dark spots on the skin before they became feverish; they recognised the black mark of the Death and they gave themselves up for lost. Labourers became very scarce. They claimed higher wages. The lords tried to drag them back into serfdom; they tried to force them by law to take the old wage.

On both sides of the Severn the labourers took arms, and waged war against their lords. The peasant war in England is called the Peasant Revolt; the peasant war in Wales is sometimes called the revolt of Owen Glendower. A change came over the rebellions in Wales. At first, the rebellions were those of Llywelyn's country; the allies who had deserted him, and then turned against Edward, like Rees ap Meredith; or his own followers, like Madoc, who said he was his son; or men he had protected, like Maelgwn Vychan in Pembroke. Later on, under Edward II. and Edward III., the rebellions were against the march lords, and the king was looked upon as a protector – such as the rebellion of Llywelyn Bren against the Clares and Mortimers in Glamorgan in 1316. But the wilder spirits went to the French wars, and fought for both sides. With the assassination of Owen of Wales in 1378, the last of Llywelyn's near relatives to dream of restoring the independence of Wales, the rebellions against the King of England came to an end. When they broke out again, it was not in Snowdon or Ceredigion; the old dominions of Llywelyn were almost unwilling to rise. The new revolts were in the march lands, and especially in the towns.

CHAPTER 2

Glyndŵr's Early Life & Family 1354-1398

OWAIN GLYNDŴR'S PARENTS & ROYAL BACKGROUND

After the assassination of Owain Lawgoch (Yvain de Galles) in 1378, on the orders of the English crown, the Royal House of Gwynedd was extinct. Owain Glyndŵr became 'un pen ar Gymru', the only head for Wales, as he was the direct descendant of, and also the link between, the dynasties of Powys and Deheubarth. Glyndŵr later symbolically adopted Owain Lawgoch's heraldic device of the four lions of Gwynedd. As his ambassador was to later tell the French King, Glyndŵr was the rightful heir of the French ally Lawgoch, the real Prince of Gwynedd and Wales. Owain Glyndŵr was to unite Wales both politically and symbolically. After the killing of the last Princes of Gwynedd, Llywelyn and Dafydd, Glyndŵr's ancestral lands had been confiscated.

However, by the early fourteenth century Owain's great-grandfather Madog ap Gruffydd had regained his own lordships of Glyndyfrdwy and Cynllaith (in Northern Powys), but now subject to the King as a feudal tenant. It was a landed estate that provided a huge income of around 300 marks. By 1300 Edward I had formally assigned the baronetcy of Glyndyfrdwy and Cynllaith to Madog. Owain's grandfather Gruffydd ap Madog almost lost the estates because of the machinations of his legal guardians, the Mortimers of Chirk, but in 1321 the King ordered that Gruffydd should regain all his lands and assumed the baronetcy. Owain's father was another Gruffydd, known as Gruffydd Fychan to distinguish him from his father. 'Bychan' (mutated to Fychan) means small, or little. The epithet works in the same way as the American habit of calling a son with the same name as the father 'junior', as in George Bush jr.

Glyndŵr's mother Elen ferch Tomas ap Prince Llywelyn of Deheubarth had a brother, Owain ap Tomas, who died childless in 1360. Elen was co-heir with Margaret, her sister, of the half-commotes of Iscoed Uwch Hirwen and Gwynionydd Is Cerdyn, Cardiganshire. Elen's mother was Elinor Goch (Elinor the Red), the daughter and heiress of Catherine, who was said to be one of the daughters of Llywelyn II. Catherine had been somehow concealed on the death of her father, later marrying Philip ap Ifor, otherwise Edward I would have imprisoned her for life. Thus, Glyndŵr had the three major bloodlines of

Gwynedd, Powys and Deheubarth, an unrivalled heritage to become Welsh leader, with no rivals as the leader of the forthcoming Welsh resistance. The contemporary poet Iolo Goch used a cywydd (a complex form of poetry, favoured by the Poets of the Nobility), to trace Owain's pedigree. In the paternal line Owain was linked back to Bleddyn ap Cynfyn, Prince of Powys (d. 1075), and in the maternal line to Rhys ap Tudur, Prince of Deheubarth (d. 1093). Iolo also said that Owain's great-grandmother Gwenllian was from the House of Gwynedd, and traced the common ancestry of these three lineages to the legendary kings of pre-Roman British tradition.

Owain succeeded to his father's estates some time before 1370-71. These consisted of the lordship of Glyndyfrdwy, land around Carrog situated in the Dee valley between Corwen and Llangollen, and a half of the commote of Cynllaith, a fertile lordship bordering the Tanat valley, to the south of the Berwyn Mountains. In Cynllaith, his manor was at Sycharth. Glyndŵr must have also inherited his mother's estates in the county of Cardigan, for his lands in both North and South Wales were declared forfeit at the commencement of war. Owain may also have owned part of the estate of his maternal grandmother at Trefgarn in the hundred of Pebidiog, Pembroke. Thus Owain Glyndŵr's claims to his ancestral lands were solid, and recognised both in English law and by the English crown. Iolo Goch, in *Owain Glyndŵr's Genealogy*, notes Glyndŵr's domains at Tref-y-Traeth (Newport) and Tref-y-Garne, and also claims he is the inheritor of Acharn (Laugharne). In the same poem, in the last five lines, he asserts Glyndŵr's descent from the Princes of Gwynedd and their court at Aberffraw, calling him 'un pen ar Gymru', the sole head of Wales:

> ... pure golden fruit of the lord of Aberffraw;
> sole head of Wales, bright form,
> and Gwynedd's one soul,
> one eye, slaughterer of slaves,
> and one hand he is to Cynllaith.'

THE LEGENDS OF GLYNDŴR'S BIRTH

Sources variously give us 1349, 1354 and 1355 for the date of Owain's birth. The most accredited date is 28 May 1354 (see Chapter 12). Among the most famous legends are that his father's horses were standing in blood up to their fetlocks in their stables on Glyndŵr's birth, and that as a baby he would cry at the sight of a weapon, and only stop when he could touch it. (However, this same tale is attached to the birth of Edmund Mortimer). Terrible storms and a comet were also supposed to have attended Glyndŵr's birth, and the legends are referred to in Shakespeare's Henry IV, Part I:

> ... at my birth
> The front of heaven was full of fiery shapes;
> The goats ran from the mountains, and the herds
> Were strangely clamorous to the frighted fields.

These signs have marked me extraordinary,
And all the courses of my life do show,
I am not in the roll of common men

There were indeed strange weather conditions surrounding Glyndŵr's childhood, although from 1349-1355 nothing of note seems to be recorded. However, the asteroid Toutatis approaches the earth every four years, and last flew close by Earth in 2004, the closest since 1353. (It is about half the size of the asteroid that sixty-five million years ago caused the last mass extinction, 'The Great Dying' of 85% of the world's species, and will not come as near again until 2562.) In 1353, with clearer skies, it would have been visible to the naked eye, and from 1350 the climate altered to a mini-Ice Age very quickly. We know of some other events in Britain at this time. Upon 25 February 1361 an aurora formed 'a cloud like fire' at night, so this may be associated with Owain's birth date. 13 January 1362 saw a great south-westerly storm known as St Maury's Wind cause terrible damage. A month-long comet was said to have appeared in March 1362 after this extreme weather. There was an exceptionally severe winter with terrible frost from September 1363 to April 1364, with European rivers from the Thames to the Rhine frozen over. In 1366, on 12 January, an aurora formed a red sky in the east at night, with red and white rays shining and flickering for hours. We could easily posit a later birth date for Glyndŵr, of around 1359-60, rather than 1349-1355, which would make his willingness to fight in 1400 more understandable.

GLYNDŴR'S CAREER

J.G. Bradley (Owen Glyndŵr) recounts:

At court, Glyndŵr soon found considerable favour and in course of time became squire of the body, or "scutiger," not, as most Welsh authorities have persisted, and still persist, to King Richard the Second, but to his cousin Bolingbroke, the future Henry the Fourth. This latter view is certainly supported by the only documentary evidence extant, as Mr. Wylie in his able and exhaustive history of that monarch points out. "Regi moderno ante susceptum regnum" is the sentence in the Annales describing Glyndŵr's position in this matter, and it surely removes any doubt that Bolingbroke is the King alluded to. In such case Owen must have shared those perils and adventures by land and sea in which the restless Henry engaged. It is strange enough, too, that men linked together in a relationship so intimate should have spent the last 15 years of their lives in a struggle so persistent and so memorable as did these two. Bolingbroke began this series of adventures soon after the loss of his wife, about the year 1390, and we may therefore, with a fair probability of truth, picture Glyndŵr at that grand tournament at Calais where Henry so distinguished himself, and poor Richard by comparison showed to such small advantage.

He may also have been present at the capture of Tunis, where English and French to the wonder of all men fought side by side without friction or jealousy; or again with Bolingbroke on his long journey in 1393 to Jerusalem, or rather towards it, for he never got there. There were adventures, too, which Owen may have shared with German knights upon the Baltic, and last, though by no means least, with Sigismund, King of Hungary, at that memorable scene upon the Danube when he was forced into his ships by the victorious Turks. Yet the tradition is so strong that Glyndŵr was in the personal service of Richard during the close of that unfortunate monarch's reign, that one hesitates to brush it aside from mere lack of written evidence. Nor indeed does the fact of his having been Henry's esquire constitute any valid reason for doing so. It is not very likely that, when Henry in 1398 was so unjustly banished by Richard to an uneventful sojourn in France, Glyndŵr, with the cares of a family and estate growing upon him, would have been eager to share his exile. On the other hand, he must have been by that time well known to Richard, and with his Pembrokeshire property and connections may well, like so many Welshmen, have been tempted later on to embark in that ill-fated Irish expedition which promised plunder and glory, but turned out to be incidentally the cause of Richard's undoing.

Glyndŵr was a royal ward and was sent as a child to study law at Westminster (records only begin in 1422, so we have no confirmation). University entrance for the nobility was at the age of eleven or twelve, and it appears that he went to Oxford or Cambridge for a short time. He then became a squire to the Earl of Arundel (whose estates bordered his) and/or to Henry Bolingbroke. Owain was around eighteen when the ten-year-old Richard II assumed the English crown in 1377.

THE HANMER FAMILY & GLYNDŴR'S 1383 MARRIAGE

In common with many Welsh families, marriage connections were established with the Anglo-Welsh families of the Marches. Owain's paternal grandmother was Elizabeth, daughter of John Lestrange of Knockin, and Owain's sister Lowri married Robert Puleston. Glyndŵr's family were part of the Anglo-Welsh gentry of the Marches, occupying important offices for the Marcher Lords while maintaining their position as 'uchelwyr' (nobles descended from the pre-conquest royal dynasties), in traditional Welsh society. Glyndŵr's parents seem to have died some time before 1370, and he was fostered at the home of Sir David Hanmer. Sir David was a Member of Parliament, King's Serjeant and King's Bench Judge from 1383, whose family had settled in Maelor Saesneg, the detached portion of Flintshire nearest England. (Flintshire used to be on either side of Denbighshire.) Hanmer's own mother had been Welsh, and he served with distinction as a lawyer under both Edward III and Richard II. Sir David seems to have wanted his ward to take a legal career, and Owain was sent to London to study law at the Inns of Court, and he may have studied as a legal apprentice for seven years.

At Westminster Owain may have met his future wife, David Hanmer's daughter Margaret. Around 1383 he returned to Wales and, in St Chad's Church, Hanmer, married Margaret, also known as Marred or Marged. David and Angharad Hanmer had at least four children: Marged, who married Glyndŵr, and three sons, Gruffydd, Philip and John. Gruffydd was the eldest son, who became the acting legal attorney to the Principality of North Wales. John held important posts in the government of Flintshire, later becoming Glyndŵr's ambassador to France, and Philip was probably a lawyer. All four children were bilingual, and all three brothers-in-law immediately sided with Glyndŵr in the forthcoming war. The Hanmer estate was forfeited to the Crown following the family's support for Owain in the war. John Hanmer was pardoned for his role in 1411, but severely fined, and he subsequently divided the estate between his own four sons.

Glyndŵr and Margaret themselves had six sons. Gruffydd, Madog and Maredudd fought for him in the war. Of Thomas, John and David we know very little – they disappear from history, probably killed during the war. There was also possibly an illegitimate son, Ieuan (1380-1430). Of Glyndŵr's seven daughters, Isabel married Adda ab Iorwerth Ddu. Alys married John Scudamore of Holme Lacey. Scudamore's other estates at Ewyas and Kentchurch in Herefordshire were bordered by the lands of Roger Monnington of Monnington, who married another daughter, Marged. Janet Glyndŵr married John Crofts of Croft Castle in Hereford, and Catrin remained at home, marrying Lord Edmund Mortimer, of which more later. Other daughters appear to have been Elizabeth (who may be Isabel) and Jane. Phylip ap Rhys of Cenarth married a daughter named Margaret or Gwenllian, and fought on for Glyndŵr long after the war ended. A praise poem, the only surviving work by the Radnorshire bard Ieuan Gyfannedd, dedicated to Phylip ap Rhys of Cenarth and Gwenllian ferch Owain Glyndŵr begins:

> Philip, a generous royal stock,
> Ap Rhys, there's mention of you,
> Lover of our song;
> And much, too, of Gwenllian;
> Honour to you and this goddess,
> Famed Arthur of Gwerthrynion.

There may also have been an illegitimate daughter named Myfanwy, who lived at Camhelig Isa after marrying Llywelyn ab Adda ap Dafydd of the House of Trefor.

GLYNDŴR IN SCOTLAND 1385

Lord of Sycharth and Glyndyfrdwy, by 1385 Glyndŵr had enlisted under the Earl of Arundel in Richard II's Scottish War, along with his brother, Tudur, and his brothers-in-law Robert Puleston and John Hanmer.

The Fitzalans, Earls of Arundel, became lords of Bromfield and Yale (from 1347) and Oswestry and Chirk, the latter including the other half of the commote of Cynllaith. (Glyndŵr was lord of one half.) Glyndŵr's grandfather and great-grandfather had served the Arundels, and the Arundel connection was strengthened by Owain's marriage to Margaret Hanmer, whose father served on the Arundel's Marcher Council in 1386-7. Owain and his brother Tudur are named among the esquires of the retinue of Richard Fitzalan, Earl of Arundel, mustered on 13 March 1387, and Owain's name headed the list of Arundel's esquires mustered for overseas service in May 1388, although he may not have served on the expedition. Glyndŵr's cousins, Rhys ap Tudur and Gwilym ap Tudur, sons of Margaret ferch Tomas, his mother's sister, and Tudur ap Goronwy of Penmynydd (near Llangefni) in Anglesey, directly served Richard II, however. Also in Scotland with Glyndŵr was Morgan Yonge, whose sons Iorwerth Fychan and Jankyn later joined Glyndŵr's cause with their own sons. An illegitimate son of Morgan Yonge was Gruffydd Yonge, later to become Glyndŵr's ambassador.

As Howeyn Glyndourde and Tedyr Glynderde, Owain and Tudur served under Sir Gregory Sais at Berwick in 1384. Glyndŵr fought for Richard II in a battle in Scotland in 1385, mentioned in the 1386 Scrope Trial at Chester. Such was Glyndŵr's standing that around 1385, the poet Gruffydd Llwyd composed a cywydd to Owain Glyndŵr (a formal poem consisting of a series of seven-syllable lines in rhyming couplets, with all lines written in cynghanedd). Llwyd complained that only three Welshmen had been knighted in recent years; 'Syr Hywel Y Fwyall' (Sir Hywel of the Axe); Glyndŵr's own father-in-law, Sir David Hanmer; and 'Grigor ail Sain Siôr Sais', Sir Gregory Sais (whom Glyndŵr fought for). (After Poiters in 1356, the Black Prince had set aside a special place of honour for Hywel ap Gruffydd's battleaxe in his royal hall. Food was ordered to be served before it daily, which was later distributed as alms. This traditional ceremony was not discontinued until the era of Elizabeth I).

When its truce with England ended in 1385, France sent an army to Scotland to make war on the English. 1,000 knights and squires in full armour, with 5,000-6,000 men, were led by Jean de Vienne, High Admiral of France. Richard II quickly moved north with an army. Archibald, Earl of Douglas led the Scots in the combined Franco-Scottish army of 30,000 men and 2,000 lancers. The English army supposedly consisted of 7,000 men-at-arms and 60,000 archers under John of Gaunt, Duke of Lancaster, which laid waste to villages, finding little to destroy. (Men-at-arms is a difficult term to explain. It may include not just dismounted armed soldiers but also armoured cavalry including knights, squires and sergeants. Heavy cavalry often fought on foot, depending on the terrain. Also included were less heavily-armoured footmen who could carry billhooks, halberds, axes or clubs. Often the term men-at-arms only referred to the armoured cavalry, and did not include their squires and footmen. As a result the actual size of armies is often difficult to estimate.)

The French wanted a pitched battle, but the Scots withdrew, preferring guerrilla warfare. Glyndŵr was present in the English army, and according to Iolo Goch in his poem *Praise of Owain Glyndŵr*:

When he reached strong manhood
he was a fierce mighty slasher,
he did nothing but ride horses.
Best time, in dark trappings,
bearing a lance, good bold lord,
a steel socket and a thick jacket,
wearing a rest and mail cap
and a white helmet, a generous man in wine
and in its peak, fine plumed summit,
a red wing [a flamingo feather] of the bird of Egypt.

For a while he was the best soldier
with Sir Gregory, he was a lord ...
Great renown for knocking down a horseman
did he win
... and felling him splendidly to the ground, with his shield in fragments.
And the second rout was a grim battle,
and his spear shattered from fur;
 this is remembered as a disgrace today,
(Glyndŵr was called) Candle of Battle, by the whole of Scotland;
some screaming, some wretched yonder,
every bad man, everyone indeed for fear of him
shouting like wild goats, he caused terror,
harsh he was to the Scots.
Great was the path through the froth of blood,
 a year feeding wolves; neither grass nor dock grew,
nor corn where he had been ...

Ernest F. Jacob recounts that Glyndŵr had a scarlet flamingo feather as his crest, and drove into the Scots bearing only the butt of a broken lance, which brought disgrace on the Scots who fled before him.

Thomas Pennant believed from an old manuscript that Glyndŵr was born in 1354, but the Scrope vs. Grosvenor trial documentation places him as being born in 1359, or possibly before, as he was stated as being twenty-seven 'et pluis'(and more) in 1386. (However, Geoffrey Chaucer was described as forty 'et pluis' in the same trial when he was nearer fifty-eight.) Upon 3 September 1386, Glyndŵr gave his evidence at Chester, as a witness in the greatest and most prolonged lawsuit England had ever experienced. The trial lasted almost five years and nearly every prominent person in the country gave evidence. 'Oweyn Sire de Glendore de age XXVII ans et pluis' and 'Tudor de Glindore', his brother, who was three years younger than Owen, gave evidence along with Robert Puleston, Owain's brother-in-law. At the sitting in 1387, Puleston was said to be aged twenty-eight, so was a similar age to Glyndŵr, whom he served in the Welsh war of independence. Another brother-in-law, John Hanmer, was also a witness.

Sir Richard le Scrope of Bolton had brought a case against Sir Robert Grosvenor of Hulme, to settle a dispute over a coat-of-arms that both of them had borne during Richard II's 1385 campaign in Scotland. The trial was presided over by the Duke of Gloucester, Constable of England. Puleston, Hanmer and the Glyndŵrs gave evidence supporting Grosvenor's claim, stating that they had seen Grosvenor bearing the coat of arms during the Scottish campaign, but the court found in favour of Scrope. Other nobles and enemies of Richard II allied themselves with the Scrope cause. This Lancastrian pro-Scrope grouping included Henry Bolingbroke, and this may have caused antagonism between him and Glyndŵr in later years. In 1386, the year Glyndŵr gave evidence, Bolingbroke's father John of Gaunt, Duke of Lancaster, left England to follow a claim to the throne of Castile.

As we have seen, Glyndŵr had served in Richard II's expedition to Scotland in 1385, and testified to this in his deposition to the above court of chivalry in 1386. He seems to have served in the retinue of Sir Gregory (Degory) Sais of Flintshire, and had been associated with Sir Gregory in a military capacity since at least 1384. Owain and his brother can be found on two muster rolls of 1384, which show that they were serving in Sais' retinue in the garrison at Berwick upon Tweed. In the only signature extant of Owen previous to his assumption of princely honours, we find him describing himself as 'Oweyn ap Griffith, Dominus de Glyn Dwfrdwy.'

Sir Gregory Sais was the only notable Welsh commander on the English side following the resumption of the conflict with France, and he lived near Owain's estates. Glyndŵr's other early military connection was to Richard Fitz Alan, Earl of Arundel, in whose retinue he soldiered on successive campaigns in the late 1380s. Two fifteenth-century chronicles also name Owain as one of the earl's esquires. Arundel and Glyndŵr were neighbouring landholders in the Marches, near the border towns of Chirk and Oswestry. Arundel probably retained the services of Owain from at least 1385, but he was possibly linked to the earl before this. It may be that Glyndŵr was one of Arundel's supporters during the Lords Appellant crisis of the late 1380s, when Arundel took up arms against Richard II's favourites. If Owain had been indented to serve the earl in peace and war, then he therefore probably joined with the earl in his defiance of the King at the battle of Radcot Bridge (December 1387).

Glyndŵr also took part in Battle of Cadzand in March 1387 when a fleet was routed off Margate. Richard Fitzalan, Earl of Arundel, attacked a Franco-Flemish wine fleet. After some German and Flemish vessels deserted to them, the English were eventually able to overcome the enemy, capturing around fifty ships and the fleet's Flemish commander. Over a dozen ships were sunk or burnt, and almost 9,000 tons of wine were captured and carried to London. Besides lowering the cost of wine in London, the victory gave the English temporary command of the Channel, and allowed the earl to raid the Flemish coast. However, he failed to achieve his aim of an anti-Burgundian uprising in Flanders, to replace Philip the Bold with a pro-English faction. Following the battle, a number of Arundel's squires were knighted, but notably Glyndŵr was not one of them. Arundel had indented with the crown to serve with 2,500 men and a fleet of 60 ships. That previous autumn, the French had intended to invade England, with 1,200 ships and 30,000 men, but Philip the Bold fell ill and the invasion was called off.

Glyndŵr was one of the Barwnaid (Welsh barons) who held their lands as Tir Pennaeth (tenants-in-chief), a condition of which was military service. This responsibility had survived from before the conquest of Wales. The King indented Arundel to muster men, and Arundel indented his lords, and they in turn indented their followers. Welsh tenants had held their land in exchange for military support of their princes, and this was still acknowledged by the English crown. Like his cousins the Tudurs in Anglesey, Glyndŵr's obligation was to the crown before Arundel. Thus military leadership was something which Glyndŵr expected. Therefore during the 1380s Owain and his supporters had served as soldiers in an English garrison force on the Scottish borders; fought in the expedition led by Richard II to Scotland in 1385; and took part in the royal expedition at the blockade of Sluys, led by the earl of Arundel in 1387.

THE LORDS APPELLANT & THE BATTLE OF RADCOT BRIDGE 1387

Richard II's enemies, the so-called 'Lords Appellant' tried to control his actions in the late 1380s. The group was called the Lords Appellant because some of the great nobles were appealing to the King for better government. They also strongly opposed his decision to make peace with France, as pillage was one of their major income streams. Their leaders were the Duke of Gloucester, the Earls of Arundel, Warwick and Nottingham, and Henry Bolingbroke, Earl of Derby. Bolingbroke was the son of John of Gaunt, Duke of Lancaster, who was in Spain at this time. Richard II's favourite and Chancellor, the Earl of Suffolk, was impeached and exiled by their council in 1386. Next, the King's uncle, Thomas of Woodstock, Duke of Gloucester, accused another of the King's favourites, Robert De Vere, Earl of Oxford, of treason. Oxford escaped to the West Midlands where he gathered together an army of 15,000 men in the winter of 1387. He marched south to try and reinforce the King's followers in London. Gloucester led the troops of the Lords Appellant north to close the roads from the Midlands. Richard II's western supporters also moved south towards London.

Richard's cousin, Henry Bolingbroke, the Earl of Derby, had taken up a southerly position, along with Mowbray, the Earl Marshal. They blocked off the route across the Thames by encamping between the Pidnell and Radcot Bridges on the Berkshire-Oxfordshire border. The Earl of Oxford's royalist army then arrived at these twin Thames bridges, only to find Pidnell Bridge had been sabotaged, and Radcot Bridge was guarded by Bolingbroke's troops. The Earl of Gloucester's men were closing in on the Earl of Oxford from the north. Many royalists turned and deserted when Bolingbroke's pikemen attacked. Oxford fled the battlefield and managed to escape, and the Lords Appellant gained control of the kingdom. Richard was now virtually a figurehead, and would have been replaced on the throne, but the lords could not agree who should replace him. This coup d'état culminated in the Merciless Parliament of 1388 in which King Richard's main allies were condemned. The Earls of Oxford, Suffolk and the Archbishop of York had escaped to France, and were condemned in their absence. Lesser supporters of Richard were hung, beheaded or exiled. It is difficult to know who Glyndŵr served with at Radcot. He owed his feudal obligation primarily to the King, rather than Arundel. Even if he had supported Bolingbroke, Glyndŵr's feelings about disloyalty may have been known to the Lancastrian. Whatever happened, somehow the two men became enemies. Different sources claim Glyndŵr fought for Arundel, Bolingbroke or the King.

In 1386-7 Glyndŵr served the Earl of Arundel in meeting the threat of a French invasion. In 1387 Glyndŵr fought at sea as an esquire in the retinue of Arundel, who led the expedition. There are three recorded entries featuring Owain. There are two for 1387, one from a retinue listing and the other from the muster roll; and one for 1388, from the muster roll. The muster roll for 1387 shows Owey'n Glyndou'dy esquire, 48th in the retinue, and the 8th squire listed of Richard Fitzalan, Earl of Arundel. In the 1387 retinue listing, Owain served in Arundel's retinue alongside his brother Tudor ap Gruffydd, who was named as Tudor de Glyndor and the 93rd listed squire, and his ally Goronwy ap Tudor listed as Grono ap Tudour and the ninety-fourth listed squire. The latter was captured and killed at the beginning of the

Glyndŵr War, in September 1400. The entry on the muster roll for 1388 shows Oweyn Glyndouerdy 33rd in the retinue and the 1st listed squire – however, crossed through, as it appears that he did not turn up for the Scottish expedition in that year.

1388 saw the Battle of Otterburn. Henry Percy (Hotspur) and the English were defeated by the Scots under the Earl of Douglas. Henry and Ralph Percy were captured (and later ransomed) but Douglas was killed. Douglas had a premonition of his death, recounted in the contemporary *Ballad of Otterburn*:

> Last night I dreamed a dreary dream,
> From beyond the Isle of Skye,
> I saw a dead man win a fight,
> And I think that man was I.

GLYNDŴR'S RETIREMENT

Owain's legal training and his Hanmer connections are shown by his appointment in 1387, as joint administrator of the Hanmer lands for the term of life of Sir David's widow, Angharad. He was also to handle the affairs of Sir David's sons. These duties were given to trustees, who then gave the responsibility to Glyndŵr. Around this time Glyndŵr seems to have semi-retired from military service to concentrate upon running his estates. However, when Richard II regained sovereign power in 1389, the Earl of Arundel fell from power (and was eventually executed in 1397) thus undermining Glyndŵr's own power base. Sir Gregory Sais's death in 1390 further weakened Glyndŵr's position.

In 1386, King Richard's uncle John of Gaunt had left England to try to gain the throne of Castile, but by 1387, Richard's misrule almost brought England to civil war. In 1389, John of Gaunt, Duke of Lancaster, had come back from Spain and helped Richard to rebuild his shattered power. John of Gaunt had acted as regent when the ten-year-old Richard II assumed the throne, and never allied with other nobles against him. (He was known as John of Gaunt, as he had been born in Ghent. His son Henry was known as Bolingbroke as he was born at Old Bolingbroke Castle, Lincolnshire.) Without John of Gaunt's return in 1389, Richard may well have died in the Tower of London.

With national stability secured, Richard began negotiating a permanent peace with France. However, the plan failed in 1393 because of the condition that the English King had to perform homage to the King of France. Instead, a 28-year truce was agreed upon in 1396. As part of the truce, Richard would marry Isabella, daughter of Charles VI. There were some misgivings about the marriage. The Princess was only six years old so was unlikely to produce an heir for many years. Meantime, the English lordships in Ireland were in danger of being over-run, and the Anglo-Irish lords pleaded for the King to intervene. In the autumn of 1394, Richard left for Ireland, where he remained until May 1395. Owain Glyndŵr probably was mustered to serve in this Irish campaign under Richard II. The expedition was a success, resulting in the submission of a number of Irish chieftains to English overlordship.

J.G. Bradley described Glyndŵr's one mansion at Glyndyfrdwy near Carrog:

This is locally known as "Glyndŵr's Mount", not because, as was probably the case at Sycharth, it was erected as a foundation for the chieftain's house, since this one here is evidently prehistoric, but merely from the fact that the house stood at its foot. Vague traces of it are still visible beneath the turf of the narrow meadow that lies squeezed in between the Holyhead Road on the upper side and the river and railroad on the lower side. Whether Sycharth was Owen's favourite home in peace or not, Glyndyfrdwy was most certainly his more natural headquarters in war ... A friend of the writer, who lived to an advanced age, was told in his youth by old men in the neighbourhood that they could remember when there was a good deal of stonework to be seen lying about. Now, however, there is little to mark the spot but the suggestive undulations of the turf ... The only surviving relic of that hero's residence is a long, narrow oaken table of prodigious thickness, which is yet treasured in a neighbouring farmhouse. A meadow below is still called "Parliament field", while the massive old stone homestead of Pen-y-bont, half a mile up the valley, contains a portion of the walls which formed, it is believed, Glyndŵr's stables.

However, the home at Glyndyfrdwy, the Valley of the Dee, at Carrog, was more of a hunting lodge than Owain's main residence at Sycharth. Glyndŵr's Mount is a motte adjacent to the main road (between Corwen and Llangollen) but below it in the meadows adjoining the river is the site of Glyndyfrdwy manor. Sycharth, in Cynllaith, was Owain's chief house, set on a motte, protected by moats, with nine guest rooms, resident minstrels and bards, fishponds, deer-park, chapel, bake-house, dovecot, vineyard, orchards, mill, wheat fields and peacocks. His income from his estates, around 300 marks (£200) a year, had enabled this faithful servant of the English Crown to settle down in 1398 with his wife Marged, and thirteen or more children. This grand house had many rooms and pillars, and a tiled roof, even boasting a chimney, a very modern feature for these times. His near neighbour, the bard Iolo Goch wrote of Sycharth as 'Llys barwn, lle syberwydd/Lle daw beirdd aml, lle da byd' (the court of a baron, a place of courtesy, where numerous bards come, a place of the good life). Sycharth was a plentiful estate, where Glyndŵr brewed his own chwisgi, and delighted in the beer from Shrewsbury. It was set in prosperous and fertile land, with many timbered buildings and nearby market towns. The bard Iolo Goch composed a poem after being invited to Sycharth, here translated by George Borrow:

Twice have I pledged my word to thee
To come thy noble face to see;
His promises let every man
Perform as far as e'er he can!
Full easy is the thing that's sweet,
And sweet this journey is and meet;
I've vowed to Owain's court to go,
And I'm resolved to keep my vow;
So thither straight I'll take my way

With blithesome heart, and there I'll stay,
Respect and honour, whilst I breathe,
To find his honoured roof beneath.
My chief of long lined ancestry
Can harbour sons of poesy;
I've heard, for so the muse has told,
He's kind and gentle to the old;
Yes, to his castle I will hie;
There's none to match it 'neath the sky:
It is a baron's stately court,
Where bards for sumptuous fare resort;
There dwells the lord of Powys land,
Who granteth every just demand.
Its likeness now I'll limn you out:
'Tis water girdled wide about;
It shows a wide and stately door
Reached by a bridge the water o'er;
'Tis formed of buildings coupled fair,
Coupled is every couple there;
Within a quadrate structure tall
Muster the merry pleasures all.
Conjointly are the angles bound –
No flaw in all the place is found.
Structures in contact meet the eye
Upon the hillock's top on high;
Into each other fastened they
The form of a hard knot display.
There dwells the chief we all extol
In timber house on lightsome knoll;
Upon four wooden columns proud
Mounteth his mansion to the cloud;
Each column's thick and firmly based,
And upon each a loft is placed;
In these four lofts, which coupled stand,
Repose at night the minstrel band;
Four lofts they were in pristine state,
But now partitioned form they eight.
Tiled is the roof, on each house-top ...
Each with nine wardrobes in its walls
With linen white as well supplied
As fairest shops of famed Cheapside.
Behold that church with cross upraised
And with its windows neatly glazed;

All houses are in this compressed -
An orchard's near it of the best,
Also a park where void of fear
Feed antlered herds of fallow deer.
A warren wide my chief can boast,
Of goodly steeds a countless host.
Meads where for hay the clover grows,
Corn-fields which hedges trim enclose,
Rise smoke-ejecting chimneys up.
All of one form there are nine halls
A mill a rushing brook upon,
And pigeon tower framed of stone;
A fish-pond deep and dark to see,
To cast nets in when need there be,
Which never yet was known to lack
A plenteous store of perch and jack.
Of various plumage birds abound;
Herons and peacocks haunt around,
What luxury doth his hall adorn,
Showing of cost a sovereign scorn;
His ale from Shrewsbury town he brings;
His usquebaugh is drink for kings;
Bragget he keeps, bread white of look,
And, bless the mark! a bustling cook.
His mansion is the minstrels' home,
You'll find them there whene'er you come
Of all her sex his wife's the best;
The household through her care is blest
She's scion of a knightly tree,
She's dignified, she's kind and free.
His bairns approach me, pair by pair,
O what a nest of chieftains fair!
Here difficult it is to catch
A sight of either bolt or latch;
The porter's place here none will fill;
Her largess shall be lavished still,
And ne'er shall thirst or hunger rude
In Sycharth venture to intrude.
A noble leader, Cambria's knight,
The lake possesses, his by right,
And midst that azure water placed,
The castle, by each pleasure graced.

Shakespeare painted Glyndŵr as a cultured, affable nobleman:

> In faith, he is a worthy gentleman,
> Exceedingly well read, and profited
> In strange concealments, valiant as a lion,
> And wondrous affable, and as bountiful
> As mines of India.

Unfortunately for Owain, this life of domestic contentment was to be disturbed by happenings in England. By 1397 Richard had become powerful enough to destroy the power of the Lords Appellant, with Glyndŵr's neighbour Arundel being executed, Oxford exiled and Gloucester murdered by smothering. At the Parliament of September 1397, Arundel was put on trial first, and after a heated quarrel with the King, he was condemned and executed. Warwick was also condemned to death, but his life was spared and he was instead exiled, as was Arundel's brother, Thomas Arundel, Archbishop of Canterbury. As the time came for Gloucester to be tried, the Earl of Nottingham brought news that he was dead. Gloucester had been Nottingham's prisoner at Calais, and it is probable that he was killed on Richard II's order, to avoid the disgrace of executing a Prince of the blood. Richard then carried out his revenge in the counties, prosecuting, fining and confiscating land from local men who had been loyal to the Lords Appellants.

A new faction now supported the King. These were men Richard could trust, lifted to positions of power, and mockingly called Richard's duketti. The loyalist Earls of Somerset, Rutland and Salisbury were rewarded with new lands and incomes. The King's half-brother and nephew were promoted from Earls of Huntington and Kent to become the Dukes of Exeter and Surrey. However, Richard made the ultimately tragic error of not punishing his cousin Henry Bolingbroke, as Bolingbroke's father was John of Gaunt, Duke of Lancaster. Without Lancaster, Richard would have probably been killed when previously imprisoned. Instead, Bolingbroke, Earl of Derby, was made Duke of Hereford.

THE CAPTURE OF RICHARD II

The House of Lancaster possessed greater wealth than any other family in England, and were of royal descent, so were among the candidates to succeed the childless Richard to the crown. Other claimants were the Percies of Northumberland and the Earl of March. A solution to one part of the problem occurred to Richard in December 1397. Henry Bolingbroke, Duke of Hereford and Thomas de Mowbray, Duke of Norfolk, violently quarrelled. According to Bolingbroke, Norfolk had claimed that the two, as former Lords Appellant, were soon to be punished by Richard. Norfolk strongly denied the charges, which amounted to treason. A parliamentary committee decided that the two should settle the matter by mortal combat. However, in early 1398, at the last possible moment Richard called off the battle and exiled the dukes instead. Norfolk was banished for life and Bolingbroke for ten years. Henry's son, Henry of Monmouth (later renowned as Prince

Hal) was summoned to court, and virtually held as a hostage to ensure his exiled father stayed out of the country. Another claimant to the crown also died in July 1398. Roger Mortimer, 4th Earl of March, 6th Earl of Ulster, Lord Lieutenant of Ireland and heir presumptive to the throne of England was ambushed and killed near Kells by an Irish clan. He left two very young sons. Suddenly Bolingbroke and his supporters could see the way open to his becoming king or regent, upon Richard's death

On 3 February 1399, John of Gaunt died. The Duke of Lancaster had been at the centre of English politics for over thirty years, and his death destabilised the nation. Instead of allowing Bolingbroke to succeed to his father's estates, Richard extended his ten-year exile to life, and had him disinherited of all lands, titles and possessions. Richard II now felt safe from Henry, who was residing in Paris, since the French had little interest in any challenge to Richard and his peace policy. Richard now left the country, feeling secure, in May 1399 for another expedition in Ireland. He took Henry Bolingbroke's young son as his hostage with him, and knighted him there. In June 1399, Louis, Duc d'Orleans gained control of the court of the 'mad' Charles VI. The policy of a long peace with Richard II did not suit Louis's political ambitions, so he allowed Henry to leave for England, obviously hoping that England would be weakened by fresh rebellion. With a small group of followers, Bolingbroke landed at Ravenspur in Yorkshire on the 4 July 1399. With him was Thomas Arundel, the exiled Archbishop of Canterbury (and brother of the executed Earl of Arundel).

Henry was met by supporters of his dead father, John of Gaunt. They were quickly joined by Bolingbroke's brother-in-law, Ralph Neville, Earl of Westmoreland, and Henry Percy, Earl of Northumberland, who had their own problems with Richard. Also present were Northumberland's son Henry 'Hotspur' Percy and Thomas Percy, Earl of Worcester. From Ravenspur their army travelled to Doncaster. Here, Northumberland compelled Bolingbroke to sign a solemn oath not to lay claim to the crown, but to be satisfied with the estates and titles of his father John of Gaunt, Duke of Lancaster. At this time Bolingbroke assured his supporters that he had no intention of taking the crown, just wishing to ensure that the realm was governed fairly. The King had taken most of his household knights and the loyal members of his nobility with him to Ireland, so Henry experienced little resistance as he moved south. A transcript from the metrical version of Chaplain William Peeris reads:

> The said Henry of Darby (Bolingbroke) after he was entered into the land
> At Doncaster in the White-friars was sworn on the sacrament,
> To the said seventh Henry, 1st Earl of Northumberland,
> And to the Lord Percy his eldest son, being there present,
> With his uncle the Earl of Worcester, that he would be content
> His own inheritance only to claim,
> Which was the dukedom of Lancaster which of right he would obtain;
> And not to usurp the crown upon his prince King Richard;
> And after he was perjured, and of his oath had no regard.

Landowners across England and Wales feared the confiscation of their lands, as had happened to the Lords Appellant, their supporters and Bolingbroke himself. Edmund Langley, Duke of York, who was acting as keeper of the realm, had little choice but to side with Bolingbroke. By 28 July the conspirators were in Bristol, arresting Richard's treasurer, William Scrope, Earl of Wiltshire. Meanwhile, Richard had been delayed in his return from Ireland, and did not land in Milford Haven, Wales until 24 July.

> When arrived at Carmarthen, he received a particular detail of Lancaster's amazing progress, the death of his favourites, the surrender of his forts, the revolt of his cities, and the defection of his subjects. His soldiers also, like the rest of their comrades, were so strongly infected with the prevalent opinion in favour of the duke of Lancaster, that his army melted away like snow before the sun; and Richard soon perceived he was in no condition to meet the enemy ... wavering and irresolute, he knew not whom to trust, nor whom to fear. At length he decided to take refuge in Wales.
> (Barnard 1783.)

He decided to head for the safety of Conwy Castle and there to take the first opportunity to escape to Ireland or France. Bolingbroke's hostage son Henry and his cousin, Humphrey of Gloucester, had been left in Ireland in safe custody in the castle of Trim. Richard II complained to Henry of his father's treachery, but accepted the boy's assurances of his own innocence. Henry joined his father at London towards the end of September.

With only part of his army, Richard found little support in Wales. He made his way to Conwy Castle, awaiting support from London or a ship to flee until the time was opportune to return. However, his bodyguard melted away as the size of Bolingbroke's support became clear, and Richard was left with a small retinue, some say including Owain Glyndŵr. Henry Bolingbroke had arrived with his forces at Chester, Cheshire being the centre of Richard's support, to stop men flocking to join Richard. Matters now become unclear, as information discrediting Bolingbroke would have been destroyed. Richard II sent his half-brother and his nephew, John and Thomas Holland, the Dukes of Exeter and Surrey, to discuss terms with Henry, and they were imprisoned. It seems that Bolingbroke next sent the Henry Percy, Earl of Northumberland and Archbishop Thomas Arundel, to negotiate with Richard II at Conwy Castle on 12 August. Northumberland and Arundel swore on oath that Richard would receive safe conduct, under the authority of Bolingbroke. Thus Richard was encouraged to leave the castle for negotiations at Flint. About five miles away, at Penmaenhead, Richard's small band was ambushed by Northumberland's men and taken to Flint Castle to meet Bolingbroke on 19 August. It appears that Northumberland expected that a peaceful settlement would be made, as in the past, with Richard giving concessions to the barons.

Richard's cousin the Duke of Aumerle, and his Royal Steward, Sir Thomas Percy seized Richard's baggage train, containing the royal regalia, ' ... pure silver, many a good horse of foreign breed, many a rich and sparkling precious stone, many a good mantle and whole ermine, good cloth of gold and stuff of foreign makes.' However, '... the Welsh who saw their treason, opposed them here and there in companies of one or two thousand, saying, "Wretched traitors, you shall advance no further this way and shall surrender all the stolen jewels you are carrying away, for the king has not given them to you . . ." thus were the English robbed by the Welsh. They kept back all the wagons and the harnesses, gold and silver and jewellery set in gold.' This was a hammer-blow to the relatively impoverished Bolingbroke, who spent years trying to recover most of it. As late as 1408, Meredith Powys of Clun was fined twelve pence for stealing a gown and doublet. Whether Glyndŵr was involved in this action is unknown.

Bolingbroke and the rest of the traitors next took the King to the Tower of London, disguised as a friar on the journey from Flint. Glyndŵr must have reflected upon how these events would impact on him. The King was imprisoned in the Tower of London on 1 September, Arundel dead, and Bolingbroke in power. (Arundel's estate pushed between Owain's two estates at Glyndyfrdwy near Corwen and at Cynllaith Owain near Oswestry.) Glyndŵr had been a loyal supporter of Arundel and was known to Richard II, Bolingbroke, the Archbishop of Canterbury and the Percies of Northumberland. Around this time Reginald de Grey, a friend of Henry IV, began occupying some of Glyndŵr's lands.

Henry had decided to take the crown, and argued that Richard, through his misgovernment, had rendered himself unworthy of being king. However, Henry was not next in the line to the throne. The heir presumptive was the young Edmund Mortimer, Earl of March, who descended from Edward III's second son, Lionel of Antwerp. Bolingbroke's father, John of Gaunt, was Edward's third son. The official account claims that Richard 'voluntarily' agreed to resign his crown to Henry on 29 September:

> In the name of God Amen! I Richard by the Grace of God King of England and of France and Lord of Ireland, quit and absolve archbishops, bishops, marquises, lords and all my other liegemen both spiritual and secular from their oath of homage. I resign my Kingly Majesty, Dignity and Crown ... and with deed and word I leave off and resign him and go from him for evermore ...

This document had been carefully drafted, containing admissions by Richard that he was unworthy to be king. After signing it, Richard was not seen again. Parliament met on 30 September, and accepted Richard's resignation.

> The Parliament took care not to examine his (Henry's) claim too closely, and therefore, without any regard to the earl of Marche, it was decreed, that Henry, duke of Lancaster, should be proclaimed king of England and France, and lord of Ireland.
> (Barnard.)

THE CORONATION OF THE USURPER HENRY BOLINGBROKE 13 OCTOBER 1399

Henry's coronation was the first time since the Norman Conquest that the monarch made an address in English. There were several bad omens during the ceremony. Henry's head, when being anointed, was swarming with lice, and he dropped the gold noble he was supposed to give to the offertory. It rolled away and was lost. Reginald de Grey, Lord of

Rhuthun, carried Henry's golden spurs which were buckled over Henry's velvet slippers, and had the right of taking away all the coronation table cloths and linen. Reginald de Grey had bought estates in Duffryn Clwyd in 1188, making him a neighbour of Glyndŵr, and after Arundel was executed had begun trying to take Glyndŵr's lands. Grey was a former Governor of Ireland, a peer in Parliament, a member of the King's Council and officiated at Henry IV's coronation. He had influence with the King and parliament – Glyndŵr had little of either.

Henry IV had become the first King of the House of Lancaster, who gained the crown through his leadership of the great nobles, not through succession. According to the King in Shakespeare's *King Richard II,* 'every stride he (Bolingbroke) makes upon my land/Is dangerous treason; he is come to ope/The purple testament of bleeding war...' Despite the backing of Parliament, Henry's dubious right to rule left him with deep insecurities, and sowed the seeds for the Yorkist-Lancaster Wars of the Roses from 1455 to 1487.

Soon after his accession, Henry IV tried to seek the goodwill of his Percy kinsmen in the north by giving them new honours. Indeed, his first signature as King was attached to a charter making Henry Percy, Earl of Northumberland his Lord High Constable, and he quickly also granted the Percies the Isle of Man. Henry 'Hotspur' Percy was granted the Wardenship of the Eastern Marches and the Justiciaryship of North Wales, and also named Governor or Constable of Berwick, Roxburgh, Bamburgh, Chester, Caernarfon and Flint. The first positive action of the new King was to take the seven-year-old Edmund Mortimer, Earl of March, and his younger brother from their safety at Wigmore Castle on the Welsh Borders, to the royal stronghold at Windsor Castle. The true heirs to the crown were thus in Henry's hands.

CHAPTER 3

Glyndŵr Falls Out of Favour with the New English King 1399

THE EPIPHANY RISING 1399-1400

Some of Richard's followers had their estates confiscated, and around Christmas 1399 a plot was hatched by the Earls of Salisbury, Huntingdon, Kent, Rutland, Baron Lumley and Baron Despenser (formerly the Earl of Gloucester). Thomas Despenser, Lord of Glamorgan, had previously tried to raise an army in Glamorgan to join Richard II after he landed in Pembroke, but men refused to join him. As a result he was imprisoned for a short time by the new King and his earldom was withdrawn. The dissatisfied nobles planned a Twelfth Night celebration in Henry's honour, at a tournament in Windsor where he would be assassinated, to restore Richard II. Henry IV and his son Prince Henry and others of the royal household were suffering from an illness which was attributed to poison, and they were still ailing when, early in January 1400, the conspiracy was discovered.

The plotters had taken Windsor Castle, but because they had been betrayed Henry did not ride to Windsor, and began to raise an army in London. The King committed his sons to the keeping of the mayor and citizens of London, but the danger was soon over. When they saw Henry's army of 20,000 men, the plotters fled westwards and tried to raise support. Lumley was beheaded after trying to seize Cirencester, where Salisbury and Kent were captured. They were also beheaded, without trial, on 7 January. Despenser escaped from Cirencester but was taken at Bristol, trying to take a ship for France, and beheaded without trial on 13 January, while Huntingdon was captured at Pleshey and likewise executed. Despenser's possessions were confiscated, but his wife Constance was granted for life the greater part of his lands, as she was a relative of Henry IV. She returns in our story as her castles in Glamorgan, such as the great Caerffili, were attacked by Glyndŵr in 1402, and because she herself later plotted against Henry IV.

TROUBLE IN CHESTER

The new King was now very nervous of past supporters of Richard, which did not seem to help Glyndŵr's case for justice against Lord Grey. The Welsh and the men of Cheshire were also always linked with Richard's strongest supporters. There was unrest in the garrison city of Chester, where Richard II's favoured regiment of archers was based. It was also full of outlaws and criminals, who had gained immunity from prosecution in return for making a plea of loyalty (an advowson) to the Earl of Chester. In this manner, the earl could always get 'volunteers' for his attacks on Wales. Henry sent his army to Cuddington, just outside Chester where it camped. Peirs Leigh, the Captain of the Chester archers, was recognised and taken as he travelled dressed as a monk, to reconnoitre the King's strength. He was immediately beheaded. On 10 January, the mob in Chester attacked its castle. Its Chamberlain, Bishop Trefor, was asked to hand over the keys but refused. The mob captured the Eastgate and took down the displayed head of Peirs Leigh, marching with it around the town, trying to gain supporters. After a week of hostilities, Bishop Trefor managed to restore order.

THE MURDER OF RICHARD II

The Duke of Gloucester had been a leader of the Lords Appellant, enemies of Richard II in the successful rebellion of 1388. When Richard managed to break their power in 1397, the Duke was imprisoned in Calais, but murdered (probably smothered) in gaol before his trial for treason. The Duke was Bolingbroke's uncle. This act had dramatically increased Richard's unpopularity amongst his nobles. (Thomas Despenser soon after killed Gloucester's son and heir.) According to Froissart, Richard II saw the murderers of Gloucester being killed, from his cell, and thus despairingly knew he would never be allowed freedom.

The Earl of Northumberland had asked how Richard should be treated, as Henry was 'resolved to spare his life' and the Lords decided unanimously that he should be kept under guard in a secure place. From the Tower, Richard was taken to Pontefract Castle, disguised as a friar, shortly before the end of 1399. The Epiphany Plot had highlighted the danger of allowing Richard to live. Early in February, the Privy Council decreed that if Richard II was still alive, he should be brought to 'a secure place', and if he was dead, his body should be shown to the people. Henry IV was unnerved by the earls' revolt and the happenings in Chester, and by 14 February, Richard II was dead in Pontefract Castle, either starved or smothered. He left no issue. One account tells us that Sir Piers Exton and eight guards bludgeoned Richard to death. Rumours persisted into the reign of Henry V that Richard was alive, however, serving as a focus for discontent against the new Lancastrian dynasty. The dead King's body was displayed in the old St Paul's Cathedral on 2 February 1400, and he was buried in Kings Langley Church on 6 March. (Henry V, to silence the rumours of Richard's survival, decided to have the body moved to Westminster Abbey in 1413, buried next to his first wife Anne).

GLYNDŴR'S DISPUTE WITH LORD GREY

In 1397, the Lord of Glyndŵr and his wife had been granted the services of a confessor 'in the hour of death' (reported in the registers of Pope Boniface IX). In 1399, Glyndŵr's estates brought in about 300 marks a year, with retainers and servants enabling a luxurious lifestyle. (300 marks, in terms of relative earnings, would be around £1.1 million pounds today.) Suddenly, in 1399, everything began to go wrong. Glyndŵr and many of his followers came from the Welsh uchelwyr, the high men or nobility, equivalent to the English squirearchy. They had generally adapted loyalty to the crown and its marcher barons, in return for settled tenancies of their hereditary estates. However, they were suffering heavy taxation, often discriminated against legally, and were always aware that their lands, theirs by right, had been taken from them by power. They knew of the creeping takeover of Wales since the Normans came, and its acceleration since the death of Llewelyn II. They also knew, from the long history of conflict with their neighbour, that they could not trust the Norman-French-English any more than the Saxons. There was a sense of 'this far, and no further' amongst the uchelwyr. Any further attempts to move them out of their lands would meet resistance.

The *Annales Henrici quarti* (written in St Albans) claimed that the Glyndŵr war was instigated by a long-running territorial dispute, which Parliament failed to redress, between the Lord of Dyffryn Clwyd 'Reynold Grey', and Glyndŵr, over lands which Glyndŵr owned called Croesau (Crosses) in the parish of Bryneglwys. Under Richard II the case had been found in favour of Glyndŵr, but on the usurpation of Bolingbroke Lord Grey again seized land at Derwen, south of Ruthin. Glyndŵr responded, registering his grievances with Parliament several times in 1399.

In 1400 a bandit named Gruffydd ap Dafydd ap Gruffydd was operating on Glyndŵr's lands at Glyndfrdwy. Bishop Trefor of St Asaf tried to lure him away with an offer of becoming master forester or bailiff on the nearby estates of the Earl of Arundel at Chirk. Gruffydd agreed to negotiate under a safe conduct in Oswestry, under the terms that he could not be arrested 'in Chirkland'. However, he was warned that he would be lured outside Chirkland and taken as a thief. The two men accompanying him stole horses from Lord Grey's park, and they managed to escape the trap. Gruffydd hid on Grey's estate at Duffryn Clwyd, carrying on robbing horses and supplies, and sheltered by Grey's Welsh tenants. Gruffydd wrote to Grey, letting him know that he would retaliate if any of Grey's tenants were hurt for aiding him. Grey responded threatening him with hanging, his letter ending:

> But we hope we shall do you a privy thing
> A rope, a ladder and a ring
> High on the gallows for to swing
> And this shall be your ending
> And He that made thee be there to helping
> And we on our behalf shall be well willing
> For thy letter is knowledging.

Details of the correspondence are in Hingeston, and interestingly Gruffydd ap Dafydd states that he is under the protection of Maredudd ab Owain, one of Glyndŵr's sons. After answering the letter, on 23 June 1400 Grey wrote to the Prince of Wales stating that he had received the Privy Seal and letters asking him to 'appease the misgovernance and the riot which is herein begun in North Wales' but asking for a 'more plainer commission than I have yet.' Grey sent copies of the letters to Prince Henry at Chester Castle, warning him that the King's officers in North Wales were 'kin to these rebels' and asking for strong action. This implicated Glyndŵr as the relevant most blameworthy King's officer, in fact a 'tenant-in-capite' to the King for the estates where Gruffydd had been active.

Parliament should have discussed Glyndŵr's case against Grey in the spring of 1400, but his case was not deemed important enough to be granted a hearing. Bishop John Trefor of St Asaf had been Richard II's ambassador to Scotland, and pleaded that it could be unwise to provoke a man as well-regarded as Glyndŵr, provoking the response 'Se de illis scurri nudipedibus non curare?' ('What care we for barefoot Welsh curs?' – 'scurri' has been translated as 'clowns' but seems to either mean 'rabble' or be cod-Latin for 'curs' or dogs.) Instead it was asked of Glyndŵr that he grant Lord Grey further concessions. Glyndŵr left London, fuming at the injustice of Parliament. Trefor was also Chamberlain of the Principality of Cheshire, so seemed to know how dangerous it could be to spurn Glyndŵr.

The *Vita Ricardi secundi* and a fifteenth-century Welsh tract also tell of the withholding by Grey of a summons to a general muster addressed by the King to Glydwr. Reginald de Grey was responsible for issuing and enforcing royal demands in the Northern March. Lord Grey commanded the general muster to fight for Henry IV in Scotland in 1400. Local barons were told to take a certain number of armed men each. However, Grey also delayed summoning Glyndŵr's levy of men for service in Scotland until the last moment, making it impossible for Glyndŵr to respond as requested, or even send an explanation for his absence. Refusal or failure to respond to an order of the King was deemed treason, so Glyndŵr's estates would be forfeit until he could prove his loyalty or receive due punishment. The King's forces returned from Scotland in September 1400, having met with little success. Talbot and Grey were now told to bring Glyndŵr to justice.

Grey invited Glyndŵr to a reconciliation meeting, by letter carried by friars. He realised that Glyndŵr would not trust him after the Gruffydd ap Dafydd affair, so the meeting was arranged at Glyndŵr's court at Glyndyfrdwy, on condition that Grey only brought thirty armed followers. Grey set off, but another heavily armed party of horsemen followed him later, dispersing into the woodlands around the manor. Glyndŵr met Grey, but the bard Iolo Goch noticed these horsemen crossing the water meadows heading to the manor. He communicated this in an englyn that bemoaned the death of Prince Dafydd, the brother of Llywelyn the Last. The verse recounted Dafydd's heart jumping out of the funeral flames and blinding his executioner. Glyndŵr realised the problem, made an excuse to the non-Welsh-speaking Grey and left the negotiations room. The oncoming men-at-arms soon attacked the house but Glyndŵr had escaped into the hills. Adam of Usk gives the date of this attempt at entrapment as 21 September 1400, but it must have been shortly before 16 September.

Owen Rhoscomyl states that Earl Talbot from Chirk was also involved in the entrapment scheme and arrived with a large force, attempting to surround Glyndŵr and clearly showing his intent. Glyndŵr escaped with his life and went into hiding, confirming himself a traitor in English eyes. Glyndŵr now decided that there was no justice from the English crown and his life would be permanently in danger from Grey of Ruthin. On 16 September, Glyndŵr Day, he raised the flag of war. King Henry soon confiscated Glyndŵr's estates, and granted them to John Beaufort, Earl of Somerset, Henry's illegitimate half-brother in 1400. (In 1404 Beaufort became Constable of England, dying in 1410 before he could ever effectively control Glyndŵr's lands.)

The harsh taxation policies, pursued by the crown and by marcher regimes in Wales, had caused opposition from both tenants and local officials. There were few opportunities for professional advancement available to Welsh laymen and churchmen, and growing resentment of more privileged English settlers, especially those in the towns of the crown lands and the marcher lordships of north-east Wales. All this helped to fuel a broader support for Glyndŵr, as well as the deposition of Richard II.

The laws of the early part of this reign were not conciliatory towards the Welsh. By stat. 2 Hen. IV. Jan. 1401, no person born in Wales of Welsh parentage could purchase land or tenement in or near the cities in the Marches of Wales: he could not henceforth receive the freedom of any city or borough. All Welsh citizens were to produce security for their conduct: they were not to be admitted to any municipal office, nor to wear armour in their town or borough. (Stat. Realm, ii. 124.) No Welshman might purchase land in England, &c. (129.) By stat. 4 Hen. IV., Sept. 30, 1402, Englishmen could not be tried by a Welsh jury in Wales; minstrels, rhymers, wasters, and other vagabonds, were condemned; meetings were not allowed; no Welshman might carry arms: Welshmen were not to have castles; the fortresses were to be manned by English; even Englishmen married to Welshwomen were prohibited from bearing office in Wales or the Marche.

(J.S. Davies, ed. *An English Chronicle* ... Written before the year 1471.)

CHAPTER 4

Rebellion of Glyndŵr,
the War Begins 1400

There was massive resentment and discontent across Wales ... 'Such parts as they (the English conquerors) left to ye ancient inhabitants of ye country to possess, being for ye most part ye barrenest soils, was permitted by some lords to be holden by ye old Welsh custom. The same account tells us how 'in the second year of Henry IV it was ordained the Lords of the Marches of Wales should send sufficient stuffing and ward in their castles to the intent that no loss, riot, or danger should come to ye King or to his realm by their tenants or other Welshman.' (*Description of the Dominion of Wales* Harleian mss141). Welshmen were prohibited by law from buying land or holding office in any English town or borough. The spirit and effect of these laws is summed up in Powel's *Cambria*:

> These laws were not ordained for their reformation but of mere purpose to work their bitter ruin and destruction. Which doth evidently appear in that they were forbidden to keep their children at learning, or to put them to be apprentices to any occupation in any town or borough of this realm. Let any indifferent man therefore judge and consider whether this extremity of law, where justice itself is mere injury and cruelty, be not a cause and matter sufficient to withdraw any people from civility to barbarism.

In early 1400, Henry IV and Henry 'Hotspur' Percy invaded Scotland to try and force the King to declare his allegiance to England. This was the expedition that Glyndŵr had missed. They took Edinburgh but failed to take Edinburgh Castle, which was defended by Archibald the Grim, Earl of Douglas and Prince David, Duke of Rothesay. The sieges of Edinburgh and Dalhousie castles were quickly abandoned when reports came that Owain Glyndŵr had revolted against England. In Davies' *An English Chronicle* we read:

> 1400 The second year of his reign, he (Henry IV) went in to Scotland, but the Scots would not meet with him; and there the earl of Dunbar became his man, and the king gave him the Count of Richmond. This same year was held a parliament at Westminster, and thither came Oweyn of Glendore, a Walshman, that was sometime a squire of the earls of Arundel; complaining how that

the lord Gray of Ruthynne had taken from him wrongfully a part of his land; but he might have no remedy. And the Bishop of Saint Assaphe of Walis counselled the lords of the parliament that they should not mistreat the said Oweyn, lest he made the Walshmen arise; and they answered and said they set nought to him.

This same year the Walshmenne began to rebel against king Harri, and also a debate began between the lord Gray Ruthyn and the forsaid Oweyne of Glendore and the Walshmen destroyed the king's towns and lordships in Walis, and robbed the kyng's people both English and Walshe; and this endureth xiv years. And the king went in to Walis with a great power, but he might not take Oweyn that was chief captain of the Walshmenne, nor spared that he came for ; and returned home again. And the lord Gray undertook for to keep the country, and soon after the said Oweyne took the said lord Gray prisoner; and he was ransomed for prisoners of the Marche. And at last Oweyn made the said lord Gray wed one of his daughters, and kept him there with his wife, and soon after he died. This same year was so great a dearth of corn, and so great scarcity, that a quarter of wheat was sold for xvi pounds.

Giraldus Cambrensis had written two centuries previously: 'The English fight for power; the Welsh for liberty; the one to procure gain, the other to avoid loss. The English hirelings for money; the Welsh patriots for their country.'

Whether Glyndŵr had been planning his war for a long time is still unsure, but certainly the deposition of Richard II, extreme laws against the Welsh, his treatment by Grey and the English Parliament, English plots against Henry and Henry's movement to Scotland seem to have pushed Owain towards setting up his standard:

It is possible that he had long intended to raise the people and strike for freedom. In fact, there is an entry in history which makes one almost sure of it, for in the summer of the same year, 1400, a certain Meredydd ap Owen, of Merioneth was planning to bring an army of Scots from the Hebrides, to land at Abermaw (Barmouth) and open a war. Now the only man, of consequence bearing that name at that date was Meredydd the son of Owen Glyndŵr himself.
(Owen Rhoscomyl, *Flamebearers of Welsh History*,1905.)

RAISING THE STANDARD AT CAERDREWYN
SEPTEMBER 1400

The unsettled state of the English government encouraged Owen Glendour, a descendant of the ancient prince of Wales, and obnoxious to the present ruling power, on account of his attachment to the late king, to set up his standard in opposition to Henry, His mind was that of a hero, his heart that of a patriot, ready to burst with indignation at the miseries of his country. His genious was enterprising, his conduct firm but cautious ...
(Barnard 1783.)

On 16 September, having escaped from Grey's trap, Glyndŵr was proclaimed as Prince of Wales at Llys Glyndyfrdwy, his court at Carrog, and began the war of independence.

The standard then raised was probably the Black Lion Rampant of Powys, rather than the Golden Dragon he later adopted at Caernarfon. The height of Caerdrewyn was chosen symbolically, on Glyndŵr's ancestral lands, overlooking Corwen. Also known as Mynydd y Gaer, it is the site of an Iron Age hill fort, the old camp of Edeyrn Edeyrnion. In 1165, the Princes of Gwynedd, Powys and Deheubarth had rallied with a great Welsh army to halt a massive invasion mobilized by Henry II.

Caerdrewyn thus represented not only the unity of Wales, but the retreat of a royal expedition out of Wales. Glyndŵr's brother Tudur and son Gruffydd attended, along with the Sycharth poet and Owain's personal priest Crach y Ffynnant. Glyndŵr's wife's brothers, Philip and Griffith Hanmer, were there along with his sister's husband, Robert Puleston. The Dean of St Asaf, Hywel Kyffin (or Gyffin), attended with his nephews Ieuan Fychan and Gruffydd ap Ieuan. Madog ab Evan (Ieuan) ap Madog from Eyton, Ieuan ap Hywel Pickhill and John Astwick were also there. Bards recounted the news across Wales, and up to 250 men gathered quickly to support Owain against the English. From Court Rolls we see that eleven men came from Grey's stronghold at Rhuthun, and 111 came from Grey's lands at Duffryn Clwyd, which were tenanted by the Lord of Brynlluarth. These 111 men styled themselves Cewri Cadfan, the giants (heroes) of Cadfan, referring to a past ruler of the Vale of Clwyd. Ten local landowners joined, including Sir Hywel ab Einion ab Hywel, eighty-one men came from the Mortimer estates in Denbigh, eleven from Glyndyfrdwy, nine from Ial (Yale), six from Edeyrnion, two from Corwen and two from Bala.

It is believed that not only the place of the declaration of war was chosen deliberately and symbolically, but also the date of 16 September. This was the birth-date of the English Prince of Wales (Prince Hal, later Henry V) at Monmouth in 1387, not 9 August as recorded by some chroniclers. It also was said to be the birthday (and later the death day) of Glyndŵr himself. On hearing of the rising, the Commons enacted legislation banning the bards and their poetry, similar to that carried out after the murder of Prince Llywelyn in 1282. Because news was carried (and memorised) by travelling bards to the people, Parliament wanted to suppress 'wasters and rhymers, minstrels or vagabonds ... for to make commorthas or gatherings upon the common people, whom by their divinations, dreams and excitations, they draw into the Welsh insurrection and rebellion.' (A cymorth is a collection of goods or money in this context, cymmortha being the plural.)

Owain Glyndŵr was a Merioneth man, and it was in Merioneth, at Caer Drewyn, that the Red Dragon, the standard of national revolt, was unfurled in the year 1401. (This should be 1400.) In June of that year the famous Hotspur, who was Governor of North Wales for the King, paid a flying visit to Dolgelley with a movable column, probably invited by Hywel Sele of Nannau, who, like many other landlords, disliked the peasant revolt at the head of which Glyndŵr stood. Dolgelley was in the heart of a country devoted to Glyndŵr, and Hotspur hoped to crush the national cause by a single blow at its very centre. A battle was fought outside Dolgelley between Hotspur's column, in which the Earl of Arundel took part, and some of Glyndŵr's adherents on the 4th June, and Hotspur sent a flamboyant report of how he had crushed his foe. The boast, however, was an empty one; for the encounter was followed by Hotspur's precipitate retreat to Denbigh, where, soon after, pleading lack

of support, he resigned all his offices, and deserted the King's cause.
(Dolgellau and Llaneltud: The Story of Two Parishes TP Ellis 1923.)

THE BURNING OF RHUTHUN & BORDER TOWNS
18-24 SEPTEMBER 1400

In English known as Ruthin, its original name was Castell Coch yng Ngwernfôr (red castle in the sea-marsh). Rhuthun Castle is built on a red sandstone ridge 100 ft above the Clwyd valley, overlooking a strategic river crossing. Formerly owned by Prince Dafydd ap Gruffydd (drawn and quartered by Edward I in 1283), it was then given to an earlier Lord Reginald Grey. Grey used the famous military architect Master James of St George (who built Edward I's Iron Ring of castles) to strengthen and extend the castle. He gave it a twin-towered gatehouse and six round towers, the northern tower incorporating a smaller Welsh one. The walls were 7-9 ft thick, and rose to 100 ft above the bottom of the moat. The castle was not to be easily taken, but its bastide, or settled town, was now in danger from the vengeful Glyndŵr. He wanted the Grey family to suffer, and could deal it an economic blow by cutting off its rentals and fees at source. The burning of Lord Grey's Ruthin was the signal for the rising to start. The chamberlain of Caernarfon saw local people selling their cattle in order to buy horses and war equipments. 'Some of hem stelleth horse,' he wrote to the King, 'and some of hem robbeth hors, and purveyen hem of sadles, bowes, arrowes, and other harnys.'

A Shropshire jury, sworn on 25 October 1400, stated that an assembly of men, including Glyndŵr's brother, his son Gruffydd, his Hanmer and Puleston brothers-in-law, Hywel Cyffin, dean of St Asaph, and Crach y Ffinnant, described as their prophet (eorum propheta), and many other Welshmen, had gathered at Glyndyfrdwy on 16 September, intending the death and dis-inheritance of Henry, King of England, and the Prince of Wales, and the obliteration of the English language. They had 'elevated ... Owain as their Prince' and had proceeded 'in warlike fashion like enemies' to the town of Rhuthun which they had plundered and burned, thence turning to attack the 'English towns' of Denbigh, Rhuddlan, Flint, Hawarden, Holt, Oswestry, and Welshpool which were also plundered and despoiled. (For his part in the rebellion, Robert Puleston's estates at Emral and in Shropshire and Cheshire were confiscated by Henry IV, but the King soon pardoned Robert and eventually restored his estates to him. In 1403, Robert was commissioned by the Prince of Wales to 'receive into his grace' all the rebels the Maelor (the area of Flintshire in which Emral was located.)

Glyndŵr's followers burnt down Oswestry and Handbridge, Chester, so frequently that they became known as Burnttowns. The Lordship's court records testify that the attack was launched on 18 September, the Saturday preceding Rhuthun's St Matthew Fair, and that some 270 men were involved of whom the largest number were drawn from surrounding Welsh lordships, notably the lordship of Denbigh. Welshmen were not allowed to live within the town walls of Rhuthun, and it was hit as it was preparing for market day. The small Welsh force marched 10 miles from Owain's mansion at Glyndyfrdwy, and waited overnight in the forest of Coedmarchan, waiting for the town gates to open. Glyndŵr's men were not properly armed – some had only homemade spears and farm sickles. Other followers were mainly archers, and few would have had swords. Rhuthun was burnt to the ground, reputedly leaving only the castle and a few other buildings standing. Cattle awaiting market were driven off, horses taken and there were no casualties. The damage was assessed at £1,400 (£570,000 today using the Retail Price Index, but £7.5 million using Average Earnings). However, fourteen Welshmen were later rounded up and executed.

Encouraged by their success, Glyndŵr's band burned the other Anglo-Norman boroughs of Denbigh, Flint, Rhuddlan and Hawarden. Then the force moved quickly on to Holt, Oswestry and Welshpool. Near Flint, an English relieving force headed by Sir John Massy, Constable of Conwy, was beaten back. Oswestry was so badly damaged on 22 September that large parts had to be rebuilt. The final target was Welshpool, but from 23 September, after ravaging Welshpool, Glyndŵr's army melted back into the hills with their loot. He had damaged Grey's lands and possessions, without ever losing men needlessly trying to take the castles.

Supposedly on 24 September, Glyndŵr's men were defeated by Hugh Burnell of Shropshire near Welshpool, or on the banks of the River Vyrnwy or the River Severn. Glyndŵr was said to have stopped at Oswestry, allowing Sheriff Burnell to send for levies to Stafford and Warwick to support his men. However, this seems unlikely – Glyndŵr would not want a pitched battle, with poorly armed supporters. Owain Glyndŵr and plant Owain (Owain's children) had other ideas and had headed for the Welsh hills. Perhaps Burnell sent a column to follow them, and captured some stragglers. These guerrilla warfare tactics were to prove to be the making of the campaign, and the English would usually invade only to find that Glyndŵr could not be found. Glyndŵr's local war with Lord Grey in north-east Wales was to become a full-scale war, threatening Henry IV's tenure as the new King of England. This year, according to Adam of Usk, brought another ill omen to Henry's rule:

> In this year, that is, in the year of our Lord 1400, a great plague prevailed through all England, and specially among the young, swift in its attack and carrying off many souls. Then died my lord John of Usk, Abbot of Chertsey, together with thirteen monks ... I was with him in his last moments, and I had his blessing, wherein I rejoice, in these words ...

FIRST ROYAL EXPEDITION INTO WALES 1400

Henry IV had sensed the importance of the revolt, racing back from his Scottish invasion. He mustered an army, and arrived in Shrewsbury on 26 September. One report is that he was alerted in Scotland that the mighty Caerffili Castle in South Wales was besieged. Glyndŵr must have known that forces were being mustered against him, so his retreat to the hills, rather than a pitched battle against Burnell and border levies, makes sense. Glyndŵr had few supporters and almost no armoury. His men were on light Welsh horses, suitable for rough terrain and carrying archers, but of no use in a pitched battle against heavily armoured men-at-arms, squires and knights on great horses. Henry had levied troops from ten counties, marching through Coventry and Lichfield, and in Shrewsbury locked up any Welshmen who would not give securities against disloyalty.

The new King left Shrewsbury with a great army on 28 September. We know that by early October he reached Bangor in north-west Wales, threatening the Anglesey lands of the Tudurs of Penmynydd (near Llangefni in the island's centre). Rhys ap Tudur and his brother Gwilym were the most powerful nobles in north-west Wales, who, being cousins of Glyndŵr, had expressed support for the revolt. They were no friends of Henry IV of Lancaster. Ancestors of the English Tudor dynasty, they had previously served King Richard II in Ireland before Richard's crown had been usurped by Henry.

Without trial, Henry took eight Welshmen and executed them as an example on 28 September. Among them, he hanged Goronwy (Gronw) ap Tudur of Anglesey. He was said to have taken part in the opening attack of the rebellion at Ruthin, and was hung, drawn and quartered and the four quarters of his body were later sent to Bristol, Ludlow, Hereford and Chester as a warning to the Welsh. It looked as if all fighting had stopped, but either Rhys Tudur or Rhys Ddu attacked Henry's army near Beaumaris Castle at Rhos Fawr. Henry was forced to flee into Beaumaris Castle for safety until his main army crossed the Menai Straits into Anglesey. According to Walsingham, Henry fought Rhys Ddu (the Black) of Erddreiniog at Beaumaris, returning via Bangor to Shrewsbury on 15 October. In reprisal, Henry and his son Prince Hal sacked and burned the Franciscan house at Llanfaes, capturing and killing friars there and elsewhere. The Royal Expedition sacked Bangor, and looted its way across North Wales, down to Harlech, returning via Mawddwy. The abbots of Bardsey Island, Maenan Abbey (near Llanrwst), Cymer Abbey and possibly Bangor went to the King and pledged allegiance, along with the Rector of Llanllechid. While Henry was busy ploughing through north-west Wales, Glyndŵr's followers were raiding English border settlements in the north-east once more.

PARDONS OFFERED OCTOBER 1400

The general population of North Wales submitted to the English but the Tudurs' guerrilla forces had harassed Henry's army, and he returned to Shrewsbury by 15 October with little to show for his efforts. Offers of pardon were made to rebels over a wide area of North Wales including the lordship of Ellesmere (where Glyndŵr's father had once acted as keeper) and the lordship of Whittington, both in Shropshire. At Shrewsbury, Henry from 23 October repeatedly offered pardons to everyone involved in the uprising except Glyndŵr and Rhys and Gwilym ap Tudur. The priest Crach Ffynnant, Glyndŵr's brother Tudur and Owain's teenage son Gruffydd accepted the pardons.

To pardon Glyndŵr would bring disgrace to Henry's friend and Privy Councillor Lord Grey, so Glyndŵr's lands in North and South Wales were declared forfeit on 8 November 1400, together with those of his kinsmen, and given to John Beaufort, Earl of Somerset (Henry's bastard brother). The estates of Gruffydd Hanmer and Philip Hanmer were given to John Hanmer. To stabilise the situation in the south, there was an order that 'the

King's lieges in South Wales should be allowed none the less to come and go into England provided they were of good behaviour.' If Glyndŵr had been allowed the return of his properties, perhaps Welsh nationalism may have died out, not allowing the Tudors to take the English crown three generations later. Owain was not betrayed, but made himself a base in Snowdonia at Llanberis, controlling access from Dolbadarn Castle. Adam of Usk says that Owain took just seven companions with him to the mountains of Snowdonia. In *The Chronicle of Adam of Usk*, Adam describes the events of 1400:

> On the day of the Decollation of Saint John the Baptist (August 29th) the king returned to England; and hearing at Leicester how Owen, lord of Glendower, along with northern Welsh who had raised him up to be their prince, had broken out into open rebellion and had seized many castles, and how he had burned on all sides the towns wherein the English dwelt amongst them, pillaging them and driving out the English, he gathered together the flower of his troops, and marched his array into North Wales. And the Welsh being subdued and driven away, their prince with seven others lay hid for a year among rocks and caves. With others who yielded peacefully the king dealt gently, slaying but very few of them, yet carrying away their chieftains captives to Shrewsbury. But afterwards he set them free, on condition of pursuing and taking those who still held out in rebellion in Snowdon and elsewhere ...

Prince Henry had accompanied his father on the expedition into Wales to repress the rebellion. The King left the Marches and was back in Shrewsbury by 15 October, but the Prince remained at Chester, apparently in a position of authority, for on 30 November all Welsh rebels were summoned to present themselves to him there. The English Parliament passed more laws to restrict the Welsh, but Welshmen in turn began to return to Wales to join the rebellion.

GLYNDŴR'S MOUNTAIN ESCAPE

It is unknown when this occurred, but it would have either been in the first or last stages of the war. Perhaps it was when Glyndŵr escaped into Snowdonia in its early days, in 1405 when for a time he was a fugitive, or even later. Rhys ap Dafydd was known as Rhys Goch Eryri (Red Rhys of Snowdon) and was an admirer and supporter of Owain, who lived at Hafod Garegog, near Beddgelert. He is known for his poems, in one of which he addressed Carnedd Llywelyn from the top of Eryri (Snowdon). In it, he predicts a renewed campaign in the next summer. Rhys Goch is supposed to have sheltered Glyndŵr, when Glyndŵr narrowly escaped capture, only succeeding in eluding his pursuers by climbing the difficult Simnai y Foel, on Moel Hebog. Journeying by night, Owain came to Rhys's house and Rhys told him he should stay as long as he wished. Rhys sent one of his men to watch the Colwyn valley, as that was the way that the King's men would come to look for Glyndŵr. After a short time Rhys's watchman galloped to the house and reported a large force approaching along the valley.

Rhys and Owain donned old cloaks and hats, so they looked like servants, and quickly left the house, scrambling up the hillside behind it. They were spotted and the soldiers gave chase, leaving their horses at the foot of the steep, wooded slope. Fortunately, there were no archers amongst them. The Welshmen could not outpace the chasing soldiers, and decided to split up as they approached the rocky outcrops. However, Rhys's hat flew off and they could see his red hair, so abandoned chasing him and began to close on Glyndŵr, who was having to skirt the rocks. Owain was older than the chasing men, so knew that time was not on his side. He then ran downhill towards the Pass of Aberglaslyn. In former times the sea came up to the western end of the pass, and Owain probably wanted to escape by boat. However, the captain of the troop guessed his intentions and sent his fastest runners to cut Owain off. He was forced to swerve back to the right, towards the mountain called Moel Hebog, 'Bare Hill of the Hawk', which stands above Beddgelert. Glyndŵr swam the tidal Afon Glaslyn at Nantmor, and climbed as fast as he could up the rough hillside. Behind him the pursuing soldiers spread out in a wide crescent to prevent him from escaping to one side or the other. Soon he was high up on Moel Hebog, with the dark cliffs that defend its summit close above him.

Owain had hoped to cross the ridge on the left and escape into Cwm Pennant on the other side, but soldiers were closing in on that side and knew he could never reach the ridge. He ran across to the right, but he was being cut off here also. Trapped, he saw the dark line of a cleft in the middle of the cliffs, and climbed up towards it at all speed. It was as steep and narrow as a chimney and 250 ft high, but it was his only chance. By the time the breathless soldiers reached the foot of the cleft he was more than halfway to the top. The soldiers could not follow, and Owain climbed out at the top of his chimney and made his way to a cave in the next mountain, Moel yr Ogof. It is so called after the cave, Ogof Glyndŵr, in which he sheltered. Rhys Goch kept him secretly supplied with food until the soldiers had left the valley, then Owen came out of hiding after six months. Another version is that the Prior of Beddgelert or Edynfed ab Aron fed Owain, and Rhys Goch himself hid in Twll Rhys Goch (Rhys Goch's Hole) at Nant y Benglog. It is thought that Glyndŵr then hid in Nantmor at the house of the poet Dafydd Nanmor, who was a friend of Rhys Goch. A modern rock-climbing guidebook to the climbing routes on Moel Hebog describes each climb and records who made the first ascent and when. One of the routes is described as 'Glyndŵr's Gully. 250 ft. First Ascent, Owain Glyndŵr, c. 1400'.

CHAPTER 5

War Across Wales 1401

THE LOLLARD ISSUE & MORE PROBLEMS FOR WALES

Henry hosted the Byzantine Emperor Manuel II Palaiologos from December 1400 to January 1401 at Eltham Palace, and a joust was given in the emperor's honour. Henry also gave him financial aid for his battle against the Ottoman Empire, believing that his troubles with Wales had ended. His agents must have told him that Glyndŵr and his kinsmen had very little support, and that he was hiding in the wilds of Snowdonia in yet another cold winter. In the light of Henry's ongoing financial problems, he would not have given assistance to the Byzantine Emperor if he had foreseen more trouble in Wales.

In January 1401, spurred by Thomas Arundel, Archbishop of Canterbury, Parliament passed the statute 'De Heretico Comburendo', giving the religious authorities the power to hand heretics over to the temporal authorities to be burned. Burning ensured that the soul would not pass to Heaven – extinction of the unbeliever was assured. To own an English translation of the Bible was to be condemned as a heretic – the church wanted no interpretation but its own. On 2 March, a Lollard named William Sawtrey was the first person to be burned at the stake, in Smithfield. Lollards were the Protestant followers of the theologian John Wycliffe, who wanted a reform of Christianity. They believed that priests should be 'pious', that the word of the Bible was more important than the word of priests, and that religious power came from piety, not priests. Lollardy demanded apostolic poverty from churchmen and a taxation of church possessions and incomes. It presented a huge threat to the Catholic Church, dependent upon incomes from power structures. Thus possession of the Bible by non-priests was dangerous.

Because of the cost of his Welsh invasion, Henry now called upon Parliament to fund him. The Common House used this opportunity to expand its powers in 1401, securing recognition of freedom of debate and freedom from arrest for dissenting opinions. In January 1401, border landowners asked Parliament for new laws against the Welsh, which were passed in February. The cost of any damage was to be borne by the Welsh, not the English in their bastides in Wales. Another law made the Welsh collectively responsible for any damage whatsoever which occurred in the course of any war. The Marcher Lords were given greater powers of repression, probably making a full-scale war inevitable. Until now Welsh lords had largely administered estates in Wales for absentee lords. This buffer was removed, forcing men to side with Glyndŵr as their livelihoods were removed when the Marcher Lords took over direct rule of their lands. No Welshman was allowed to be a JP, chief forester, chancellor, receiver, constable of a castle etc. All these posts were immediately given to Englishmen. The Welsh Civil Service was broken up and punitive taxes imposed. Welsh could not marry English people, and court and all other proceedings were to be in a foreign language, English. This set of new legislation ensured that more men now thought about joining Glyndŵr – they had nothing to lose.

In February, the Common House was warned that a massive rebellion was likely in Wales, and that bards were spreading tales that Glyndŵr's coming was prophesied by Merlin. Even more laws were passed against the Welsh. Englishmen were to be protected from the 'malice' of Welsh juries, and the Marcher Lords were told to equip and garrison their castles more strongly. Parliament heard that Welsh scholars at Oxford and Cambridge were leaving their studies to join Glyndŵr, and Welsh labourers in England were likewise returning to Wales and preparing for war. Bradley informs us:

> Oxford, particularly, sent many recruits to Owen, and this is not surprising, seeing how combative was the Oxford student of that time and how clannish his proclivities. Adam of Usk, who has told us a good deal about Glyndŵr's insurrection, was himself an undergraduate some dozen years before it broke out, and has given us a brief and vivid picture of the ferocious fights upon more or less racial lines, in which the Welsh chronicler not only figured prominently himself, but was an actual leader of his countrymen. He 'was indicted,' he tells us, 'for felonious riot and narrowly escaped conviction, being tried by a jury empanelled before a King's Judge. After this I feared the King hitherto unknown to me and put hooks in my jaws.' These particular riots were so formidable that the scholars for the most part, after several had been slain, departed to their respective countries. In the very next year, however, 'Thomas Speke, Chaplain, with a multitude of other malefactors, appointing captains among them, rose up against the peace of the King and sought after all the Welshmen abiding and studying in Oxford, shooting arrows after them in divers streets and lanes as they went, crying out, 'War! War! War! Slay Slay Slay the Welsh dogs and her whelp; who so looketh out of his house he shall in good sooth be dead,' and certain persons they slew and others they grievously wounded, and some of the Welshmen, who bowed their knees to abjure the town, they led to the gates with certain indignities not to be repeated to ears polite.

> We may also read the names of the different halls which were broken into, and of Welsh scholars who were robbed of their books and chattels, including in some instances their harps. It is not altogether surprising, therefore, that Welsh Oxonians should have hailed the opportunity of Owen's rising to pay off old scores. We have the names of some of those who joined him in an original paper, in the Rolls of Parliament, which fully corroborates the notice of this event; Howel Kethin (Gethin), 'bachelor of law, duelling in Myghell Hall, Oxenford,' was one of them; 'Maister Morres Stove (Morris Stove), of the College of Excestre,' was another, while David Brith, John Lloid and several others are mentioned by name. One David Leget seems to have been regarded as such an addition that Owen himself sent a special summons that he 'schuld com till hym and be his

man.' So things in Wales went from bad to worse; Glyndŵr's forces gaining rapidly in strength and numbers, and actively preparing in various quarters for the operations that marked the open season of 1401.

To try and prevent fresh support for Glyndŵr, Prince Henry and Henry 'Hotspur' had taken control of the North Wales campaign and convinced the King to issue a general pardon for North Wales. On 10 March 1401 a pardon was granted to various rebels at Prince Henry's request, 'to all the King's lieges for all treasons and insurrections, except Owyn Glendowrdy, Rees ap Tudour, William ap Tudour and those who have been captured, detained in custody or persisted in rebellion'. On 10 May this pardon was extended to, 'the men of Oswestry hundred in Wales' and the following week to 'the men of the lordship late of John Lord Lestrange of Knockyn decd. of The Hundred of Ellesmere in Wales.' Interestingly, both Oswestry and Ellesmere are firmly placed in Wales. Several petitions emphasized the gravity of the situation in Wales and six punitive statutes were enacted, followed on 18 and 22 March by further supplementary measures taken on account of 'the late insurrection in North Wales'. On 21 March the Council authorised Prince Henry to discharge any constables of castles who had not performed their duty. At the same time there was bitter fighting on the Scottish borders, with George Dunbar, the Scottish Earl of March leaving the Scots and joining Northumberland. Across Britain, there was a shortage of food in a severe winter and spring.

THE 'IMPREGNABLE' CONWY CASTLE FALLS 1 APRIL 1401

Because of fresh English oppression, widespread starvation and the destruction of the infrastructure of Welsh tenancies and laws, support for Glyndŵr's rebellion was again growing. Rhys and Gwilym ap Tudur ap Goronwy were cousins and supporters of Owain Glyndŵr. Henry IV had tortured their brother Gronw ap Tudur to death a few months previously. With a company of just forty men, they tricked their way into the walled town of Conwy. (Conwy and its castle were part of the Iron Ring of fortresses built by King Edward I in the thirteenth century in an effort to subdue the Welsh.) Some say they were disguised as workmen, or just mixed with the country people entering the town to trade at the market. On Good Friday, they knew that the small garrison of fifteen men-at-arms and sixty archers under Constable John Massy would be at prayer in the parish church of St Mary's. One source states that a Glyndŵr supporter walked into the castle dressed as a carpenter, with a toolbox that contained weapons. He then strangled the two unsuspecting warders on the gate, allowing the war party to get in. They quickly overcame the remaining guards and captured the castle. Once in control they demonstrated that with just a few dozen men this magnificent castle could be easily defended against massive forces. Massy and his men raced back from the church, as the town had been set ablaze, and the smoke alerted his men. Safe inside the castle, the Welsh burned all the records of the town's Exchequer. Also, the town gate had been destroyed, and the King's Justiciar's quarters were burnt along with the Chamberlain's lodgings.

1401 William ap Tudor and Rhys ap Tudor, brothers, natives of the isle of Anglesey, or Mona, because they could not have the king's pardon for Owen's rebellion, on the same Good Friday (April 1st) seized the castle of Conway, which was well stored with arms and victuals, the two warders being slain by the craftiness of a certain carpenter who feigned to come to his accustomed work; and, entering therein with forty other men, they held it for a stronghold. But, straightaway being besieged by the prince and the country, on the twenty-eight day of May next following they surrendered the same castle, cowardly for themselves and treacherously for their comrades; for, having bound nine of their number, who were very hateful to the prince, by stealth as they slept after the night watches, they gave them up, on condition of saving their own lives and the others' lives. And the nine thus bound and yielded up to the prince they straightaway saw drawn, disembowelled, hanged, beheaded, and quartered.

(The Chronicle of Adam of Usk.)

Henry Percy (Harry Hotspur) was furious, galloping from Chester to the royal castle with 120 men-at-arms and 300 archers. Immediately he put Massy under house arrest and deprived him of all his lands. Massy was to die, trying to retrieve his reputation, at Shrewsbury two years later. The Welsh held out against siege engines, inflicting heavy casualties on the 500 men of Prince Henry and Hotspur for weeks, until the English decided to try to starve them out instead of fighting. Importantly, the Welsh now knew that the 'impregnable' Iron Ring of castles could be taken. Hotspur, Justiciar of Chester and North Wales, was helpless. He knew that he would have to agree terms with the rebels, as the longer they held out, the more support could grow across Wales and lead to all-out war. Richard Yonge, Bishop of Bangor since 1399, along with John Perant, wrote to the King, stating that the Bishopric would pay some of the siege expenses, and stating that Howel Vaughan (Hywel Fychan) was one of the defenders as well as the Tudur brothers.

FIGHTING BREAKS OUT ACROSS WALES

From May onwards, North Wales, Powys, Ceredigion and Builth all began supporting Glyndŵr, with support also building in Brecon and Carmarthen. There were reports of malefactors in Breconshire and defections of entire communities in Buellt to the rebels. The people of Llanrwst people suffered much hardship at this time, and Aberconwy Abbey and Maenan Abbey also had problems.

A pardon was granted 'to the supplication of the King's firstborn son Henry, Prince of Wales' ... 'to all who have taken part in "treasons and insurrections" in the counties of Denbigh, Carnarvon, Anglesey, and Merioneth in the first year of the King's reign. On 6 May there is special mention of this pardon as applying to the King's lieges of the lordship of Thomas, Earl of Arundel, of Chirke and Chirkland in Wales'. (David Powel's *History of Cambria*.) On 17 May, Hotspur sent a letter to the King complaining of the expense involved in policing North Wales. He told Henry that the country was virtually pacified – 'the country of North Wales (le paiis de Northgalez); was well intendant and obedient in all points to the law', except for rebels in the castle of Conwy, and that the people of the counties of Caernarfon and Meirionydd were prepared to submit and to pay substantial payments for pardon.

In this letter Hotspur wrote:

> ... excepting those rebels who are in the castles of Conway and Rees, which is in the mountains, and whom I hope will be well chastised, if God pleases, by the forces and authorities which my redoubtable brother the Prince has sent there, as well of his council as of his retinue, to hold the siege before the rebels in the said castles; which siege if it can be continued until the said rebels are taken, will be at great ease and comfort to the governance of this country in time to come. And also Reverend Fathers in God and our very dear Brethren, the peasantry of the said country of North Wales, that is to say the counties of Caernarvon and Merioneth, have just presented themselves before me and humbly thanked my redoubtable brother, the Prince, for his very great kindness in supplicating our lord the King for his gracious pardon, and they humbly beg for the confirmation of this under his seal, offering to give him of their own will (beside the usual dues) and without any other request, as great a sum as they have to King Richard when he was King and Prince, as the bearer will fully declare to you ... And you will remember how many times I have besought you for the payment of the soldiers of the King in the City of Berwick and the Marches of England, who are in such great poverty that they cannot bear arms for the want of their pay, and for them you are supplicated to order that they be paid in manner as was promised between the Treasurer and myself at out last meeting, if better payment cannot be obtained for them. For otherwise I must come to you for the said payment, everything else being of minor importance ...

Hywel Fychan was in Conwy Castle with Gwilym Tudor, and perhaps Rhys Tudur had left, as the correspondence was held with William Tudor, and Rhys is mentioned as being in the mountains of Snowdonia.

Percy probably minimised his problems to prove to Henry that he deserved money for putting down the rebellion. However, Henry had little money, and ignored the letter. Anything that weakened the power of the most powerful family in his realm - the Percies - was in the King's interest in the end. They kept his northern borders secure also at great cost. The signs of ill feeling between the new made King and the House of Percy were becoming serious. Hotspur urged the strengthening of Carlisle and Berwick castles as protection against possible invasion by the Scots, but the King again took no notice of his appeal. When he wrote yet again to the King requesting funds to pay for his endeavours, pleading that he 'cannot bear them any longer than the end of the month' the King refused to pay anywhere near the full amount. Instead the Privy Council sent a letter to each Marcher Lord to upgrade the defence of their castles. Again Hotspur replied pleading for the money telling his Majesty that his troops remained unpaid. It seems that Hotspur could have hunted down Glyndŵr, who had retreated to the mountains with few men. Spies were sent to Meirionnydd, Llyn and Eifionydd to find Glyndŵr.

In 1403 the King accused Hotspur of meeting secretly with Glyndŵr at this time in 1401. Possibly Hotspur had done so as he was wracked with guilt from the Percies' promise of safe passage to Richard II, not believing that Bolingbroke would usurp the crown as Henry IV. The Percies also owned, as well as all of the March which separated England from

Scotland, huge areas of Wales and the Isle of Man. Perhaps Hotspur felt that Henry IV was more of a threat to his estates than Glyndŵr, a man of unparalleled honesty. Certainly, the Percy and Mortimer possessions in Wales were never raided as much as those of the other Marcher Lords.

FRESH REVOLT

There were random attacks across Wales – it seems that warbands arose spontaneously across the nation. English property was destroyed and livestock taken. These were guerrilla attacks, among the first in modern European history. The Welsh knew they had no chance in open battle, with just lightly-armed horsemen and archers and no cannon. The English levies contained skilled Welsh archers from the borderlands, so the archers would cancel each other out. In close combat, the Welsh horsemen would be cut to pieces by the spears of English men-at-arms and heavy cavalry. Their chief opportunity lay in surprise and mobility, always having a secure retreat for hiding in the forests and mountains.

The English were well-equipped with armour, necessary protection in battle. However, it gave no protection against either heat or cold. It was worn over a felt-like material designed to absorb the impact of blows, and either became oppressively hot, exhausting the wearer, or simply absorbed the cold, leading to the loss of body heat and possible hypothermia. The Welsh rain entered through armour, and the soldier soon became soaked in a mixture of rainwater and sweat. The armour chafed the body and sores developed, often becoming infected. On normal campaigns, where the enemy was not immediately present, it was not necessary to wear it, or most of it, all the time. Armies marched to a battleground, and spent some days preparing for battle. However, in the Welsh wars, where the enemy might appear at any moment, it had to be worn nearly all the time, sometimes even when sleeping.

Glyndŵr was an experienced warrior, and had no wish to fight pitched battles against the impressive English army. He used the hilly terrain and river crossings to engage guerrilla warfare against small bodies of the English army in the valleys. His archers picked off the slow-moving army from a distance where there was an easy retreat. The English might control a valley, but were subjected to constant and demoralising attacks by an unseen enemy. Glyndŵr took the initiative to decide when and where to attack or ambush. Prince Henry reacted by forming small parties of men to take the war to Glyndŵr's men, going to the hills and seek them out, but was only partially successful. Wales was the original home of the most formidable infantry weapon of the time, the six-foot longbow. The English had later adopted it and were proficient in its use, but it was a weapon that was ideally suited to Glyndŵr's guerrilla campaign.

The English gained intelligence that Glyndŵr was near Machynlleth, and a triple attack had been devised to cut him off. Prince Hal, aged just fourteen, led an army from the north, heading down from Harlech. From the east, a force under John Charleton, Lord Powys, approached from Welshpool, probably following the Severn through Newtown. From the south-west, an Anglo-Flemish army headed north. Glyndŵr would have no escape except by sea. There were next two confusing actions – difficult to disentangle because of conflicting reports.

Prince Henry and Hotspur now moved south on 30 May to the Mawddach River and the Cader Idris area near Dolgellau. On 31 May, Hotspur claimed to have been ambushed by Glyndŵr at Cader Idris, but he and Arundel beat him off. On 4 June, Hotspur recorded that he and Arundel had defeated Glyndŵr at Dolgellau. They then tried to secure the submission of the counties of Meirionnydd and Caernarfon. John Charleton Lord of Powys claims to have ambushed Glyndŵr at 'M' (probably the Mawddwy Valley or possibly Machynlleth) or Llanberis (much further north) or Dolgellau at that same time. Glyndŵr was said to have escaped south with just 120 men.

Perhaps Hotspur had secretly met Owain Glyndŵr, under the cover of a skirmish, while Charleton had fought with Tudur Glyndŵr, who bore a marked resemblance to his brother. Possibly Charleton's men came across the small contingent that Glyndŵr had left in Snowdonia, under the command of his brother Tudur. (It may be that Hotspur met Glyndŵr in mid-May, telling him that he was in danger of being surrounded, and then wrote to the King that he had been ambushed.) Whatever went on, we will probably never know, but on 4 June Hotspur wrote to the king that he had beaten a Welsh force near Cader Idris, and that he had just heard from Charleton that he had wounded several of Glyndŵr's men.

It was claimed that the Welsh suffered a heavy defeat at the hands of Charleton, who according to his letter to Prince Henry of 4 June 1401, had 'discomfited Glyndŵr'. It is said that a 'magic relic', a banner 'painted with maidens with red hands' was taken in the fight with Glyndŵr, and made into nightshirts for Henry IV and Prince Henry. One wonders if this was a relic brought by the soldiers of Owain Lawgoch (Red Hand) from France. Charleton wrote:

> ... last Monday (May 31) I was on chevauchée with my men on the mountains of the county of Powys and sent some of them into various parts of M with 400 archers. When they were approaching that area they had seen Owain and his people in the mountains, where my spies had reported their presence beforehand ... where they are now I do not certainly know at present, but some say towards K. (Kermerdin was the English spelling of Caerfyrddin, Carmarthen.) In this chase were taken some armour of the said Owain, some horses and lances, and a drape of cloth, also his henchman, whom I intend to send to our lord the King, your father. That night I lodged with my other troops at M., in order to govern that area and to prevent the aforesaid rebels from returning.

A chevauchée was a particularly destructive kind of military raid especially prominent during The Hundred Years War. Rather than besieging a castle or conquering land, soldiers on a chevauchée aimed to create as much destruction, carnage and chaos as possible, to both break the morale of enemy peasants and deny their rulers income and resources. They would burn crops and buildings, kill the population and steal anything valuable before enemy forces could challenge them, often systematically laying regions to waste and causing great starvation. The chevauchée compares to the modern concept of Total War, as practised in Vietnam and other arenas. Each of the six royal expeditions into Wales was a chevauchée.

Reports that Glyndŵr had been in two battles at once confirmed his magical qualities. Glyndŵr had headed south away from the forces of Prince Henry and Lord Powys. On 26 May, Henry had summoned troops from fourteen counties to Worcester, to head for Carmarthenshire because of Glyndŵr's assumed presence there. However, he cancelled the campaign, seeming to have been lulled into security by John Charleton's report that Glyndŵr had been defeated.

In late May, Glyndŵr sent a letter to Henry Dwn (Don), a leading landowner, soldier, and administrator of the Lancaster lordship of Kidwelly, exhorting him to join in the movement to liberate the Welsh. (However, it may belong to late May 1403.) The letter, known only from a late manuscript, was sent by Glyndŵr styling himself Owain ap Gruffydd, Lord of Glyndyfrdwy. The Privy Council noted Glyndŵr's appearance in the Marches of Carmarthen before the end of May, which may have meant that he met Henry Dwn, who became his leading supporter in the south. This signified a fresh sphere of hostilities and an escalation of the rebellion into a war:

> We inform you that we hope to be able, by God's help and yours, to deliver the Welsh people from the captivity of our English enemies who, for a long time now elapsed, have oppressed us and our ancestors. And you may know from your own perception that now their time draws to a close and because, according to God's ordinance from the beginning success turns towards us, no one need doubt that a good issue will result, unless it be lost through sloth and strife.

From about 1105, Henry I had encouraged settlements in Wales to expand Norman power, to conquer the country piecemeal. The most prominent group of colonists in the south of Pembroke and the Gower area were Flemings. Sir William Beauchamp had been named Justiciar of South Wales by Henry IV. In response to raids, Beauchamp had taken an army of mainly south Pembrokeshire men towards Glyndŵr's force, completing the pincer movement. Glyndŵr was moving south to avoid further confrontation with Hotspur, Arundel, Prince Henry and Charleton. He left a small band in Snowdonia, taking his other men down the west coast, intending not only to escape, but to spread the rebellion in the south-west.

THE BATTLE OF HYDDGEN JUNE 1401

1400 Henry went to Scotland and with him a great host. While he was unoccupied there, one of his lords told him he had better have faithful men in Wales, for he said that Owain ap Gruff would wage war against him. Therewith Lord Talbot and Lord Grey of Ruthin were sent to make sure of Owen and they undertook the task. But the man escaped into the woods; the time was the feast of St Matthew in autumn (September 21). The following summer (1401) Owain rose with 120 reckless men and robbers and brought them in warlike fashion to the uplands of Ceredigion; and 1,500 men of the lowlands of Ceredigion and of Rhos and Penfro (Pembroke) assembled there and came to the mountain with the intent to seize Owain. The encounter between them was on Hyddgant (Hyddgen) Mountain, and no sooner did the English troops turn their backs in flight than 200 of

them were slain. Owain now won great fame, and a great number of youths and fighting men from every part of Wales rose and joined him, until he had a great host at his back.
(Peniarth MS 135)

As the rebellion started and spread, it is estimated that Owain's force at this stage amounted to just 500 men. Some records, such as Gruffydd Hiraethog's *Annals of Owen Glyn Dwr*, written in 1550 and based on lost earlier accounts, put his force at just 120 men by the time he reached Hyddgen near Pumlumon. In June 1401, the English settlers of the south of Pembrokeshire (the Englishry) and settlers of Flemish descent from the same area, were supported by a large force of English soldiers and Flemish mercenaries, making a small army of 1,500 – 2,000 men. Glyndŵr's out-riders came across the Anglo-Flemish force, heading north from Aberystwyth, and led them into the wilds of Pumlumon in the Cambrian Mountains. Glyndŵr seems to have led them into the remote Hyddgen Valley, constantly harassing them with archers and attacks. In a surprise onslaught, Glyndŵr's army finally beat back the attack, killing 200, chasing the main force away and taking scores of prisoners for ransom. This was the end of what seems to have been a running battle, situated around where the Nant-y-Moch reservoir is today. (There are plans to despoil this remote and remarkable landscape with yet more wind turbines.) Without this key battle of Mynydd Hyddgen, it is doubtful if the revolt would have spread into a full-scale war across Wales.

The Annals of Owen Glyn Dwr record that 'Owen now won great fame, and a great number of youths and fighting men from every part of Wales rose and joined him, until he had a great host at his back.' The dead were probably buried in mass graves at Esgair y Ffordd, Mynydd Bychan, Nant y Moch and Bryn y Beddau, the 'Hill of Graves'. Two white quartz blocks are known as Cerrig Cyfamod Glyndŵr (Glyndŵr's Covenant Stones), and may be the site of final battle, or of a meeting before the battle. Glyndŵr's reputed camp is at Siambr Trawsfynydd. Near there, Glyndŵr's men would have the advantage of being above their opponents – probably hiding on the reverse slope of the ridge – only revealing themselves at the last moment. Their opponents would have been in a boggy valley, unable to use horses properly and easy targets for archers. There is a tradition that the dead of the battle were buried further north and marked by a cairn.

The Flemings whom Owain distressed most of all raised 1500 men and went against him, being full of confidence that they would either kill or take him. They hemmed him in on all sides so that he could not possibly get off without fighting at a great disadvantage. He and his men fought manfully a great while, in their own defence, against them. Finding themselves surrounded and hard put to it, they resolved at last to make their way through or perish in the attempt; so, falling on furiously, with courage whetted with despair, they put the enemy, after a sharp dispute, to confusion; and they pursued so eagerly their advantage, that they bade them give ground, and in the end to fly outright, leaving 200 of their men dead on the spot of the engagement. This victory rendered Owain considerable renown and was the means to bring many to his side, that his number was greatly increased.
(Robert Vaughan of Hengwrt, fifteenth century.)

This famous victory in the uplands of Ceredigion was such a success that it transformed Owain's fortunes; 'a great number of youths and fighting men (direidwyr) from every part of Wales rose and joined him, until he had a great host behind him.' Sir William Beauchamp, leader of the English forces at Hyddgen, was relieved of his duties as Justiciar but allowed to retain the earldom of Pembroke. His duties were given to Hotspurs' uncle Sir Thomas Percy, Earl of Worcester and Lord of Haverfordwest. Percy spent the years 1402-1403 restocking castles in Pembrokeshire as a bastion against Welsh assaults. Sir Thomas now suffered the same problems as his nephew Hotspur, writing to the Privy Council on 3 July 1401, begging for monies to pay for his troops and supplies.

THE DISENCHANTMENT OF HOTSPUR

On 4 June, Hotspur had sent a letter to the King, with news of a victory, but making it plain that he was no longer willing to fight for nothing and was intending to return to Northumberland:

> I see much pillage and mischief in the country, that good and hasty measures ought to be immediately adopted by sea as well as by land. All the country is without doubt in great peril of being destroyed by the rebels if I should leave before the arrival of my successor, the which will be an affair of necessity; for I cannot bear the cost that I am put to without ordering from you. And touching this that has been done by my very honoured uncle (Thomas Percy, the Earl of Worcester) and other forces in his company, I hope that he has been certified to you and of my doing this (illegible) by land and sea for my soldiers' pay and my own expenses, and for the journey I had on May 13th last to Cader Idris, God Be Praised. The bearer John Irby was with me and can acquaint you with the particulars. Monsieur Hugh Browe was with me, 12 lances and 100 archers of my right honourable cousin the Earl of Arundel, without any other aid, at my proper charges; and by such governance as you may see meet to order for this answer; for I do not here await your answer by the aforesaid James Strangeways of the under-mentioned and other matters; and please to know that news has reached me this day from the Sieur of Powis, as to his combat with Owen de Glyndyfrdwy, whom he hath discomfited, and wounded many of his men on his way to my much honoured uncle and myself as he certified, for which I thank God.

Hotspur resigned later that autumn, as the King had sent no monies to Denbigh for his efforts. He returned to Northumberland, unhappy – he had helped Henry Bolingbroke since his landing in England, seen his word broken to Richard II when he enticed him out of Conwy Castle to meet Henry, helped his new King fight the Scots and taken his own men to fight in Wales, with neither gratitude nor payment. It is a strong possibility that he may have met and negotiated directly with Glyndŵr in the spring of 1401. Perhaps this involved negotiations involving the pardoning of Glyndŵr's Tudur cousins in return for the surrender of Conwy Castle. Glyndŵr was at this time still hoping for a peaceful settlement, and hostilities stopped for a time. In July John Massey, the Constable of Conwy, was pardoned by Henry IV for the taking of Conwy Castle. He had been sent to the King by

Prince Henry, and such was his standing that many of the King's men had wished to stand bail for him so that he could be involved in the siege of Conwy.

Perhaps in June, a small force of Glyndŵr's men came across Hotspurs force and attacked it at Cadair Idris near Machynlleth, but this may be another account of the previous skirmish in May. Both sides claimed victory. Also in June, spies were again sent to the uplands of Nant Conwy and Traeth Mawr looking for Glyndŵr. Prince Henry was in Chester, giving out huge fines to the Welsh, legislating new ordinances against them and ordering increases in garrisons across Wales as soon as the Exchequer could release any money. There were actions around Harlech and Aberystwyth castles. Still in June, the Scots landed on Ynys Enll (Bardsey Island) and attacked English shipping off the Welsh coast.

THE SURRENDER OF CONWY CASTLE 24 JUNE 1401

Hotspur had been under pressure from Henry since the taking of the castle. Negotiations began, and the Tudurs wanted free pardons for them and their followers. They also wished to be freed from any reparations for the immense damage done to Conwy. Hotspur knew that tradesmen and house-owners, under the protection of the English, would be furious if there was no compensation, and that Henry IV would not permit these terms. Hotspur also did not want to cause any great damage to the royal castle by mining it. He offered six months immunity, followed by a trial with a mixed jury of English and Welshmen. The Welsh agreed, but the King had written to Prince Henry in late May refusing the terms:

> ... you have signified to us how that between our most dear and faithful cousins Henry de Percy('Hotspur') and our dear and faithful Arnald Savage and others of your council, on the matters touching Rees and William ap Tudor, and other our rebels, their adherents, certain treaties have been settled; and how, to what result the said William, Howel Vaughan and all other companions and persons who are rebels with him at the castle of Conway have finally arrived by their offer and supplication of which we have seen a copy. Considering the good arrangement of archers, and works, which you and your cousin ('Hotspur') have made for the siege of the said castle, giving us your advice that 120 armed men and 300 archers should remain upon the said siege, until the feast of St Michael or the feast of All Saints next coming, to the end that the rebels be punished according to their deserts, or that we should at least have some other treaty which should be agreeable to us and more honourable than was any one of the offers of the aforesaid rebels; the which, as seems to your sage counsel, and that of our said cousin, are not at all honourable to us, but a matter of most evil precedent ...

Sir Arnold Savage was Steward of the Household for Henry IV, and Speaker of the House of Commons from 1400-1402, so was obviously present at the negotiations to ensure the King's voice was heard. Unfortunately the terms finally agreed, which included full pardons to the Tudurs, were not favourable to all the Welshmen, with nine of the rebel soldiers being executed as part of the deal. The King was furious that most of the rebels were pardoned, including the ringleaders, but Percy had found the long siege extremely costly and did not wish to damage the King's castle:

> ... on 28 of May next following the Welsh surrendered the said Castle, cowardly for themselves and treacherously for their comrades. For having bound 12 of their number who were very hateful to the prince, by stealth as they slept after the night watches, they gave them up on condition of saving their own and others' lives. And the 9 thus bound and yielded up to the prince they straight away saw them drawn, disembowelled, hanged, beheaded, and quartered ...
> (Adam of Usk.)

Adam of Usk has the date of surrender incorrect. On 24 June the Tudurs returned Conwy to Hotspur and Prince Hal, and in July Rhys ap Tudur, Gwilym ap Tudur and their surviving followers were pardoned. Some sources state that the men who were executed were volunteers. Among those pardoned were the landowners Dafydd ap Gruffydd Fantach of Dwygyfylchi and Hywel Fychan ap Madog ap Hywel. From 10 July, the Prince was given extra monies (which had been withheld from Hotspur, who decided to return to Northumberland). Throughout July and August Prince Hal raised men, and was forced to send a fast relief force from Chester through Bala, to re-supply the besieged Harlech Castle.

WAR ACROSS WALES SUMMER-AUTUMN 1401

In August, Abbey Cwm Hir was burnt, thought to be in revenge for the sacking of Llanfaes Abbey by Henry, but as Llywelyn ap Gruffydd, the last Prince of Wales, was thought to be buried there, it could have been English destruction. Cistercians usually sided with the Welsh princes against the Normans. Leland wrote 'Al the Howse was spoiled and defaced by Owen Glindour' after visiting Wales in the 1530's. Bishops' Castle was then destroyed, and Glyndŵr took New Radnor Castle and ravaged the east of Radnorshire. At New Radnor Castle near Llandrindod Wells around sixty to seventy survivors from the castle were said to have been beheaded and hung from the walls in retaliation for the executions at Conwy:

> Radenor was partely destroyed by Owen Glindour, and the voice is there that he wonne the Castel, he took a iii score men that had the Garde of the Castel, and caused them to be beheaded on the Brinke of the Castel Yarde, and that there since a certain Bloodwort growth there where the Bloode was shed.

In 1845 the medieval church at New Radnor was demolished and many skeletons were found, so 'proving' the slaughter of the garrison, but they could equally have been Welsh captives. At this time bodies were usually buried within the church, under the earth floor, unless a crypt was available. Whether the story of the beheadings was made up to secure more funding for defences is unknown, but certainly the castle was not thoroughly dismantled at this time. Cymer Abbey was also despoiled, as its Abbot had submitted to Henry. Owain went on to take Montgomery Castle, the town and the area. The castle was only partly repaired and its defenders were to panic the following September, fearing another attack. Welshpool Castle held out under the Charletons, but the area around Y Trallwng (Welshpool) was devastated. Its 'Red Castle of Powys' was too strong and its constable John Charleton chased off the raiding party. Through the autumn, Hay, Abergafenni, Grosmont and Usk were taken with hit and run tactics. Others like Clifford Castle may have been destroyed but many events are unrecorded or the records have been lost. Many Welsh castles fell into disuse around this time, possibly because they were sacked or damaged. It seems that Castell Dinas near Talgarth was destroyed at this time also.

Intelligence sent to Henry IV in Chester mapped Glyndŵr's route:

> ... it had been confirmed that Owain of Glendour and R de B with a great number of rebels were yesterday at the burial of two knights of the Lordship of C who were killed on your last journey into Wales and they lay with their host last night one league from this part of the B. Their purpose is to come and destroy my lands together with the Lordship of D and the Lordship of C, I do not know which for certain. (R de B could be Ryhs the Black).

After asking for aid, the letter went on:

> If the rebels want to drag themselves further into South Wales or into another estate your council will have sufficient knowledge of the places where they can be found ...

On 30 August, Prince Henry, based at Chester, was ordered to advance again against the rebels, and in October the King joined him. On 26 May at Worcester Henry had desperately wanted to attack Wales again, and had ordered a new invasion. However, he had been poverty-struck and cancelled it, believing that Charleton had seen off Glyndŵr's men. Now, after heavy borrowings and threats he rode to Worcester with enough promised funding and support for another invasion. He wrote to Prince Henry in September:

> Owen Glendower and other rebels of our land in Wales, now recently risen against us and our majesty have assembled in great numbers and from one day to the next commit many grievances and destructive deeds against our faithful subjects who do not wish to concur with their evil purpose. And by such coercion a large part of our aforesaid country has been given over to the rebels and, according to our reports, all the remaining parts of our said country and the Marches will surrender to the said rebels if we are not there in person to resist their evil.

SECOND ROYAL EXPEDITION INTO WALES 1 OCTOBER 1401

A summons to twenty-two counties, dated 18 September 1401, to a general muster at Worcester on 1 October, stressed that Owain Glyndŵr and other 'rebels' had risen to great numbers. Many landowners of crown lands in south-west Wales had appealed for the King's help. Henry used his Knights of the Household and Knights of the Shire to recruit men-at-arms and archers, soldiers able to wear the royal livery. These men were given arms from the Great Wardrobe in the Tower of London. Henry's twenty personal squires also recruited clerks, paymasters, surgeons, cooks, chaplains, trumpeters, pipers, fiddlers, drummers, physicians and gunners. There were bowyers to make bows and fletchers to make and fit the arrow flights. A master musician commanded the musicians. Merchant ships were impressed into royal service in Bristol, and the carpenters sent to place forecastles on merchant ships for fighting. Cannon were taken from the Tower for the ships. Master gunners from Germany were employed, and there was even a 'stuffer of basinets' to stuff and pad the helmets of the nobles. Clerks to the Stable looked after provisioning horses, and men were appointed to the Spicery, the Scullery and the Poultry.

The logistics of such an undertaking were immense. There were no roads, just muddy tracks through forest and over hills, except where some Roman roads were still under some state of repair. Carts were laden with 26-stone cheeses from Cheshire and barrels of salted beef, mutton, and pork. Stockfish and salted herring were loaded, with bags of wheat, oats, peas and beans. Potatoes were not to reach Britain for another 200 years, so a large circular loaf of bread served as a plate. Other carts were filled with tents, ropes, forges, horseshoes, nails, scythes, axes, arrows, daggers, swords, lances, shields, saddles, spurs, leather goods, tents, tent poles, spare wheels, spades, sickles and stoves. Apart from camp followers, mobile inns and brothels also kept up with the army. Sometimes herds of cattle, spare horses, flocks of geese and turkeys accompanied the army, dependent upon where they were foraging. A large army did not move quickly, and cost a fortune if it did not recover its costs through pillage – and there was very little to loot in Wales except in its churches and monasteries. Glyndŵr knew that Henry was not a rich King. His barons and earls had lesser lords who held land from them. In return these lords had to supply professional soldiers on contracts, mercenaries, often for nine weeks, whenever required. Also, any criminal would be pardoned if he served a year in the army, so murderers and outlaws filled up to ten per cent of the ranks. Keeping discipline was never easy.

If Glyndŵr did not want to meet an English army, it could never catch him. Glyndŵr knew this, and constantly sent warbands using guerrilla tactics, with night attacks, firing fusillades of arrows from overhead rocks, cutting down trees to block paths and the like. Longbowmen could fire twelve arrows a minute, with excellent accuracy on targets 250 yards away. Long flight arrows were used at distance, and shorter sheaf arrows could pierce armour at short distance. Crossbowmen, however, could only release three iron quarrels in the same time, and their bows were often useless in wet weather. Glyndŵr's only way to win the war was not to be captured or badly beaten, so he never risked everything, preferring to irritate the English into retreat, often relying on the Welsh weather. The English had light cavalry like Glyndŵr's, as well as heavy cavalry to carry the armoured knights, but Glyndŵr usually used the tactic of surprise and knew the terrain (and escape routes) better than the English mercenaries. Attacking in Wales in the autumn was folly, with heavy rains and later snow and ice.

The tragedy of trying to defend Wales as a nation had always been its geography. North to south routes were difficult, but east to west, from England to Wales, there were three relatively easy lowland routes: along the north coast; along the south coast, and straight through Powys to Aberystwyth in the middle of Wales. Then it was relatively easy to link up all along the west coast. Wales also had a coastline with plenty of harbours on its southern, western and northern extremities. With a different geography, one where the main lines of communication were north to south, it is difficult to say if Wales would ever have been conquered. This time the main English army attacked with extra troops from the garrisons of Shrewsbury and Hereford, through central Wales. From Shrewsbury and Hereford, they drove through Powys toward the Abbey of Strata Florida.

THE DESECRATION OF STRATA FLORIDA (YSTRAD FFLUR)

The Cistercian house was known to be sympathetic towards Owain, and Henry intended to remind them of their loyalties and prevent the revolt from spreading any further south. After terrible weather and constant harassment by the Plant Owain he reached the abbey. At least nine Welsh princes are buried at Strata Florida, and Henry's troops camped in the building itself. Relics were stolen, monks executed and others taken captive, and hundreds of Welsh children were led back to England in chains. Henry himself gave orders for the knights' horses to be stabled at the high altar, while his men spent two days getting drunk on the abbey wines before destroying the great church. Another English force also marched from Worcester into South Wales, confiscating properties and executing many rebels. This southern army marched to Brecon, then down the Ystrad Tywi to Llandovery, where Henry IV took the grand army to meet up.

THE SLAUGHTER OF LLYWELYN AP GRUFFYDD FYCHAN

At Llandovery, one man was granted a pardon on the scaffold if he would betray the whereabouts of Glyndŵr, but refused. The Monk of Evesham commented, 'We Englishmen should follow this example, and depart this life faithfully unto death, keeping our counsel and secrets.' After the execution, the Lord of Caeo, Llywelyn ap Gruffydd Fychan, was coerced into leading Henry towards Glyndŵr, and led his army on a wild goose chase for several days. His punishment was gruesome. A wonderful stainless steel statue commemorates him today where he was killed, outside the ruins of Llanymddyfri (Llandovery) Castle. Adam of Usk mentions Llywelyn as 'a man of gentle birth and bountiful who yearly used 16 tuns of wine in his household' (around 15,000 litres of wine). The army looted and raped its way back to England after this event. Crops were burned, land confiscated from Welsh gentry, captives executed without trial, and children taken into a life of slavery in England.

Bradley wrote:

> Henry did his best to bring Owen to action, but the Welsh chieftain was much too wary to waste his strength on a doubtful achievement which hunger would of a certainty accomplish for him within

a few days. An eminent gentleman of the country, one Llewelyn ab Griffith Vychan of Cayo, comes upon the scene at this point and at the expense of his head relieves the tedium of this brief and ineffectual campaign with a dramatic incident. His position, we are told, was so considerable that he consumed in his house no less than sixteen casks of wine a year; but his patriotism rose superior to his rank and comforts. He offered to guide the royal troops to a spot where they might hope to capture Owen, but instead of doing this he deliberately misled them, to their great cost, and openly declared that he had two sons serving with Glyndŵr, and that his own sympathies were with them and their heroic leader. He then bared his neck to the inevitable axe of the executioner, and proved himself thereby to be a hero, whose name, one is glad to think, has been rescued from oblivion. The King, having attended to the mangling and quartering of this gallant old patriot, crossed the Montgomery hills with his army and hurried down the Severn valley, carrying with him, according to Adam of Usk, a thousand Welsh children as captives. Beyond this capture, he had achieved nothing save some further harrying of a land already sufficiently harried, and the pillaging of an historic and loyal monastery.

Adam of Usk also describes this sorry Royal Expedition:

1401 In this autumn, Owen Glendower, all North Wales and Cardigan and Powis siding with him, sorely harried with fire and sword the English who dwelt in those parts, and their towns, especially the town of Pool (Welshpool). Wherefore the English, invading these parts with a strong power, and utterly laying them waste and ravaging them with fire, famine and sword, left them a desert, not even sparing children and churches, nor the monastery of Strata Florida, wherein the king himself was being lodged, and the church of which and its choir, even up to the high altar, they used as a stable, and pillaged even the patens; and they carried away into England more than a thousand children of both sexes to be their servants. Yet did the same Owen do no small hurt to the English, slaying many of them, and carrying off the arms, horses, and tents of the king's eldest son, the prince of Wales, and of other lords, which he bare away for his own behoof to the mountain fastnesses of Snowdon ... in those days, southern Wales, and in particular all the diocese of Llandaff, was at peace from every kind of trouble of invasion or defence ... among those slain by the above inroad of the English, Llewellyn ap Griffith Vaughan, of Cayo in the county of Cardigan, a man of gentle birth and bountiful, who yearly used sixteen tuns of wine in his household, because he was well disposed to the said Owen, was on the feast of Saint Denis (October 9th), at Llandovery, in the presence of the king and his eldest son, and by his command, drawn, hanged, and beheaded, and quartered ... at this time, about Michaelmas, a quarter of wheat all of a sudden rose in price from one noble to two, and in some parts of England to three nobles ... throughout all Wales the strongholds were repaired in walls and ditches ...

Fuming, Henry IV left the blood-soaked carcass of Llywelyn ap Gruffydd Fychan at Llandovery to march to Carmarthen, before travelling along the west coast to the castles of Cardigan and Aberystwyth. This second expedition returned to England through Builth and Painscastle. Henry left extra garrisons at all his castles. However, he failed to engage Owain's forces in any large numbers. Plant Owain (the children of Owain) harassed him and engaged in hit-and-run tactics on his supply chain but refused to fight in the open.

Henry was forced slowly to retreat. As he did so the weather turned. The army was nearly washed away in floods. Wet, starving, and dejected, his grand army returned to Hereford with nothing to claim for their efforts except around 1,000 crying, bewildered children and some gold and silver stolen from abbeys.

> When the season permitted, he *(Henry)* again entered Wales; but the very elements fought against him, and nature seemed to have abandoned her ordinary course in favour of Owen. Such dreadful storms arose, that the common people in that age of ignorance believed they were raised by the magic of Glendour, whose activity and success, and above all his retirement into parts almost inaccesible, made them consider him as something more than human. Henry was unable to regain any of the vast plunder taken from the English, and forced to abandon an expedition, in which his disappointment was heightened by the great hopes he had entertained of success.
> (Barnard 1783)

By 15 October, the King was back at Shrewsbury, where he arranged for the administration of Wales. Prince Henry was to have Anglesey with £1,000 yearly out of the estates of the Earl of March, and Thomas Percy, Earl of Worcester, was appointed as the Prince's tutor. The young Earl of March was held by Henry IV, so was in no position to complain about the huge revenues appropriated from his estates. There was talk at this juncture, possibly encouraged by the Percies, that Glyndŵr was prepared to enter into a treaty, but no peace was concluded. During the autumn of 1401 the King's Parliament considered peace but, probably due to the influence of Reginald de Grey, nothing came of it. Hotspur had written to the King several times warning him that serious trouble might result from lack of payment to his soldiers. Finally, in September, Hotspur resigned his post of Justiciar of North Wales and military governor. He rode north in October to assist his father, the Earl of Northumberland, to try to preserve peace with the Scots, which ended in failure. In October, Hotspur's uncle, Thomas Percy, Earl of Worcester was appointed Royal Lieutenant in South Wales, in command of the royal armies and garrisons. He immediately ensured that all castles were more strongly garrisoned, especially those at Cardigan and Aberystwyth.

In October, Glyndŵr attacked Welshpool again and captured the baggage train of Prince Henry, as it was heading north to Chester. For the first time in eighty years, Builth Castle and Brecon Castle had serious military garrisons, twenty men-at-arms and forty archers in each. On 19 October John Charleton, Lord of Powys, died, possibly in the skirmish where the baggage train was attacked. His brother Edward became Lord Powys.

BATTLE OF CAERNARFON (TWT HILL) 2 NOVEMBER 1401

Owain now raised the flag of King Arthur's father Uther Pendragon, a golden dragon on a white shield, on Twt Hill overlooking Caernarfon Castle. The flag symbolised that he was now the Pendragon, Chief Prince, and King of the Britons. Back in North Wales, with a second invasion force repelled, he attempted to lay siege to the great castle and its English bastide. In a sally, John Bolde's garrison and the English settlers in the town fought against Glyndŵr's men. Around 300 men were lost on each side, and the English retreated to the safety of the castle to await reinforcements. Both sides claimed victory, as eventually Glyndŵr withdrew his men, realising that the castle could not be taken without siege engines and more attackers. By this time, Glyndŵr had regained his lost territories at Carrog and Cynllaith from the forces of Lord Grey of Rhuthun.

Adam of Usk recounted:

> On the morrow of All Hallows *(2nd November)* Owen, seeking to lay siege to Caernarvon, there, in the midst of a great host, unfurled his standard, a golden dragon on a white field; but, being attacked by those within, he was put to flight, losing three hundred of his men ... Owen and his men cruelly harried the lordship of Ruthin, in North Wales, and the countryside with fire and sword, on the last day but one of January, carrying off the spoil of the land and specially the cattle to the mountains of Snowdon; yet did he spare much the lordship of Denbigh and others of the Earl of March, having at his beck the two counties of Cardigan and Merioneth which were favorable to him both for government and war.

At this time England was fighting on four fronts: a force under the King's second son crossed to Ireland to subdue a rebellion; the Earl of Rutland had been despatched to repulse a French invasion of Gascony; Robert III and the Scots were at war with England and the Percies of Northumberland; and Prince Henry and Thomas Percy were fighting Owain in Wales. Glyndŵr seems to have decided that it was time for a united effort against England.

Because of fears of the revolt spreading south, the following castles were regarrisoned, with 'lances' (men-at-arms) being paid twelve pence a day, and archers six pence a day. The King promised to pay Thomas Percy, Earl of Worcester, these expenses, but failed to do so. Each man-at-arms had up to six of his own armed servants, so the garrisons would be higher than seems from the following figures. Percy had to levy the following men for three months service: Cardigan fifty men-at-arms and one hundred and twenty archers; Carmarthen twenty and forty; Aberystwyth thirty and forty; Builth (captained by Sir John Oldcastle) twenty and forty; Brecon twenty and forty; and Llandovery ten and twenty. Cardigan, Carmarthen and Aberystwyth were owned by the Prince of Wales, Builth and Brecon by the King, and Llandovery by Lord Audley.

WELSH AMBASSADORS TO FRANCE, IRELAND AND SCOTLAND

Glyndŵr sent emissaries to the Irish chieftains at war with England, to Robert III of Scotland and Charles VI of France. Adam of Usk tells us that the bearers of the letters to Ireland and Scotland were taken in Ireland and beheaded. (Later in the war, Adam took refuge with Owain.) Unable to take the Caernarfon Castle, the administrative and military headquarters of English rule in the crown lands of North Wales, Glyndŵr needed external alliances, addressing letters in French to the King of Scotland and in Latin to the Gaelic lords of Ireland. Sadly both letters were intercepted and the messengers beheaded, almost certainly after torture to discover fresh intelligence about Glyndŵr's whereabouts, strengths and plans.

T.P Ellis referred to the ambassadors:

In November, Glyndŵr's arch-enemy, Lord Grey, was taken prisoner; and, as on the 29th November Glyndŵr was in Dolgelley, it is possible that his illustrious captive was with him. It was on that date that Glyndŵr despatched letters from Dolgelley to the King of Scotland and various chiefs ill Ireland, bidding for support from those countries against the common foe. Again referring to the tyranny and bondage under which his people had suffered, he appealed for help in the name of common ties of blood, and because from this tyranny and bondage the "prophecy saith that I shall be delivered by the aid and succour of your royal Majesty". In the Irish letters he points out that he is fighting their war as much as his own, and that his success means "welcome peace and calm repose for them". Unfortunately, the letters went astray; the messengers bearing them were seized in Ireland, as they were trying to find their way to Scotland, and they were beheaded.

The Chronicle of Adam of Usk gives us the content of the letters to Scotland and Ireland:

From Owain Glyndŵr to the king of Scotland
Most high and mighty and redoubted lord and cousin, I commend me to your most high and royal majesty, humbly as beseemeth me, with all honour and reverence. Most redoubted lord and right sovereign cousin, please it you and your most high majesty to know that Brutus, your most noble ancestor and mine, was the first crowned king who dwelt in this realm of England, which of old times was called Great Britain. The which Brutus begat three sons, to wit Albanact, Locrine and Camber. From which same Albanact you are descended in direct line. And the issue of the same Camber reigned royally down to Cadwalladar, who was the last crowned king of my people, and from whom I, your simple cousin, am descended in direct line; and after whose decease I and my ancestors and all my said people have been, and still are, under the tyranny and bondage of mine and your mortal foes the Saxons; whereof you, most redoubted lord and right sovereign cousin, have good knowledge. And from this tyranny and bondage the prophecy saith that I shall be delivered by the aid and succour of your royal majesty. But, most redoubted lord and sovereign cousin, I make grievous plaint to your royal majesty and right sovereign cousinship, that it faileth me much in men at arms. Wherefore, most redoubted lord and right sovereign cousin, I humbly beseech you, kneeling upon my knees, that it may please your royal majesty to send unto me a certain number of men at arms who may aid me and may withstand, with God's help, mine and your foes aforesaid; having regard, most redoubted lord and right sovereign cousin, to the chastisement of this mischief and of all the many past mischiefs which I and my said ancestors of Wales have suffered at the hands of mine and your mortal foes aforesaid. Being well assured, most redoubted lord and right sovereign cousin, that it shall be that, all the days of my life, I shall be bounden to do service and pleasure to

your said royal majesty and to repay you. And in that I cannot send unto you all my businesses in writing, I despatch these present bearers fully informed in all things, to whom it may please you to give faith and credence in what they shall say unto you by word of mouth. From my court. Most redoubted lord and right sovereign cousin, may the Almighty Lord have you in his keeping.

From Owain Glyndŵr to a lord in Ireland

Greetings and fullness of love, most dread lord and right trusty cousin. Be it known unto you that a great discord or war has arisen between us and our and your deadly foes, the Saxons: which war we have manfully waged now for nearly two years past, and which too, we purport and hope henceforth to wage and to bring to a good and effectual end, by the grace of God our Saviour, and by your help and countenance. But, seeing that it is commonly reported by the prophecy that, before we can have the upper hand in this behalf, you and yours, our well-beloved cousins in Ireland, must stretch forth hereto a helping hand; therefore, most dread lord and right trusty cousin, with heart and soul we pray you that your horsemen and footmen, for the succour of us and our people who now this long while we are oppressed by our said foes, as well as to oppose the treacherous and deceitful will of those same our foes, you do despatch unto us as many as you shall conveniently and honourably be able, saving in all things your honourable estate, as quickly as may seem good to you, bearing in mind our sore need. Delay not to do this, by the love we bear you and as we put our trust in you, although we may be unknown to your dread person, seeing that, most dread lord and cousin, so long as we shall be able to wage manfully this war in our borders, as doubtless is clear unto you, you and all the other chieftains of your parts of Ireland will be in the mean time have welcome peace and calm repose. And because, my lord cousin, the bearers of these presents shall make things known unto you more fully by word of mouth, may it please you to give credence unto them in all things which they shall say unto you on our behalf, and as it may be your will, to confide in full trust, unto them whatsoever, dread lord and cousin, we your poor cousin may do. Dread lord and cousin, may the almighty preserve your reverence and lordship in long life and good fortune. Written in North Wales, on the twenty-ninth day of November.

NEGOTIATIONS WITH HOTSPUR & THOMAS PERCY

Late in November, Glyndŵr sought a negotiated settlement with Hotspur and his uncle Thomas Percy, Earl of Worcester. Both Percies had been impoverished by the costs of war, and previously Glyndŵr may have negotiated with Hotspur before his departure from Wales. On the other hand, Henry IV was raising monies for his own costs from the Commons, from the Church, from foreign bankers and from moneylenders such as Richard Whittington, Mayor of London. 'Dick' Whittington had also helped finance Richard II and was later to finance Henry V. The Percies were obviously annoyed that Henry was not passing monies on to them. They knew that Glyndŵr now had no sources of finance except what he captured, so there was probably some empathy between him and the Percies. All were losing in this prolonged war. There is a story that Glyndŵr refused to attend a meeting with Thomas Percy in person, as he had intelligence (possibly from Hotspur), that he was to be captured and executed.

Henry IV's advisors later criticised both Percies for not trying to kill Glyndŵr by any means. Hotspur responded saying that Glyndŵr would not break his word of honour to 'an honourable and noble opponent' and that Glyndŵr was not planning 'the genocide of the English' of which he was accused. (There were only about 150,000 inhabitants of Wales at this time, including Flemings and English settlers amounting to perhaps 150-200,000 people. Over 2 million lived in England.) After his failure at Caernarfon, Glyndŵr must have reflected that he could not take great castles except by prolonged siege or trickery, and that living as a guerrilla could not bring about nationhood for Wales. He was grey-headed and old for his times, sometimes referred to by the bards as Owain Llwyd (Grey Owain). If a man lived to be twenty-three, he could expect to live until fifty-nine, and he was around fifty-three years old now. He wanted safety for his wife, children and extended family including the Hanmers and Pulestons. Thomas Percy passed on Glyndŵr's offer to negotiate, to Prince Henry in Chester Castle:

> May it please you to know that the envoys have come from Owen Glendower telling me that the said Owen wishes to parley with representatives of my people, upon which I sent him to know his intent saying that if he would submit with our conditions to the Lord our King, I would make it my task to beg for his life, without promising him anything. He has replied that he dare not come for anything to England because he has heard that the commons of England have slain some great lords against the wishes of the King our Lord without being brought to justice ...

In the rest of the letter, Worcester planned for responding strategically to the threat from Wales:

> ... I suggest that the castle of Pole (*Powys Castle*) would make a good garrison, that Sir Edmund Mortimer and the foot soldiers from this country could reach it on a good route into North Wales and at the same time your garrisons of Chester and Harlech would make another good route for entering different parts. I suggest that I with the people of this country should come towards the borders of North Wales. Mortimer should be informed and one group should meet the others at a chosen spot. It seems to me that this would be one way of dealing with your enemies ...

Eventually Prince Henry seemed to agree that Glyndŵr could be pardoned and his rights of inheritance secured, to stop the war. The Prince agreed that the Earl and Hotspur should carry on negotiating with Glyndŵr. However, Prince Hal carried on planning for three separate armies to make a third expedition against Wales. The Privy Council met in November and asked the King his feelings. Glyndŵr only wanted his life to be spared and the return of his properties. It seems that Henry IV was agreeable, and a meeting was arranged between Glyndŵr and Northumberland's kinsman, Edmund Mortimer. It seemed that the war was ending.

John Kynaston of Stocks was Hotspur's kinsman, and one of the earliest supporters of Glyndŵr. It seems that he was the intermediary in these discussions, as he was later, regarding the 'Tripartite Indenture'. Madoc Kynaston of Stocks would later die fighting for Hotspur against Henry at Shrewsbury, along with many of John Kynaston's tenants.

CHAPTER 6

The Rise of Wales 1402

REGINALD GREY BLOCKS RECONCILIATION JANUARY 1402

In January 1402, the Privy Councillor Reginald de Grey petitioned to block reconciliation between Henry IV and Glyndŵr, alarmed by the attempts of the Percies, and possibly Mortimer, to come to a settlement. Grey wanted revenge, because of his costs in prosecuting war and his losses of livestock and rentals. The Welsh had continually attacked his lands in Duffryn Clwyd, including in that January when Grey was in London, while sparing the neighbouring estates in Denbigh belonging to Hotspur and most of those belonging to Mortimer. Also, Lord Beaufort had been given Glyndŵr's lands and did not wish to return them, so he sided with Lord Grey. The January Privy Council ruling was that 'it neither was nor could be honourable and befitting the King's majesty to remit such a malefactor his offence.' Some of the council, probably led by the treacherous Grey, wished to carry on the negotiations and seize Glyndŵr, but Northumberland refused, saying 'It is not in keeping with my rank to use the oath of fealty as a means of deception.' Glyndŵr was safe, as long as he only trusted the Percies, not Henry IV, Prince Henry, Warwick, Grey or Beaufort.

THE DEATH OF HYWEL SELE

We are unsure of the date, but Hywel Sele (Selyf), 7th Baron Nannau and a supporter of Henry IV, tried to assassinate his cousin Glyndŵr. The Abbot of Cymer was said to have tried to reconcile the two and had arranged the meeting. While out hunting together early in 1402 (although other sources give 1404 and 1406), Hywel Sele drew his bow to shoot Owain, but Glyndŵr cut him down in the act of firing. Realising the repercussions from the Abbot and the followers of Hywel, Owain concealed the body in the hollow of an ancient oak tree. The tree was known as Derwen Ceubren yr Ellyl (The Hollow Oak of the Devils). Then, he fired the mansion of Hywel Sele, leaving Hywel's two-year old son, Meurig Fychan, to be brought up by his uncle, Gruffydd Derwas. Thomas Pennant, writing in 1778, inspected the oak, which was then 27ft 6ins in girth, but 'in its last stages of decay and pierced by age into the form of a gothic arch'. The oak was struck by lightning and brought down in 1813, at which moment an artist was conveniently sketching. The body of Hywel Sele was said to tumble from the stricken tree. However, it seems that Hywel had been laid to rest, with 'nine robed monks in attendance', in nearby Cymer Abbey, rather than entombed in a tree.

Sele's cousin (or son-in-law) Gruffydd ap Gwyn of Ardudwy was alerted that Hywel Sele's manor was being fired by Glyndŵr, and arrived to rescue Sele and put out the fire in the manor, but was killed at Llanelltud Bridge with sixty of his 200 men. Glyndŵr then burned Gruffydd's own manors of Cefn Coch and Berthlwyd. T.P. Ellis gave this version of events:

> In the meantime, Glyndŵr was dealing with Hywel Sele (*Lord of Nannau, outside Dolgellau*). As he was a dangerous man to be at liberty, Glyndŵr determined on capturing him; and in the beginning of 1402 he collected a few men together, attacked Nannau suddenly, and made Hywel Sele a prisoner. Returning to Dolgelley by the road north of Moel Cynwch, and down the Ganllwyd valley, Glyndŵr found his way blocked at Llanelltyd bridge by Griffith ap Gwyn, the son-in-law of Hywel Sele, who had come down by a short cut with 200 men to rescue the captive. A terrible fight took place on the bridge, Owain Glyndŵr eventually cutting his way through his interceptors, of whom some 60 were left dead on the field. The worthy Abbot of Cymmer, whose sympathies were entirely with Glyndŵr, appears to have intervened then, and to have patched up an arrangement under which Hywel Sele agreed to support Glyndŵr, or, at any rate, not to oppose him, and he was set at liberty in consequence.
>
> A short while after Glyndŵr visited Nannau, probably to discuss terms of support, and he and his former captive went out into the woods together. While out walking, a deer was espied, and Hywel Sele, pretending to draw upon it, wheeled round suddenly and shot his arrow at Glyndŵr. Thanks to his coat of mail, the latter escaped injury, and, in revenge for the treacherous assault, he slew Hywel Sele on the spot, and, carrying the corpse a little distance, he thrust it into the hollow trunk of an old tree, inside which it remained for something like 40 years. For centuries after the tree was looked upon as haunted, and was known as Ceubren yr Ellyll, the Hollow Tree of the Ghost, and no one would go near it at night. It was blown down at last in a terrible storm on the night of the 13th July, 1813, when its trunk, three feet from the ground, was found to measure 27 feet in circumference. Its site, in the kitchen garden of Nannau, is still marked by a sundial and a brass plate, on which is engraved a sketch of the tree, made the very day it fell.

HOSTILITIES RESUME FEBRUARY 1402

Hotspur was ordered to return to North Wales at the end of March, and orders were given to the King's Chamberlain in Chester to prepare for another invasion. Hotspur's uncle the Earl of Worcester had been made Royal Lieutenant in South Wales. Again the Percies had been sent to bear the costs of the King's affairs in Wales. Edward Charleton took over from his dead brother John in Powys. The Bishop of St David's, Guy de Mona (Mone), was placed in command of Brecon, Llandovery and Carmarthen. Sir John Oldcastle was sent to Builth Wells with an extra twenty men-at-arms and forty archers for the garrison.

The Earl of Warwick, Richard Beauchamp, reinforced Aberystwyth, Llandovery, Painscastle and Aberystwyth. From North to South Wales, the country was again on a war footing shortly after the peace negotiations failed.

Early in 1402, according to Adam of Usk, a second attack was launched on the town of Rhuthun on 30 January:

> Owen and his men cruelly harried the lordship of Ruthin in North Wales, and the countryside with fire and sword on the last day but one of January, carrying off the spoil of the land and specially the cattle to the mountains of Snowdon; yet did he spare the lordship of Denbigh and others of the Earl of March, having at his back the counties of Cardigan and Merioneth which were favourable to him both for government and war.

Lord Grey had been appointed one of Prince Henry's five lieutenants in North Wales, and was forced to return to his beleaguered lordship by 21 February.

THE GREAT COMET & THE PERSECUTION OF THE FRANCISCANS

From 21 February to 10 April, the perihelion of a great comet was seen day and night across Britain and France, and its appearance helped to convince people of Glyndŵr's almost magical powers. The comet was seen by the Welsh as a sign of their forthcoming deliverance from bondage, reinforcing the star that had proclaimed the birth of Owain. Iolo Goch wrote the cywydd *Y Seren* to commemorate the blazing star, lines of which translate as:

> See ye that blazing star
> The heavens look down on Freedom's War
> And light her torch on high –
> Bright upon the dragon's crest
> It tells that glory's wings will rest,
> When warriors meet to die.
> Let earth's pale tyrants read despair
> And vengeance in its flame –
> Hail! Hail! Ye bards, the omen fair
> Of conquest and of fame,
> And swell the rushing mountain air
> With songs of Glyndŵr's name

The star was also noted in the following documents, which showed the Franciscan monks (friars minor) were a perpetual cause of trouble to the new King, still unsure that his kingdom was free of internal rebellion:

> 1402 The iii year of king Harri, anon after Cristemasse, was seen and appeared a star in the west, flame ascended upward, that was called 'the blazing star,' and by clerks it was called, 'stella te comata-comata.'

And about this time the people of this land began to grouch against king Harri, and bore him heavy, because he took their goods and paid not therefore; and desired to have again King Richard. Also letters came to certain friends of king Richard, as they had be sent from himself, and said that he was alive; whereof many people were glad and desired to have him king again. And a friar minor of the convent of Aylesbury came to the king, and accused a friar of the same house, a priest, and said that he was glad of king Richard being alive; and he was brought to the king, and he said to him: 'Thou hast heard that king Richard is alive, and art glad thereof.'

The friar answered and said, 'I am glad as a man is glad of the life of his friend, for I am beholden to him, and all my kin, for he was our furtherer and promoter.' The king said 'Thou hast noised and told openly that he liveth, and so thou hast excited and stirred the people against me.' The friar said, 'Nay.' Than said the king to him, 'Tell me truth as it is in thy heart; if thou sawest king Richard and me in the field fighting together, with whom wouldst thou hold?' 'Forsooth,' said the friar, 'with him, for I am more beholden to him.' Then said the king, 'thou wouldst that I and all the lords of my realm were dead?' The friar said, 'Nay.' 'What wouldst thou do with me,' said the king, 'if thou had the victory over me?' The friar said, 'I would make you duke of Lancaster.' 'Thou art not my friend,' said the king, 'and therefore thou shalt lose thine head.' And then he was damned before the justice, and drawn and hanged and beheaded ...

1402 After this came another friar minor to the king, that owed no good will to a brother of his, asking mercy and grace, and said that men secular and religious were accorded to meet together upon the plain of Oxenforde on Midsomer eve, and go forth to seek king Richard, 'and Y and X of my fellows of the convent of Leycestre arrayed us for to go with them: and there is in that convent a master of divinity, an old man, that speaketh evil of you, and saith that king Richard shall fight against you, and so it is prophesied, as he saith.' The 8 friars and the master of divinity were brought bound unto London, and the others that were accused could not be found.

And the aforesaid friar accused many other friars of divers convents, but they fled away. The king called the archbishop and other lords, and the friars were brought before them; and some of them were young, and some old and simply lettered and their accuser stood by and steadfastly accused them, and they answered unwarily. Then said the king to the master, 'These be lewd men, and not understanding; thou shouldst be a wise man, sayest thou that king Richard liveth?' The master answered, 'I say not that he liveth, but I say if he live, he is verily king of England.' The king said, 'He resigned.' The master answered, 'He resigned against his will in prison, the which is nought in the law.' The king answered, 'He resigned with his good will!' 'He would not have resigned,' said the master, 'if he had been at his freedom; and a resignation made in prison is not free.' Then said the king, 'He was deposed.' The master answered, 'When he was king he was taken by force, and put into prison, and spoiled of his realm, and ye have usurped the crown.' The king said, 'I have not usurped the crown, but I was chosen thereto by election.' The master answered, 'The election is nought, if living is the true and lawful possessor; and if he be dead, he is dead by you, and if he be dead by you, ye have lost all the right and title that ye may have to the crown.' Then said the king to him, 'By mine head thou shalt lose thine head.' The master said to the king, 'Ye loved never the church, but always slandered it ere ye were king, and now ye shall destroy it.' 'Thou liest,' said the king; and bade him exit, and he and his fellows were led again unto the tower. Then asked the king for counsel, what he should do with them; and a knight that loved never the church said, 'We shall never cease this clamour of king Richard till these friars be destroyed.' The minister of the friars went to the king, and said that he had commanded all his brethren that they had not seen or spoken in prejudice and offence of his person, and asked grace for them. The king said to him, 'They will not be chastised by thee, and therefore they shall be chastised by me.' Then they were brought to Westminster before the justice, and the justice said unto them 'You are indicted that ye in hypocrisy and flattering and false life, have preached false sermons; wherein ye said falsely that king Richard liveth, and have excited the people to seek him in Scotland.

Also, ye in your hypocrisy and false life, have heard false confessions, wherein ye have enjoined to the people way of penance, to seek king Richard in Wallis – Also, ye with your false flattering and hypocrisy, have gathered a great sum of money with begging, and sent it to Oweyne of Glendore, a traitor, that he should come and destroy England – Also, ye have sent in to Scotland for men to be ready upon the plain of Oxenford on Midsomer eve to seek king Richard. How will ye excuse you? I counsel you to put you in the king's grace.' The friars answered, 'We put us upon the country.' And neither men of London nor of Holborne would damn them; and then they had an inquest of Yseldon, and they said 'Guilty.' Then the justice gave judgement and said, 'Ye should be drawn from the tower of London unto Tyburne, and there ye shall be hanged, and hang a whole day, and afterward be take down, and your heads smitten off and set on London bridge.' And so it was done.

And the master at Tyburne made a devout sermon with this theme, 'In manus Tuas Domine,' and swore by his soul that he trespassed not against king Harri, and forgave them that were the cause of his death. And another friar when he should die said, 'It was not our intent, as our enemies say, to slay the king and his son, but for to make him duke of Lancaster, as he should be.' On the morrow about evensong time, one came to the warden of the friars, and said he might get away the bodies and bury them; and when they came they found them cast into ditches and beggis, and the heads smitten off, and they bore them home to their convent with great lamentation. And afterward, men that damned them, came to the friars praying them of forgiveness, and said, 'But if they had said that the friars were not guilty, they should have be slain'.
(An English Chronicle, ed. Davies.)

THE CAPTURE OF LORD GREY

AD 1401 The unsettled state of the English government encouraged Owen Glyndour, a descendant of the ancient prince of Wales, and obnoxious to the present ruling power, on account of his attachment to the late king, to set up his standard in opposition to Henry. His mind was that of a hero, and his heart that of a patriot, ready to burst with indignation at the miseries of his country. His genius was enterprising, his conduct firm but cautious. Owen contented himself at first with attacking the estates of the earl of Ruthin. He was always successful in these skirmishes, and at last took that nobleman prisoner (1402).
(Barnard's History of England 1783.)

In mid-April 1402 Glyndŵr led his men to once more attack Rhuthun Castle, which was strongly defended by Grey, his personal army and royal troops. The Welsh were repulsed, and seemed in confusion, and the main body withdrew. Glyndŵr, with a small force, lingered out of bowshot range from the castle. Lord Grey, almost definitely urged on by sympathizers of Glyndŵr, led a charge from the castle to finally vanquish his weakened enemy. Glyndŵr rode off quickly, and Grey led his force straight into an ambush by the rest of Glyndŵr's men in the forest of Coedmarchan. The legend is that Grey's men were in hot pursuit, when they spied a huge force in front of them in the woods. However, these were captured cloaks and helmets set on poles. Grey's men wheeled around to escape, fleeing straight into a Welsh ambush. Not only were there archers on either side, but Grey's retreat was cut off.

The English were sure that the main Welsh force would be coming at them from the false army in the woodland, and desperately tried to fight their way back to the safety of Rhuthun Castle. Glyndŵr focused on Grey and his bodyguard, possibly forcing them to Bryn Saith Marchog, the Hill of the Seven Knights. It is supposedly named as Grey and six others were cut off there. Nearly all of Grey's force had died in the fight. However, Grey was too important to be killed, so he was captured and taken away for a valuable ransom. He may have been held at Dolbadarn Castle, but by tradition his prison was at Llansanffraid. Thomas Pennant left an eighteenth century description of it as a room 13 ft square and 10 ft 6 in high. We must remember that Owain had no resources to pay, feed or equip his followers in the War of Independence, so Grey was of inestimable value to his campaign. Glyndŵr sent his ransom demand of 11,000 marks to Parliament, with a deadline of a month to pay. Otherwise Grey, the perpetrator of all his troubles, would be executed.

> 1402 Owain and his host went and attacked in the neighbourhood of Ruthin and Dyffryn Clwyd, and Reginald Grey, lord of that region, took the field against him. And Lord Grey was there captured and long held a prisoner by Owain in wild and rocky places: at last he was ransomed for 11,000 marks.
>
> (Peniarth MS 135)

John Hardyng (1378-1465) fought for Hotspur at Shrewsbury, so obviously knew both Glyndŵr and Lord Grey, and in his *Chronicle* records his disdain for Grey:

> The lord Graye Ruthin did him great wrong
> Destoyed his land, and did him the same ...
> So on a day the lord Graye and he met
> With great power upon either side,
> Where then they fought in battle sore bet,
> And took him then his prisoner that tide,
> And there the field he had with muckle pride,
> Great people took and slew, and home he went,
> The lord Graye he ransomed at his intent.

The weather was foul that spring, and yet again people believed that Glyndŵr was controlling the weather. The rebellion was gathering momentum, especially after the successes at Hyddgen and the capture of the hated Grey. Angered, Henry IV executed more people in Wales, including several monks. However, Henry also sent eleven knights to negotiate the ransom with Glyndŵr. These men were Grey's allies who included Sir William de Willoughby, Sir Hugh Hals, Sir Richard de Grey, Sir William de Roos and Sir William de Zouche. Six thousand marks were to be paid within a month, and then Grey's eldest son was to replace him as surety for the balance. The Bishop of London was granted power of attorney to sell Grey's manor at Harleigh in Kent to raise the monies, in mid-1402. The King also gave Grey some tax allowances on his Irish holdings.

Lord Grey then would have been expected to repay the amount over time as best he could, and any outstanding debt would be borne by his family. The family did in fact sell the lordship to Henry VII in 1508 when their fortunes and favour declined. (Eleven thousand silver marks ransom for Lord Grey are worth today c.£2,300,00 (RPI) or c.£41,000,000 adjusted for Average Earnings, a mark being worth 2/3 of a pound (13 s and 4 d in old money). Gold marks would be worth nine times as much. There is a story that the ransom was paid by Grey's agents in false gold, but they were discovered and punished, before the correct ransom was paid. *Hardyng's Chronicle* recounts Grey's ensuing poverty:

> Soon after was the same Lord Greye in field,
> Fighting, taken and holden prisoner
> By Owayne, so that him in prison helde,
> Till his ransome was made and finance
> Ten thousand mark and full paid were dear
> For which he was so poor all his life
> That no power had he to war nor strike.

Grey swore never to bear arms against Glyndŵr again, and Adam of Usk, working in the Vatican, seems to have exaggerated when he recounted 'The Lord Grey of Ruthin being taken prisoner by the said Owen with the slaughter of 2000 of his men was shut up in prison; but he was set free on payment of 16000 pounds in gold'.

At this time, Henry IV received a calculated insult when the title of Duc de Guyenne was given to Louis (1397-1415), the infant son of Charles VI, as Henry had already bestowed that title upon the Prince of Wales. However, Henry IV was at war with France, Scotland and Wales so he had to try to build bridges. In April, he married Joan of Navarre, widow of Duke John IV of Brittany, and sister of Charles III of Navarre. This was highly unpopular among the Francophobe nobles and people. It was rumoured that Queen Joan practised necromancy, and she was actually convicted of witchcraft in 1419, in the reign of Henry V, her stepson.

Hotspur had spent the spring strengthening defences and garrisons across North Wales, and naval patrols operated from Chester. In June Hotspur returned to Chester, with the primary aim of supporting the English castles in the Marches and Wales. A force of 100 men-at-arms and 400 archers was rushed to Harlech to save it from surrendering, and a Scottish fleet was sighted off Caernarfon. Hotspur also quickly indented Sir William Stanley and Sir John de Pole with twenty-four lances and forty-eight archers for a tour at sea.

Throughout the spring Glyndŵr had been in Maelienydd (Radnorshire), taking castles belonging to the Mortimers including Cymaron (Cwm Aran, Valley of the Aran), Knucklas (Cnwclas, Green Knoll), Bleddfa and Cefnllys (Ridge of the Court). These were all in disrepair, unlike the great royal castles. Churches paying tithes to the English were also sacked. He seemed to be heading towards Herefordshire, but heard that Edmund Mortimer was on the move. Mortimer (1376-1409) was the second son of the 3rd Earl of March, and had a better claim to the throne than Henry Bolingbroke. Young Mortimer had been appointed the King's chief lieutenant in the Marches, and his retaliation was expected by Glyndŵr. (His nephew, the other Edmund Mortimer of Wigmore, Earl of March was the real heir to the crown, with a prior claim to this Edmund Mortimer or Henry IV, but was held by Henry.) Mortimer raised an army of around 2,500-3,000 men at Ludlow, led by the sheriff of Herefordshire, Sir Kinard de la Bere. Lord Kinnersley supplied troops, as did Sir Walter Devereux of Weobley and Lyonshall castles, Sir Robert Whitney of Whitney-on-Wye Castle and Sir Thomas Clanvowe. Mortimer's archers also assembled at Ludlow, and seem to have been infiltrated by hundreds of Glyndŵr's men among his tenants.

The Earl of Northumberland had suggested a three-prong attack through Wales, and the middle prong of 500 men had reached Harlech to relieve it. Hotspur could have attacked the north and Anglesey from Chester, and Mortimer's forces could have left Hereford and Ludlow to head south. Hotspur was said to have come to an earlier agreement with Glyndŵr on Cader Idris, and Percy and Mortimer lands had been hardly touched in the revolt. (Strangely, Mortimer's Denbigh Castle was never attacked, although it was an easier target than Harlech, Aberystwyth or Caernarfon.) Thus, of the planned three-fold attack, Mortimer's army of up to 3,000 men left Ludlow to find Glyndŵr, while a second force relieved Harlech, but Hotspur's third contingent (because of collusion?) stayed at Chester. The following battle is hardly known in British history books.

THE BATTLE OF BRYN GLAS, OR PILLETH, 22 JUNE 1402

Glyndŵr, alerted of the oncoming army of Lord Mortimer, halted his raiding in Maelienydd (north-eastern Radnorshire) at Pilleth, bear Knighton and Presteigne. At the church on the side of the hill of Bryn Glas, Owain prayed at its exterior holy well, which can still be seen. The church of St Mary's is mentioned in the Domesday Book, and there may have been a church here since the fifth century. It was originally a church dedicated to Cynllo, belonging to the 'clas' of Llangunllo, but rededicated like hundreds of churches in Wales by the Normans to saints Mary, John, Michael etc. It dates from the time when England and the rest of Europe was barbarian – the Dark Ages – and Wales by contrast was in the midst of The Age of Saints. The holy well can be seen just to the north of the church, and was used to cure eye problems. Throughout the Middle Ages, St Mary's was a place of pilgrimage to its statue of the Virgin.

Owain's second-in-command, Rhys Gethin of Cwm Llanerch (near Conwy) could see the English approaching up the wide valley of the River Lugg, and took a defensive position on the hill, with half his force hidden. Glyndŵr's sons were captains in his army – Gruffydd,

Maredudd, Madoc, Thomas and John. Glyndŵr and Rhys Gethin placed around 700-800 archers at the foot of Bryn Glas, and as the English approached, they retreated to a position about two-thirds up the slope. The other 700-800 men-at-arms and infantry were hidden by thick woodland cover in a gulley behind the blazing church. Mortimer's army formed up and began loosing volleys of arrows into the Welsh. They fell short, owing to the steep gradient, but the Welsh fire from up the hill was deadly at such short range.

The English men-at-arms waited for the order to attack, which Mortimer had to give before his force was wiped out. The order to charge was accompanied by his Welsh longbowmen defecting, firing direct volleys into the English army. Glyndŵr's own archers now took up spears and charged downhill into the advancing English, who had been significantly reduced in numbers. Simultaneously, Glyndŵr's banner appeared and his men emerged from cover to attack. The English had ordered a cavalry charge of their horsemen in the valley, but the steepness of the hill meant that their horses were exhausted well before they could reach the fighting. The remaining English foot soldiers were forced backwards, and the battle broke into two parts. The English at the foot of the hill were now charged by the Welsh cavalry, and the English battling on the hill were decimated by Welsh spearmen and archers.

Mortimer's exhausted troops collapsed and broke. The Welsh had won their first major victory in open warfare against the English forces. It is said that immediately after the battle, many English corpses were mutilated by Welsh women camp followers, in revenge for Henry IV's expedition of 1401 and its accompanying rape and capture of children. The English Parliament was desperate to portray the Welsh as savages – how else could they beat an English army? Perhaps 1100 to 1500 of men of the Herefordshire levies died, and the Welsh had gained enormous numbers of weapons. In Shakespeare's *Henry IV: Part I* we read:

> But yesternight: when all athwart there came
> A post from Wales loaden with heavy news:
> Whose worst was, that the noble Mortimer,
> Leading the men of Herefordshire to fight,
> Against the wild and irregular Glendower,
> Was by the rude hand of that Welshman taken,
> A thousand of his people butchered ...

The clump of Wellingtonia fir trees up the hill to the left of the church was planted in the nineteenth century by a local landowner, Sir Richard Green-Price. It marks where he found the bones of some of the slain. At the time of the battle, Cwmhir Abbey and Pilleth, Cascob and Bleddfa churches were burnt. Walford Wynne-Jones, in his 1989 pamphlet *A Guide to the Church of Our Lady of Pilleth*, invokes the English propaganda of the day, which has no basis in fact, that 'After the battle the Welsh female camp followers mutilated the corpses of the English and demanded payment before the bodies could be buried; not a very praiseworthy action.' The anti-Welsh Monk of Evesham and Walsingham both wrote of these atrocities. A simple explanation for the opinion that the dead had been mutilated by women is that the camp-followers will have stripped not just arms but the jerkins, boots, and armour – everything useable – from the dead. This was usual and expected at all battles. Possibly only the Welsh were buried, as Glyndŵr's men quickly marched on south to take advantage of their victory. The Welsh slain were more likely to have been concentrated on the hill.

The English dead would have been scattered all the way up hill and over the plain below, with some of the fleeing men being ridden down and killed. By the time these English bodies would have been found, weeks later, by wary English search parties, the foxes, ravens, buzzards, wild dogs, badgers and kites would have done their worst. There is no evidence of any such barbarity except in the propaganda of Parliament – as ever, history is written by the eventual victors. The *Peniarth MS 135* records the battle thus:

> Owain arose with a great host from Gwynedd, Powys, and the South, and made for Maelienydd; where the knights of Herefordshire gathered together against him. The battle between them was fought near Pilleth, and there Sir Robert Whitney and Sir Kinard de la Bere were slain and Sir Edmund Mortimer and Sir Thomas Clanvow were captured and most of the English host slain. In the following August Owain came to Glamorgan and all Glamorgan rose with him; Cardiff and Abergafenni were burnt.

Sir Robert de Whitney, Sir Walter Devereux and Sir Kinard de la Bere were killed. Sir Thomas Clanvowe was soon ransomed. Edmund Mortimer was the brother-in-law of Sir Henry Hotspur Percy, and taken prisoner. Glyndŵr offered him for ransom, hoping for even more money than he had received for Lord Grey. However, to Hotspur's fury, Henry did not want to ransom Mortimer, and forbade any attempts to do so. Henry even suspected Mortimer of treachery after the defeat, as well as becoming increasingly unsure of the loyalty of Hotspur.

> 1402 And this same year, Oweyn of Glendore took sir Edmund Mortymer in Walis, and because he might not pay his ransom, he would never be under king Harri, but wedded one of Oweyne's daughters. In the birth of this Edmund full many wonders tokened; for out of the floor of his father's stable came out blood, and welled up so high that it covered the horses' feet: and all the sheaths of swords and of the daggers in the house were full of blood, and all the axes with red of blood; and when the said Edmund lay in his cradle he might not sleep, nor cease from crying, till he saw a sword: and when he sat in his nurse's lap he would not be still until he had some instrument of war to play with.
>
> (An English Chronicle, ed. Davies.)

An article in *The Daily Telegraph* of 12 February 2002 tells us that Peter Hood farmed Pilleth Court for almost 50 years – and every day he would have seen on the hill the four great redwood trees, planted in the patch of cleared ground where a plough turned up a mass grave at the end of the nineteenth century. Hood said

> Only two things are known for certain... The church was set on fire by Glyndŵr, and the Welsh archers on the English side changed sides. And this is what I think happened: Owain is a hit-and-run

expert, he does not have the men to do anything else, so it has to be an ambush for him to destroy such a big army. The old road into Wales is across the river, and the English, coming down that, see the church burning. So they cross to investigate. At that point, below an old Norman fort, a causeway crosses the marsh. So they move uphill, and the trap closes. In 1402 the hill wouldn't have been ploughed, so Glyndŵr's archers rise up out of the bushes.

Paul Watkins said: 'The Welsh archers on the English side would suddenly have seen Glyndŵr's flag. And that would have been it, they would have known who was up there.'

Martin Marix Evans knows the land. 'For me, the clue is that the hill is not continuous, and behind the church is a gully where 600 or so men could have hidden. So the English army sees the men on the hill, and thinks: 'We can take those Welsh bastards.' And then, when they are committed and on the actual slopes, the others appear.'

Adam of Usk overestimated the death toll:

On the day of Saint Alban (June 22nd), near to Knighton in Wales, was hard battle between the English under Sir Edmund Mortimer and the Welsh under Owen Glendower, with woeful slaughter even to eight thousand souls, the victory being with Owen. And alas!, my lord the said Sir Edmund, whose father, the lord of Usk, supported me at the schools, was by fortune of war carried away captive. And, being by his enemies in England stripped of all his goods and hindered from paying ransom, in order to escape more easily the pains of captivity, he is known by common report to have wedded the daughter of the same Owen; by whom he had a son, Lionel, and three daughters, all of whom, except one daughter, along with their mother are now dead. At last, being by the English host besieged in the castle of Harlech, he brought his days of sorrow to an end, his wonderful deeds being to this day told at the feast in song.

In this year also the lord Grey of Ruthin, being taken captive by the same Owen, with the slaughter of two thousand of his men, was shut up in prison; but he was set free on payment or ransom of sixteen thousand pounds of gold. Concerning such an ill-starred blow given by Owen to the English rule, when I think thereon, my heart trembles. For, backed by a following of thirty thousand men issuing from their lairs, throughout Wales and its marches he overthrew castles, among which were Usk, Caerleon, and Newport, and fired the towns. In short, like a second Assyrian, the rod of God's anger, he did deeds of unheard-of cruelty with fire and sword.

On hearing the news of Pilleth, Henry IV abandoned his plans to invade Scotland, and levied massive fines on the border counties because border Welshmen had helped Glyndŵr. However, throughout Wales, rents and fines went unpaid as they could not be enforced except in areas around heavily defended castles. All garrisons were placed in high alert. Yet more men flocked to Owain's banner. Franciscan monks across Britain, the Friars Minor who supported Richard II, still urged men to rise up and throw out the usurper, Henry IV. After Pilleth, Glyndŵr's swollen army headed south.

In August 1402 Sir Robert de Whitney's castle at Whitney-on-Wye in Herefordshire was destroyed by Glyndŵr, as Whitney had fought him at Pilleth. In 1404 Henry IV gave the castles and lordships of Clifford and Glasbury to his son Sir Robert Whitney because 'his property has been burnt and destroyed by our rebels of Wales, so that the same Robert has not any castle or fortress where he can tarry to resist and punish our aforesaid rebels'. These castles and lordships belonged to Edmund Mortimer, who by then had joined Glyndŵr's supporters. Whitney Castle was eventually rebuilt, but was destroyed again, washed away by the River Wye in 1730 when it changed course.

Adam of Usk mentions that after Pilleth, Glyndŵr attacked and burned the castles of Usk, Caerleon, Cardiff and Newport. Intriguingly, in the following year, on 13 September, John Pers of Usk was given a pardon for having joined the Welsh forces. The pardon was made on the supplication of Joan, the wife of William Beauchamp, Lord of Abergafenni. Adam of Usk recorded the story of John fitz Peers, the same man, when he was seneschal of Usk Castle in 1401, so he presumably had joined Glyndŵr in preference to exile. Adam tells us that Pers was accused of an affair with the prioress of Usk, who was a sister of Sir Edward Charleton (who succeeded in 1402 as Lord of Powys when his brother John was killed).

1401 At this same time certain burgesses of the town of Usk, secretly leaving the church during the service of the passion of our Lord, craftily entered into the castle, and breaking prison set free one John fitz Pers, late seneschal therein, who, having been accused by evil report of adultery with a certain lady, had been, to all men's wonder, condemned to death by sir Edward Charleton, who was her natural brother, and now lay naked undergoing punishment, and they delivered him to the Lord of Abergavenny in his castle of Abergavenny, to their great delight, although for this reason on account of seduction he was afterwards exiled by the king.

Around this time, the Lord of Abergafenni deputed Sir William Lucy of Richard's Castle, Hereford, to hang three villeins for theft, on the holy day of the Festival of the Ascension. Flights of arrows prevented the execution and the men escaped. Law and order was breaking down everywhere near the border.

There was a large group of Welsh students at Oxford University, and Howel Kyffin (Gethin), the Dean of St Asaf (Llanelwy) was sent there to raise support for the war. He was Glyndŵr's Chancellor, unknown to the English at this time. By July 1402 Henry was forced to send a commission to deal with the problem, seeking delinquent Welshmen and placing them under guard. Along with Howel Kyffin, they arrested 'Clerks of Wales' Owen Conway and David Lekebreth, plus Wilfred Taylor, David Peyntour, William Laurence, William Taylor and Emmota Taylor, David Lekebreth, John Bastard and Owen Conway's 'companion' William. The suspects were brought to court on 5 August, accused of being collaborators of Glyndŵr in his treachery. Wilfred Taylor and Emmota Taylor were charged with separate offences. Owen Conway had previously been brought before Henry IV in 1401 for allegedly preaching rebellion against the 'unrightful' king. Wilfred Taylor turned 'King's Evidence' and became the main accuser. Owen challenged him to trial by battle, and a date was set for 13 November, but Taylor refused to fight, admitting he had made up evidence, and was hanged. All the defendants were set free.

In the summer of 1402, Breton pirates in channel and Celtic sea were cooperating with the Welsh against the English. There is a tale that David Perrott of Tenby landed former Welsh followers of Owain Lawgoch and Bretons, flying Lawgoch's flag. They buried Lawgoch's heart in Llandybie Church before supporting Glyndŵr. Glyndŵr besieged

Brecon, and had taken Abergafenni, Usk, Caerleon, Newport and Cardiff. Iolo Morganwg placed the following actions in 1400 but they more likely occurred in 1402 to 1404:

> In 1400 Owen Glyndŵr came to Glamorgan and won the castle of Cardiff and many more. He also demolished the castles of Penlline, Landough, Flemingston, Dunraven of the Butlers, Tal-y-van, Llanbleddian, Llanqian, Malefant, and that of Penmarc ... and many of the country people joined him of one accord, and they laid waste the fences and gave lands in common to all. They took away from the powerful and rich, and distributed the plunder among the weak and poor. Many of the higher orders and chieftains were obliged to flee into England.
> (See the account of Stalling Down in 1403.)

These castles are all in the Vale of Glamorgan, on Owain's route along the old Roman road from Carmarthen to Cardiff and Newport. Penllyne is just north of the road, near the walled bastide of Cowbridge, which was also said to have been attacked. Llandough Castle is just south of Cowbridge, as are the remains of Flemingston Castle (where Iolo Morganwg lived in a cottage). Dunraven (Dyndrafan) overlooked Southerndown Beach, and was rebuilt as a mansion, now sadly destroyed. Talyfan is north of Cowbridge, and St Quintin's Castle at Llanbleddian is on the southern outskirts of Cowbridge. Llanquian Castle remains are on Stalling Down outside Cowbridge, where Glyndŵr later (or now) fought the English, and the remains of Malefant Castle are in Llanmaes (previously named Llangattwg) are north of Llantwit Major. Penmark is in the central Vale of Glamorgan, south-west of Cowbridge. Glyndŵr was also said to have destroyed West Orchard Castle in St Athan in the Vale of Glamorgan. Coity Castle at Bridgend had to be relieved twice between 1402 and 1405, and the 'knighting chamber' at Ogmore (Ogwr) Castle was destroyed, along with its farm-buildings at Blackhall. Glamorgan was invaded by Glyndŵr in 1402 and 1404 (with the French), and it is difficult to know which events happened in which year. The Battle of Stalling Down may certainly have happened at this time, but has been placed later in this narrative.

The principal event was the capture of and burning of Abergafenni and then Cardiff, and Gruffydd Hiraethog mentions them being burnt in 1402. In the *Eulogium* we read about Cardiff:

> Owain took the town and burned it, except for the street in which the Friars Minor lived, which for his love of friars, together with their convent, he allowed to stand. In addition, he took the castle and destroyed it, and took away many valuables which had been deposited there. When the Friars Minor asked him for their books and silver which they had deposited in the castle he replied: 'Why did you put your goods in the castle? If you had left them at home, they would have been safe.'

Certainly the victorious Welsh made a 'Great Raid' along the border, heading down from Pilleth into Monmouthshire and then through Newport and Cardiff and into Vale of Glamorgan. Many men and camp followers joined, and Glyndŵr's speedy raiding force became a lumbering army. Glyndŵr knew he had to move his loot away from any invading force. From the Vale, there were strong English castles west at Ogmore and Coity, north at Llantrisant and Caerffili, and England lay to his east. There was also the danger of a naval attack on his southern flank from Bristol. Men could be landed almost anywhere in the 70 miles of coastline between Newport and Swansea. Some records suggest that Llantrisant Castle had already been attacked by the men of Glamorgan and vacated by the English. If this was true then the best way to safety was marching up the river valley of Y Rhondda, towards the wilds of Penrhys. Another alternative was to leave via Pencoed north of Bridgend (Pencoed has an 'Ogof Glyndŵr' folk story when Glyndŵr sheltered in a cave in the woodlands there). From Pencoed, Owain could head up toward Mynydd y Gaer, helped by the Welsh of the Ogwr (Ogmore) Valley.

Aware of the English mustering armies for a fresh invasion towards South Wales, Owain headed west, attacking the great castles of Aberystwyth, Harlech and Caernarfon, then cutting back to his homelands in north-east Wales to attack Ruthin and Duffryn Clwyd. Rhys Gethin (Rhys the Fierce) was left in charge of his forces in the south. There are surviving cywyddau to Rhys and his brother Hywel Coetmor. Rhys is called 'a warrior with a yellow spear, like Owain, jewel of the glen.' In North Wales the Tudur brothers, Gwilym and Rhys, had raised a large force of spearmen to help the cause. Robert Meredith of Cricieth sided with Glyndŵr, while his brother Ieuan was the co-defender of Caernarfon with John Bolde; such was the effect on families across Wales. Glyndŵr also had effected a system of intelligence across England and Wales, for instance the priest John ap Howell of Rhos-on-Wye, who was accused of passing information to Glyndŵr, and using 'little Welsh beggar boys as agents'.

THE THIRD ROYAL EXPEDITION INTO WALES 3 SEPTEMBER 1402

Hardyng's Chronicle relates:

> The King Henry thrice to Wales went
> In the haytime and the harvest, divers years
> In every time were mists and tempests sent
> Of weather foul that he had never power
> Glendower to know; but o'er his carriage clear
> Owen had at certain straits and passages,
> And to our hosts did full great damage.
> The King had never but foul tempest and rain
> As long as he was e'er in Wales' ground –
> Rocks and mists, winds and storms certain
> All men trowed that witches made that stounde *(stounde=fate)*
> The commons, all of them on England's ground,
> Cursed his going to Wales every year
> For hay and corn were lost, both in fear.

Henry appointed his son commander of an army called to muster at Lichfield on 31 July.

He planned the tripartite attack which had been recommended by Northumberland, to be directed from Shrewsbury, Chester, and Hereford. It was set in motion, but left Glyndŵr free to move into South Wales. Men of eighteen counties were summoned. There seems to be a payment for this expedition recorded on 17 July 1403, noted in Wylie. Wages of £8,108 were paid to four barons, twenty knights, 476 esquires and 2,500 archers.

The Prince of Wales led an army into North Wales from Chester. Henry IV marched into central Wales from Shrewsbury. The Earls of Warwick, Stafford and Arundel were to strike at South Wales from Hereford. A Welsh traitor, William Whitiford, claimed he knew where Glyndŵr hid, and promised to bring the King's army to meet Glyndŵr's main force.

Spies and agents were sent out in advance of any royal expedition. Also scouts ranged the area around the progress (front, sides and rear) in case of ambush. Guides, often local forced men, were used to analyse the best river crossings, paths across hills and so on. There was no opposition in North Wales – Llanrwst and other towns were torched and killing, raping and looting of civilians was common. In later histories, the burning of Llanrwst was uniformly blamed on Glyndŵr, for obvious reasons, but Henry IV massacred its inhabitants. The abbey at Maenan was looted and buildings burned, the Abbot who openly supported Glyndŵr reporting that books, vestments, chalices and ornaments had been carried away. Glyndŵr's army avoided pitched battles with the English but continued harassing the enemy.

On 7 September, a tornado was recorded in Wales, which threw down 'the king's lances' and 'pierced armour'. The huge wind blew down Henry IV's tent, inflicting such damage that had the King not been sleeping in his armour he would have been killed, crushed by a giant tent-pole. By the end of the month he has returned to London, abandoning his campaign against the Welsh, and leaving Owain effective ruler of Wales. Once again the elements appeared to back Glyndŵr as the weather turned, with storms destroying the English armies' morale. Henry returned to England in disarray. It was thought at the time that Glyndŵr could command the elements, as well as possessing a magic 'Raven's Stone' that made him invisible – even the English troops ascribed magical properties to this guerrilla partisan. Again, this is referred to in *Henry IV Part 1*:

> Three times hath Henry Bolingbroke made head
> Against my power. Thrice from the banks of the Wye
> And sandy-bottomed Severn have I sent
> Him bootless home, and weather-beaten back.

A 1402 entry in *Annales Henrici Quarti* records that Glyndŵr 'almost destroyed the King and his armies, by magic as it was thought, for from the time they entered Wales to the time they left, never did a gentle air breathe on them, but throughout whole days and nights, rain mixed with snow and hail afflicted them with cold beyond endurance.' Britain and Europe suffered such a severe winter that wolves from Norway crossed the sea ice into Jutland. On 22 September Henry returned to London, and as soon as the royal expedition left, in late September Glyndŵr again raided Grey's possessions in Dyffryn Clwyd. The body of William Whitiford, the spy, had been found outside his blazing home – whether killed by the king or Glyndŵr's men is unknown. In August and September, the navy had sent fresh men and supplies to Harlech, Caernarfon and Beaumaris castles. Harlech and Caernarfon also had land reinforcements to prevent them falling to the Welsh. Parliament, when it assembled on 30 September 1402, enacted a series of statutes prohibiting public assemblies, the bearing of arms by the Welsh, the importation of victuals or armour, and the keeping of castles or the holding of office by Welshmen. Especial mention was made of those of the amity or alliance of 'Owen ap Glendourdy, traitor to our sovereign lord and King', who, together with Englishmen married to Welshwomen, were likewise denied office in Wales. Henry's armies, of perhaps 30,000 men, had been forced to return to England and re-supply – there had been little left to plunder, and few livestock alive to feed his men.

> Owen (was) still more illustrious in the eyes of the Welch, who now considered him as born to be the deliverer of the country. The earl of Marche (Edmund Mortimer), who had armed his followers in favour of Henry, was defeated and taken prisoner. He was suffered to remain in captivity; nor would the king, notwithstanding his loyalty, permit the earl of Northumberland to ransom him, though he owed his crown to the assistance of that powerful nobleman. But notwithstanding his indifference to his cousin (Mortimer), Henry ordered all his forces to advance to the borders of Wales. Owen, who was in no condition to oppose a royal army, commanded by the ablest and most fortunate prince of the age, in the open field, pursued that conduct which true policy dictated, and his ancestors had found successful. He retired behind Snowdon-Hills, and left the English monarch, in severe season, to wreak his vengeance on an already desolate country. By this prudent step, Henry was compelled to return to England, without having affected anything of consequence against the enemy.
>
> 1402 – When the season permitted, he (Henry) again entered Wales, but the very elements fought against him, and nature seemed to have abandoned her ordinary course in favour of Owen. Such dreadful storms arose, that the common people in that age of ignorance believed they were raised by the magic of Glendour, whose activity and success, above all his retirement into parts almost inaccessible, made them consider him as something more than human. Henry was unable to regain any part of the vast plunder taken from the English, and forced to abandon an expedition, in which his disappointment was heightened by the great hopes he had entertained of success.
> (Barnard's History of England 1783.)

THE BATTLE OF HOMILDON HILL 14 SEPTEMBER 1402

A large army of Scots had crossed the border into England in August. Archibald, Earl of Douglas, had invaded to avenge the killing and capture of prominent Scottish nobles in the Battle of Nesbit Moor. His army was returning from pillaging Northumberland, and suffered complete defeat at the Battle of Humbleton Hill (or Homildon Hill). The Scots chronicler Walter Bower records:

> ... the English bowmen, advancing towards the Scots, smothered them with arrows and made them bristle like hedgehogs, transfixing the arms and hands of the Scots to their own lances. By means of this very harsh rain of arrows, they wounded others and they killed many.

The Percies captured no less than five Scottish earls, but Henry IV gave orders that they were not to be ransomed. This severely angered the Percies, to whom the King already owed £10,000 and led to rebellion, of which more later. Bower was Abbot of Incholm, and in his 'Scotochronicon' strongly sympathised with Glyndŵr's attempts to unite the Scottish (the Alban people) and Welsh (the Britons) against the English:

> The Britons shall flourish, in alliance with the Alban people;
> The whole island will bear its ancient name
> As the eagle proclaims, speaking from the ancient tower,
> The Britons with the Scots rule their fatherland.
> They will rule in harmony and quiet prosperity,
> Their enemies expelled, until the day of judgement.

THE STORY OF LLANRWST

Llanrwst is an interesting example of what had happened across Wales before and during the War of Independence. Wales had been severely depopulated by the plague. The Black Death arrived at Llanrwst around 1350, and not one person survived. Llanrwst was a major market town and important crossing, so there was a daily influx of hundreds of people, half of whom may already have contracted the disease. Persistent crop failures had left its people hungry and weak. Families native to Llanrwst and the Conwy Valley returned to repopulate the town after the plague, and the town became a focus of Welsh rebellion against Plantagenet rule in Wales. In 1390 the parson died and the Bishop of St Asaf had tried to force an Englishman, William Brown into the benefice, but the local lord, Hywel Coetmor of Cwm Llanerch expelled Brown as he was a non-Welsh-speaker and outsider. The Coetmor family was in possession of Gwydir castle during this period (Hywel's son Dafydd later sold Gwydir to the famous Wynn family). Hywel Coetmor was of a noble Welsh family, the illegitimate great-grandson of the last native Prince of Wales Dafydd. (Illegitimacy was not a stigma under Welsh Law. Illegitimate children had exactly the same status and rights as other children.)

Hywel Coetmor's armoured effigy lies in St Grwst Church. Hywel was a veteran of several campaigns against the French, including Poitiers, and his brother Rhys Gethin became Glyndŵr's most trusted lieutenant. Upon his return from the continental wars, Hywel had resumed his role as squire until the Glyndŵr rebellion, when he became one of its principal leaders. Sir John E Lloyd wrote:

> When Owain Glyndŵr's rebellion shook the country, the Conway Valley was under the sway of two brothers who espoused his cause. Hywel Coetmor and Rhys Gethin, who from their eyrie in Cwm Llanerch near Betws y Coed, so harassed the town of Llanrwst that grass grew in the market place and the deer fed in the churchyard.

Sir John Wynn had earlier written:

1. 'Owain's Motte' overlooking the site of burnt Glyndŵr's mansion at Carrog in the Dee Valley.

2. Owain's rolling, fertile estates around Glyndyfrdwy, between Llangollen and Corwen. His ancestral title in Powys Fadog was Baron of Glyndyfrdwy and Lord of Cynllaith, before he was crowned Prince of Wales.

3. Bwrdd y Tri Arglwydd – The stone 'Table of the Three Lords', where the boundaries of the estates of the Lords Glyndŵr, Grey and Arundel met, and disputes were traditionally settled.

4. Moat at Glyndŵr's great mansion at Sycharth in the lordship of Cynllaith in the Berwyn Mountains, south-east of his other lordship of Glyndyfrdwy.

5. Whittington Castle in Shropshire, attacked by Glyndŵr. Pardons were offered to the citizens of Whittington as early as 1400, because of their support for the rebels. Many people in Shropshire still considered themselves Welsh at this time.

6. Scenery around the battlefield of Hyddgen. The outnumbered Welsh fought a running battle through the hills around what is now the Nant-y-Moch Reservoir. The site is threatened by massive wind turbines and hundreds of pylons.

7. Plaque commemorating Owain's victory at the Battle of Hyddgen, June 1401, overlooking the Nant-y-Moch Reservoir, and unveiled by Gwynfor Evans upon 16 July 1977. Without this seminal victory, the war would probably have ended after just a year of fighting.

8. After the failed assassination attempt by Hywel Sele, Lord of Nannau, in 1402, the men of Gruffydd ap Gwyn of Ardudwy were defeated by Glyndŵr at Llanelltud Bridge, near Cymer Abbey.

9. The remains of Cymer Abbey, despoiled by Glyndŵr after its abbot had pledged his allegiance to the usurper Henry IV in 1400. The abbot later tried to reconcile Hywel Sele and Glyndŵr, and the King's men-at-arms and archers were garrisoned here later in the war.

10. Llyn Padarn in Snowdonia, where Glyndŵr may have imprisoned Lord Grey in Dolbadarn Castle in 1402. Dolbadarn overlooks Llyn Padarn and was built by Llywelyn the Great to guard the strategic Llanberis Pass through Snowdonia.

Left: 11. This Holy Well at St Mary's Church, Pilleth, was covered over in medieval times, and was said to cure eye ailments. Glyndŵr drank here when he prayed before the Battle of Pilleth, on St Alban's Day, 1402.

Below: 12. Pilleth Church, on the hill of Bryn Glas, which was set alight before the battle where Edmund Mortimer's royalist army was defeated on 22 June 1402.

13. The Wellingtonia fir trees on the hill to the left of the church were planted in the nineteenth century by a local landowner, Sir Richard Green-Price, to mark a mass grave. The bones were reburied in the church.

14. The mighty Carreg Cennen Castle, on a crag 300 ft above the Cennen River. It was surrendered by Sir John Scudamore in July 1403, after his wife was refused safe conduct.

Above: 15. This remarkable stainless steel statue of Llywelyn ap Gruffydd Fychan stands outside Llandovery Castle (Castell Llanymddyfri), at the place where he was slowly hung, drawn and quartered on 19 October 1401 for refusing to betray Glyndŵr.

Left: 16. Gatehouse of Caernarfon Castle, built by Edward I as headquarters for the Justiciar of North Wales, and one of the most impressive castles in Europe. Glyndŵr almost captured it in the sieges of 1403-1404.

17. The gatehouse of St Quintin's Castle, Llanbleddian, which overlooked Cowbridge and was destroyed by Glyndŵr's forces in 1403.

18. Fortified Norman Church of the Holy Cross, within Cowbridge's thirteenth century town walls. The market town was probably sacked when Llanbleddian Castle fell and Glyndŵr won at Stalling Down (Cowbridge Common).

19. The view across the battle site of Stalling Down, 1403, from the remains of Llanquian Castle towards Stalling Down.

20. Gatehouse of the Bishop's Palace outside Llandaf Cathedral, Cardiff. This castellated palace was burnt and ruined by Glyndŵr, but the nearby cathedral was spared.

21. Cardiff Castle – the great Norman motte inside the later walls, on the site of the Roman fort alongside the River Taff. The town of Cardiff was burnt by Glyndŵr at least twice, and the castle taken at least once.

22. 'Barber-surgeon' at Cardiff Castle – all armies needed these injury specialists among their camp-followers. Without immediate and prolonged attention, Prince Henry would have died after the Battle of Shrewsbury.

23. The great gatehouse at Castell Cydweli, which was rebuilt by the Lord Rhys around 1190, and repeatedly besieged by Henry Dwn and Glyndŵr's southern forces.

24. The Mayor of Carmarthen (Caerfyrddin) hands over the keys of Carmarthen Castle, in a ceremony commemorating the 600th anniversary of its surrender in 1405.

25. The magnificent fourteenth century interior of the Medieval hall-house of Cefn Caer, on the site of a Roman fort, where the Pennal Policy was drafted in 1406.

26. View from the monastic fishponds to Valle Crucis Abbey, near Glyndŵr's estates around Llangollen. Edward I first despoiled it, and its abbot is said to have told the ghost of Glyndŵr that he had been born 100 years too early.

27. Woodbury Hill, where Owain's Franco-Welsh army camped near Worcester to face Henry IV in August 1405. After eight days of single combat between knights, Henry retired to Worcester rather than fight a pitched battle.

28. The ruins of the royal Grosmont Castle, situated between Hereford, Abergafenni and Monmouth, and the site of fighting in March 1405.

Above 29. Presentation of Glyndŵr's Cleddyf
y Genedl (Sword of the Nation) to Mayor
Tecwyn Jenkins at Machynlleth in June 2004. To
commemorate the 600th anniversary of the first
Welsh Parliament at Machynlleth, it was based on
the sword on Glyndŵr's Great Seal, handcrafted by
master blacksmith Jason Gardiner, and is now on
display in Y Plas, Machynlleth.

Right: 30. This marble statue of Owain Glyndŵr,
by Alfred Turner, is at Cardiff City Hall. It is one of
'eleven Welsh heroes' in the marble hall, dating from
the early twentieth century and each by a different
sculptor.

31. Close-up of statue of Glyndŵr at Corwen. The 2007 bronze statue stands 14.7 ft (4.5m) high, and is on a plinth of eight tons of Welsh granite.

32. Coron Glyndŵr, now in Cefn Caer, Pennal given on 21 June 2004, the 600th anniversary of the coronation of Owain IV. Based on the crown on Owain's Great Seal, it was made by the master silversmith, the late A.H. Lewis, who also crafted many eisteddfod crowns. The bolts denote the practice of bolting crowns to helmets whilst in battle.

All the whole countrey then was but a forrest, rough and spacious, as it still is, but then waste of inhabitants, and all overgrowne with woods, for Owen Glyndŵr's warres beginning in anno 1400, continued fifteen years, which brought such a desolation that greene grasse grew on the market place in Llanrwst, called Bryn y botten, and the deere fled into the church-yard, as it is reported.

When Henry IV led his force from Shrewsbury into North Wales in September 1402, but was pushed back by the weather, on his return he entered Llanrwst and destroyed it completely, as a 'rebel stronghold'. A century after Glyndŵr's war, some people from Llanrwst still lived in a cave, Ogof Carreg Gwalch in Gwydir forest. (In 1947 Llanrwst Town Council applied for a seat on the United Nations Security Council, on the basis of its special status as an 'independent town state'.)

MORE FRANCISAN PERSECUTION

Eight Franciscan friars in Leicester were accused of collecting revenues for the Glyndŵr rebels, and after being allowed to go free by two juries, a third was picked, not so squeamish about executing men of religion. All eight were hanged. An old Franciscan friar in Cambridge was also charged. William Clark of Chester, who was a writer at Canterbury, had his tongue ripped out for having 'uttered against the king vicious words', then his writing hand was cut off, then he was beheaded in the Tower of London. William Sawtre, a chamberlain, chained in a pile of faggots ready to be lit, told the Archbishop of Canterbury that the King and clergy all would die, and 'the tongue of a strange people shall hold sway in the land'. Sir Roger Clarendon, Richard II's half-brother was hung, with his squire and valet, after trying to build support for those who believed that the King was still alive. Henry IV was uneasy on the throne all through his reign, but never more so than at this time.

On the third Royal Expedition the Cistercian Margam Abbey had been despoiled by the King's troops, and as late as 1440 Henry VI made a grant to recompense it for rebel damage. Its Abbot had been given a pardon after the war had ended, so it is uncertain if he supported Glyndŵr. Certainly some Cistercian foundations did, but the fortified Benedictine priory at Ewenni under Hugh Morton, a daughter house of Gloucester, did not rally to Glyndŵr's cause. However, it suffered from both the depredations of the King's forces and those of Glyndŵr. The Grey Friars of Cardiff, the Franciscans, supported Glyndŵr, who spared their house from being looted, and the remains of their monastery are just west of the castle, in Bute Park. He had spared Llandaff Cathedral but burnt the Archdeacon's house and destroyed the Bishop's Palace there. In 1428 the Bishop complained that because of the rebellion and pestilence the cathedral was becoming ruinous. Tintern Abbey, Abbey Cwm Hir and Neath Abbey suffered during the revolt, and the small priories at Llangenydd and Cardiff did not survive for long after. In October 1402 Parliament passed even more anti-Welsh Laws. The Welsh people were even more supportive of Owain, and his forces were fortified by the defection of hundreds of experienced Welsh archers from service in England.

EDMUND MORTIMER MARRIES CATRIN GLYNDŴR
30 NOVEMBER 1402

Sir Thomas Clanvowe, captured at Pilleth, had been ransomed and released by this time, and promoted by the King. Around this time the second instalment of Reginald Grey's ransom was paid and his eldest son and heir, John (1387-1439), was released. The first installment had ensured Grey's release and his replacement by his son. (Reports that Reginald or John Grey married a daughter of Glyndŵr appear to be untrue.) For Mortimer to see Grey, Grey's son and Clanvowe leaving captivity must have been galling. Henry's reason for refusing Hotspur's requests to ransom Mortimer was that he 'would not use royal revenues to strengthen my enemies against us.' The Mortimers were seen as rivals to Henry IV for the English throne, so Henry IV refused to pay any ransom for Edmund. Hotspur had violently argued over this and left for Northumberland.

On 30 November Edmund Mortimer and Catrin Glyndŵr married. The Percies had been negotiating with Glyndŵr, and must have told Mortimer of the King's repeated refusal to ransom him. Some time over the winter, John Lloyd of Denbigh, Hotspur's Welsh squire met Glyndŵr, and presumably Mortimer. The meeting may have been at Glyndŵr's camp on Cader Idris in Snowdonia. The next spring, it was known that Lloyd was in Northern England with the Percies. As well as Mortimer marrying Catrin, Glyndŵr married three of his other four daughters into Herefordshire families. Alice married Sir John Scudamore, of Kentchurch and Holme Lacy; Janet married John Croft, of Croft Castle; and Margaret wed Roger Monnington, of Monnington. His other daughter, Gwenllian married a Welshman, Phylip ap Rhys of Cenarth.

Mortimer now wrote a letter on 13 December to the gentry along the borders, including Sir John Greyndour, guardian of the Mortimer lordship of Radnor. Mortimer expressed his adherence to the cause of Glyndŵr, his intention of placing the Earl of March on the throne if Richard II was dead, and of restoring to Glyndŵr his right in Wales:

> My very dear and well-beloved John Greyndor, Howel Vaughan, and all the gentles of Radnor and Prestremde *(Presteigne, Llanandras in Welsh, once the county town of Radnorshire)*. I greet you very much and make known to you that Owen Glendwr has raised a quarrel of the which the object is, if King Richard be alive to restore his crown: and if not, that my honoured nephew (the infant Earl of March), who is the right heir to the said crown shall be king of England, and that the said Oweyn will assert his right in Wales. And I, seeing and considering the said quarrel to be good and reasonable, have consented to join in it, and to aid and maintain it, and by the grace of God to a good end, Amen. I ardently hope from my heart that you will support and enable me to bring this struggle of mine to a successful issue.
> (Written at Melenyth (Maelienydd) the 13th day of December.)

As related, Edmund Mortimer's nephew, another Edmund, the 5th Earl of March, had been taken into the 'protection' of Henry IV, after his father's death when campaigning in Ireland in 1398. This Edmund (1391-1425) and his brother Roger briefly escaped but were recaptured in 1409, and Roger died soon after. Roger was possibly killed by Henry IV to keep Edmund quiet. He dared not risk killing the heir-presumptive after killing the rightful King. The 5th Earl of March was never able to build enough of a power base to challenge Henry V (probably afraid after the death of his brother), although there was another plot to make him ruler in 1415. With the death of these two brothers, Glyndŵr's ally, Edmund Mortimer, if he had lived, would have been the real heir to the throne, not Henry V. His children by Catrin, as his nephew Edmund died in 1425, could have inherited the throne of England.

Edmund had written from Maelienydd, an upland lordship and cantref of great strategic significance in Radnorshire, east central Wales, stretching from the River Teme to Radnor Forest and around Llandrindod Wells. Sir John Greyndour (d.1415 or 1416) held St Briavels, Abenhall manor in Gloucestershire and part of Mitcheldean manor in the Forest of Dean, and did not turn to fight for Mortimer. He was later to fight the Welsh at Pwll Melyn. Greyndour was a highly esteemed member of the households of both Henry IV and V, who accompanied Henry V to France in 1415, and would have been a huge asset to Glyndŵr's forces. Greyndour took with him a company of 150 Forest of Dean Miners to France, who were instrumental in undermining the walls of the town of Harfleur, which later surrendered. In return for this service he was granted the crest of the Forest of Dean Miners. (The Miner has a pick in his hand with which to loosen the iron ore, a wooden hod on his back to carry it, and in his mouth he holds a candle.)

Note: Glyndŵr's family connections. We have seen that Owain's daughter Catrin married Edmund Mortimer, and that his kinsman John Kynaston was related to the Percies. According to J.Y.W. Lloyd of Clochfaen, Glyndŵr's sisters married as follows. Lowri married Robert Puleston of Emral. Isabel married Adda ab Iorwerth of Llys Pengwern. Morfudd married Sir Richard Croft of Croft Castle then David ab Ednyfed Siam of Llys Pengwern. Gwenllian married Gruffydd Fychan ap Gruffudd. This may be the Gruffudd Fychan who fought for Glyndŵr. Intriguingly he names 31 illegitimate children of Glyndŵr, and states that Glyndŵr had a daughter Jane, who married Henry, Lord Grey of Ruthin.

CHAPTER 7

Constant Warfare 1403

Ever more laws were passed against the Welsh, including the more rigid enforcement of the Welsh and English being unable to marry, and forcing Welshmen replaced in their posts to pay for the hire of Englishmen to replace them. By the end of 1402 the war had become truly national. The King's men raised fresh taxes to deal with the war, and especially plundered Flintshire in November and December, trying to break Glyndŵr's support. Guerrilla warfare did not cease throughout the winter of 1402-03. The traditional mould of warfare was broken. Plant Owain constantly attacked not only the great castles of Aberystwyth, Caernarfon, Beaumaris and Harlech, but any supply trains heading towards them, and raided Shropshire.

PRINCE HAL'S INVASION MAY 1403

Upon 22 February the town of Hope (Yr Hob) in Flintshire was burned, with Glyndŵr present. It is just a few miles south-west of Chester, the centre of English power in the Marches. More and more men defected to Glyndŵr, especially from north-east Wales. Hotspur had been spending vast sums since Richard ordered him again to subdue Wales, but in spring Parliament withdrew his commands and lands that had been allocated to him. Hotspur had been attacked in Parliament for not capturing Glyndŵr, preferring to negotiate. Fuming, Hotspur had left Parliament without Henry's permission and headed home to Northumberland.

Over the winter Prince Hal, Henry of Monmouth, had been organising yet another invasion of Wales. On 8 March, he was made Royal Lieutenant in Wales, and as Commander-in-Chief was given a new army of 2,500 archers, 500 men at arms, 20 knights and 4 barons. It is little wonder that Hotspur was disillusioned that the King could find men and financial support from the Exchequer for his son, but Hotspur had been starved of funding and had policed Wales using his own fortune. At Chester Castle, the Prince of Wales now commanded 3,800 archers and 1,100 men-at-arms. The promise of even more funding did little to assuage the grave military position, however.

In May, Glyndŵr's supporters attacked and (with French aid) almost captured Caernarfon Castle, and Bretons were attacking English ships. In early May, however, Prince Henry's preparations were complete. He rode out from his muster-point at Shrewsbury with veterans of the French, Welsh and Scottish fighting, and a huge contingent of the famed Chester archers, to find and destroy Glyndŵr. Aware that an army was slow and unwieldy, he took no wagon train of any substance. Although there was little to plunder for food in Wales, his men-at-arms carried their own food in saddlebags. The army destroyed and burned Glyndŵr's house at Sycharth, and proceeded to Glyndyfrdwy, where the lodge and park were also razed. The expedition then advanced to 'the fine and well-inhabited land of Edeirnion' which met a similar fate before the army returned to headquarters at Shrewsbury.

The purpose of the mission, in the event of Glyndŵr not defending his mansions and estates, was simple, bloody destruction. The Prince wished to be the man to break the will of the Welsh to fight; now his father had given him total command in Wales. He was only sixteen years old, and wanted desperately to prove himself fit to command, writing to his father from Shrewsbury, on 15 May 1403:

> We have among other matters been lately informed that Oweyn de Glyndowdry has assembled his forces and those of other rebels adhering to him in great numbers; purposing to commit inroads and in case any resistance be made to him by the English, to come to battle with them, or so he vaunted to his people ... wherefore we took our force and marched to a place of the said Oweyn, well built, which was his principal mansion, called Saghern (Sycharth), where we thought we should have found him if he had any inclination to fight in the manner he had said, but on our arrival we found nobody; and therefore caused the whole place to be burned and several other houses near it belonging to his tenants.
>
> We then marched straight to his other place of Glyndourdy to seek him there and we caused a fine lodge in his park to be destroyed by fire and laid waste all the country around. We there halted for the night and certain of our people sallied forth into the country and took a gentleman of the neighbourhood who was one of the said Oweyn's chief captains. This person offered £500 for his ransom to preserve his life and to be allowed two weeks for the purpose of raising this sum; but this offer was not accepted and he received death, as did several of his companions who were taken on the same day ... we then proceeded to the commote of Edeyrnion in Merionethshire and there laid waste a fine and populous country; thence we went to Powys, and there being want of provender in Wales for horses we made our people carry oats with them and pursued our march.

The only solid evidence of Prince Henry's invasion was the burning of Glyndŵr's mansions at Sycharth and Glyndyfrdwy. (Excavations at Sycharth in the early 1960s revealed the presence of two timber halls on the flat-topped mound, one being 43m in length, with evidence of burning.) Rebel supporters were captured and executed during the campaign, and bards were again outlawed.

Lord Beaufort had been granted Sycharth and Glyndyfrdwy, so will not have been pleased at Prince Hal's impetuous actions in destroying 'his' properties. It is surprising that the Prince did not accept the offer of £500 ransom. It is worth between £180,000 (RPI) and £2,700,000 (Average Earnings) today. To keep his force of 2,500 men in the field for a month would have cost well over £500,000 a year in today's terms, and the following letter was sent only a fortnight after his previous missive. In it, he complains that his troops were on the point of mutiny because of lack of pay or plunder:

> ... our soldiers desire to know whether they will be paid for the 3rd month of the present quarter and tell us that they will not wait here unless the are soon paid their wages according to their indentures. We pray you very clearly that you will order our payment for the said month or otherwise let us know and take order promptly for the safety of these marches. For the rebels hear every day if we are paid, and they know well without payment we cannot continue, and they strive to raise all the forces of North Wales and South Wales to over-ride and destroy the March and the counties adjoining thereto; and there is no resistance here, so they can well accomplish their malice; and when our men shall have retreated from us, it is necessary that we should by all means retreat into England, there to be disgraced forever ... at present we have very great expenses and have made all the pawning we may of our little jewels to defray them, for too our castles of Aberystwyth and Harlech are besieged and have been for a long time, and we must rescue and provision them within 10 days and besides defend the March around us with our third body against the entry of the rebels.
> (Dated 30 May 1403)

Throughout May and June, Marcher lands were reinforced in expectation of Welsh attacks, and the garrisons of Radnor, Brecon, Builth, Aberystwyth and Harlech continually wrote for help. English soldiers in Welsh garrisons wanted to be paid or else posted somewhere less hostile. Radnor was relieved, and Harlech and Aberystwyth reinforced. Harlech alone had another 1,300 men posted there in June. On 15 June, supporters in the Tywi Valley rebelled, and on 3 July Jenkyn Havard, the Commander of Dinefwr Castle, wrote that Henry Dwn (Don) of Cydweli had raised his standard and led his men against the castle. Henry Dwn had been exasperated by the constant legislation against himself and the Welsh nation – he had been treated as a traitor despite being loyal to the crown. On 16 June the sheriffs of the border counties were ordered to send troops to Prince Henry's assistance, and on 10 July the King ordered £1,000 to be sent to Prince Henry 'with all speed', to keep his troops together. By 24 June 1403 the Welsh of Brycheiniog again attacked Brecon castle, but the siege of Brecon was broken by John Bodenham, Sheriff of Herefordshire, who wrote in a letter to the King dated 7 July: 'On the Sunday last (1 July) ... we were at Brecon and broke the siege; and there were killed ... the number of 240 and upwards.' Glyndŵr had headed to South Wales again, probably to meet Henry Dwn and other gentry. On 14 June 1403, twelve leading Welshmen from the Flintshire commotes of Coleshill, Prestatyn and Rhuddlan were ordered to appoint watches against the invasion of England by the Welsh. All but one soon defected to the cause of Glyndŵr and his new ally, Hotspur. From various sources we learn that July 1403 is the time when the men of Flintshire turned to Glyndŵr's cause – 'the men of the county of Flint became rebels to the lord and joined Glyndŵr'.

JULY 1403 GLYNDŴR'S COUNTER-OFFENSIVE

Over the summer of 1403 the activities of Glyndŵr are better known, not through official accounts, but because of a flurry of undated letters, generally ascribed to July. We only know of these events from surviving letters sent to London and archived there, for instance the letter from Kingeston that on 1 July. Brecon had been besieged, and the attack beaten off. However, the violence of this attack, so soon after Prince Henry's great mission into Wales to 'seek and destroy' the rebels, alerted every garrison across the nation. Owain Glyndŵr had led his main army towards Llandovery, but went on with a vanguard of 300 men to attack and take Llandovery. He had been expected there on 16 June, on account of his 'want of victuals', and its garrison alerted. By 2 July, Owain had appeared in person to put new heart into the Welsh rebels of the Tywi valley, on his ride to south-west Wales. They had risen upon 15 June and now hurried to join him, swearing oaths of fealty.

Llanymddyfri (Llandovery) was besieged and taken on 3 July before the patriots moved westwards towards Dinefwr Castle. Glyndŵr was accompanied by his commanders Rhys Gethin (Rhys the Fierce of Llanrwst in the Conwy Valley) and Rhys Ddu (Rhys the Black of Aberteifi). They then camped at Llandeilo (near Dinefwr Castle), where Glyndŵr was joined by men from the Conwy valley, Ceredigion, and Cydweli. The Welsh then marched on to Dryslwyn the following day, recruiting more men as they marched. Eight thousand two-hundred-and-forty men are said to have made up the Welsh army. Prominent men from South Wales flocked to Owain's golden dragon banner. Now named as his supporters in letters of the time were Henry Dwn of Cydweli, his son, Rhys ap Gruffydd ap Llywelyn Foethus (the constable who threw open the gates of Dryslwyn Castle to Glyndŵr) and William Gwyn, who had been previously loyal to the King. At Newton, Llandeilo, Glyndŵr's vanguard had been met by the Chamberlain of Carmarthen, who after some losses, fled back to Carmarthen Castle. Glyndŵr next captured Castell Newydd Emlyn (Newcastle Emlyn), Dryslwyn, the mighty Carreg Cennen, Carmarthen and Llansteffan.

A letter written by John Faireford, receiver of the lordship of Brecon, referred to news from Jenkyn Havard, constable of the castle of Dinefwr outside Lladeilo. He relates that Glyndŵr with a following of 300 men laid siege to the castle of Llandovery on Tuesday 3 July, and was assured of the men of the district, except for those in the castle. Owain had then spent the night at Llandeilo where the people of the county of Carmarthen and the lordships adjacent were 'assured and sworn' to him. There was a ten day assault on the castle and borough of Dinefwr during July 1403. Our knowledge of Llandeilo and Dinefwr is based on a series of letters sent by Jenkyn Havard, to his 'dear friend', John Faireford, when Glyndŵr's forces, many of them new Carmarthenshire followers, were attacking Dinefwr. Glyndŵr rode to plan the siege of Dinefwr Castle around 3 July, while the bulk of his great army prepared to march to Carmarthen and Cydweli.

On 4 July, Faireford reported Havard's desperate situation to the sheriffs of Herefordshire, pleading for assistance for Dinefwr as quickly as possible. Another messenger also arrived in Hereford from Lord Audley's lieutenant at Llandovery Castle with more bad news. On 3 July Glyndŵr and 300 rebels had surprised Llandovery's garrison, which offered little resistance, and that night they lodged at Llandeilo. Faireford's reports were also passed to

Sir Hugh Waterton, a councillor of King Henry IV, and Steward of Brecon, Monmouth and the Duchy of Lancaster lands in Herefordshire. The messenger noted that the towns of Llandovery and Newton (both next to Dinefwr) had been burned by the rebels, who were believed to be heading towards Cydweli. Only severe flooding was temporarily hindering their progress. The Chamberlain of South Wales had been driven into Carmarthen, and some of his men had been killed.

Another march towards the town of Brecon was feared by its inhabitants, but Glyndŵr's presence at Dryslwyn Castle (in the Tywi Valley between Llandeilo and Carmarthen) is attested on 4 July. Its constable, Rhys ap Gruffydd, surrendered to Owain's massive force and joined his army. At this time a contingent of Glyndŵr's army had marched from Llandeilo to nearby Carreg Cennen Castle, one of the most impressive of all Welsh castles, rather than join the main army on its route to Dryslwyn and Carmarthen. Its keeper, John Scudamore, visited Glyndŵr to seek a safe conduct for his wife and mother-in-law out of the castle, and was refused. The inhabitants of Carreg Cennen were terrified, and the women had been trapped within the castle by Glyndŵr's swift advance. John Scudamore had replaced his brother Philip [Philpot] as Constable of Dryslwyn, as Philip had joined Glyndŵr's forces.

Around this time, Scudamore's wife died, possibly owing to the siege, but within a year he had secretly married Alys, the daughter of Owain Glyndŵr. (It was illegal at this time for an Englishman to marry a Welsh woman). From henceforth John Scudamore seems to have played a double-game. Perhaps he had been an ally of Glyndŵr even before this. His brothers were leading supporters of Glyndŵr, so he may have been 'loyal' to the King in order to retain the family estates if Glyndŵr lost. Equally, if Glyndŵr won, the estates would have been be secured. Carreg Cennen is one of Wales' most evocative castles, perched over a 300-foot drop, and Sir John Scudamore (Skydmore) wrote:

> I may not spare any man from this place away from me, to certify neither my king nor the lord my prince, in the mischief of the countryside about, nor no man pass by anyway, hence I pray you and require you that you certify them how all Carmarthenshire, Kidwelly, Carnwaltham and Yskenyd were sworn to Owain yesterday. And he lay tonight in the castle of Drosselan (Dryslwyn) with Rhys ap Griffith and there I was on truce and prayed for a safe conduct under his seal to send home my wife and her mother and her train, but he would not grant me. This day he is about Carmarthen and thinks to abide there until he may have town and castle; and his purpose then is to go into Pembrokeshire for he holds all the castles and towns in Kidwelly ... Gowersland and Glamorgan for the same countries have undertaken the siege of them until they be won ... excite the king's advisors that they should excite the king here in all haste to avenge himself on some of his false traitors he has cherished overmuch, and to rescue the towns and castles in these countries for I dread full sore there be few to maintain them ...

There is an indenture from Henry IV to 'John Skydmore, Steward of the King's lordships of Kidwelly, Carn Waltham and Iskenny ... the grantee is to receive 12d. a day for two "hommes d'armes" and 6d. a day for 10 archers for the safe keeping of the castle of Kidwelly.' The Hundred of Iscennen includes Llandybie, Llanarthne, Llanddarog etc., and the Hundred of Carnwallon includes Llanedi, Llanelli, Llangennech and Llannon.) In his letter above, Scudamore indicates that Glamorgan and Gower were already under attack, the war having spread across South Wales. The last sentence seems to indicate that he knows he will fall under suspicion, not only because of his brothers but because news of his secret marriage might be discovered.

There was another series of panicked letters from Faireford, the Herefordshire sheriffs, knights, commons and wardens, to inform King Henry that his castles were besieged, attacked and very vulnerable. On 7 July, Faireford, as Receiver of Brecon, passed on Havard's pleas for help to the King, writing that the 'traitors' were 'daily reinforced.' 'If assistance comes not speedily, all the Castles and Towns, and your loyal subjects in them, are in great peril, and on the point if being utterly ruined, for default of succour and good governance ... written at Brecon on the seventh day of July, at the hour of midnight.' (Similar letters are contained in Hingeston's *Royal and Historical Letters of Henry IV.*)

Archdeacon Richard Kingeston of Hereford wrote:

> Letters are arriving from Wales containing intelligence, by which you may learn that the whole country is lost, if you do not go there as quickly as possible. For which reason it may please you to prepare to set out with all the power you can muster, and march night and day for the salvation of these parts. And may it please you to reflect that it will be a great disgrace as well as a loss, to lose or suffer to be lost, in the beginning of your reign a country which your noble ancestors have won and for so long a time peaceably possessed. For people talk very unfavourably ...
> Your lowly creature, Richard Kingeston
> And for God's love, my liege Lord, think on yourself.

The army marched on to Carmarthen from Dryslwyn, where other loyalists and the contingent that took Carreg Cennen joined Glyndŵr Their followers swelled the numbers of the rebel army, which displayed an intimidating solidarity to those who were defending strategic, but isolated, positions in the locality. The Keeper of Newcastle Emlyn, Jenkin ap Llywelyn, chose to surrender without a fight between 4 and 7 July. This opened up an easy route back to the North, if the English should send an army after Glyndŵr through the Vale of Tywi. It also meant that the Englishry of Pembrokeshire was cut off from the rest of Wales. The Welsh forces increased their attacks on Carmarthen town and castle, secure that the road was safely held in the rear should they need to withdraw quickly. On 6 July, Owain took Carmarthen, where about 50 inhabitants had died, and the castle's keys were handed over by its castellan, Wigmore. He could see it was futile trying to resist such an army, without the promise of quick support. With Owain's army now over 8,000 strong, the royal castle of Carmarthen's surrender represented the almost total collapse of English rule in Wales.

On 7 July, the embattled Havard reported from Dinefwr to John Faireford, the King's Receiver in Brecon, that the Newcastle Emlyn had surrendered, the rebel leaders had forced Carmarthen castle to capitulate, and the Welsh had burst into the borough of Carmarthen, set fire to its buildings and slain over fifty of its inhabitants:

Dear Friend, Oweyn Glyndour, Henry Don, Rhys Ddu, Rhys ap Griffiths ap Llywelyn, Rhys Gethin have won the town of Carmarthen, and Wygmor Constable of the Castle, has yielded up the castle to Oweyn who has burned the town and slain the men of the town, more than 50 men and they are in purpose to be in Kidwelly and a siege has been ordered of the castle that I keep and that is a great peril for me and all that are here with me, for they have made a vow that they will kill us all; therefore I pray that you will not boggle us but send us a warning within a short time whether we shall have any help or not, or if there be no help coming that we must steal away by night to Brecon ... Written in haste and dread.

Dinefwr castle still held out, in increasingly desperate straits: 'a siege is ordained at the castle that I keep and that is great peril for me, and all that be within; for they have made their vow that they will all yet have us dead therein.' If speedy aid were not forthcoming, Havard and his men would have to escape to Brecon under cover of darkness 'because that we fail victuals and men, and especially men'. John Faireford of Brecon sent the Havard letter above to the Herefordshire authorities, with this covering letter believing that Glyndŵr would attack him in Brecon:

Rees ap Griffith, of the county of Carmarthen, William ap Philip, Henry Don and his son with many of their adherents were on Monday last treasonably rising in the plain country, against the King our most sovereign Lord and have laid siege to the Castle of Dynevor with a great force of rebels. And moreover it was certified to me by Raulin Moninton and others who were in the castle of Llandovery that Owen Glyndŵr and his false troops were in Llandovery on Tuesday and that the men there being surprised ... the said castle (is) assured and secured to him, and 300 of the rebels were at their ease, lying round in siege of the same castle and at night were lodged in Llandeilo; at which time the men of the said county and of other Lordships around were also assured and sworn to him. And that this same Wednesday the same Owen, and all other rebels are on their march towards this town of Brecon for the destruction of the town, which God avert, and after they purpose to make a diversion against other parties in the March if they be not resisted.

And you will know that all the Welsh nation being taken a little by surprise is adhering to this evil purpose of rebellion and they are assured thereunto, how fully, from one day to another by the support they give to it, clearly appears more openly; and I pray you, please to ordain the most speedy resistance against the rebels that you can and if any expedition of cavalry can be made, be pleased to do this first in these Lordships of Brecon and Canref-Sellyf ... written at Brecon this Wednesday afternoon and in great haste.

On 6 July, Henry IV had been marching north to deal with problems with the Percies and the Scots, unaware that Hotspur had marched south to take Chester, or that Glyndŵr's spearmen had taken Carmarthen. 7 July 1403 saw John Bodenham, Sheriff of Herefordshire, relieving Faireford at Brecon Castle, but hearing of Glyndŵr's forces in the Tywi Valley, he marched quickly back to the safety of Hereford, and appealed to Henry IV as Hereford had been the target of previous raids. Brecon's commander, John Faireford now wrote to Henry IV that 'all the castles and towns and your loyal subjects within them are in great peril and on the point of being utterly ruined for default of succour and good government'. Richard

Kingeston, Hereford's Archbishop, again reinforced these pleas: 'You may learn that the whole country is lost if you do not go there as quickly as possible...' We can thus see that both Brecon and Hereford expected imminent attacks from Glyndŵr. These towns are at least thirty miles apart, whether accessed via Hay-on-Wye or Abergafenni.

While he was still at Carmarthen, Glyndŵr, consulted a 'maister of Brut', the seer Hopcyn ap Thomas ab Einion (fl. 1337-1408) of Ynysdawe near Clydach. Hopcyn forewarned Owain of his imminent capture, under a black banner, between Carmarthen and Gower. Whatever Hopcyn's belief or motivation, his actions saved Gower's Flemish occupants from Glyndŵr's depredations. Instead of heading east towards Glamorgan, Glyndŵr proceeded west to camp at St Clears on 9 July. In a meeting, Glyndŵr had tried to get Thomas, Lord Carew, to give up Laugharne Castle, expecting the same surrender as at Newcastle Emlyn and Carmarthen. Glyndŵr's consequent delay in heading west and then north had huge repercussions for the Percies and the English crown.

Jenkyn Havard at Dinefwr was still besieged, but must have felt relief when Glyndŵr pressed on to confront Lord Carew, but possibly Glyndŵr made an unrecorded agreement with Carew and returned to Carmarthen. Once again Havard pleaded for relief, for the rebels 'have goods and victuals plenty, for every house is full about us of its poultry, and yet wine and honey enough in the country, and wheat and beans, and all manner of victuals'. At the same time, he was forced to parley daily with besiegers 'and now will ordain for us to leave that castle for there casts to be encircled thence'. Both besiegers and besieged were well aware of the historical significance of Dinefwr Castle for long-term control of Ystrad Tywi, 'for that was the chief place in old time'. 'God of Heaven save you and us from all enemies', Havard concluded on behalf of himself and John Faireford at Brecon. It is not recorded whether Dinefwr actually fell in the summer of 1403.

The threat was suddenly lifted, partly as a result of the ambush of a rebel band by Lord Carew during the night of 11-12 July, and partly because the news of the Percy uprising was announced at Chester on 10 July. However, the damage caused at Dinefwr was considerable. By 1409 £89 was being spent on repairs to the castle and on the construction of new buildings there. The towns of Llandeilo Fawr and Newton were also largely destroyed in the month of July 1403. A Glyndŵr force possibly suffered heavy losses at Lacharn (Laugharne) yet still remained strong – it is unsure whether Laugharne and St Clears were taken or merely attacked. The Laugharne defeat may be propaganda from Lord Carew, who possibly beat off a scouting party. He claimed to have beaten or killed 700 men on 11-12 July but there is no proof – all that is known is that he immediately returned to the safety of Laugharne Castle. A letter to the burgesses of Monmouth from the burgesses of Caerleon tells us of a battle at Laugharne Castle on 12 July:

> There was this day a battle between the worthy baron of Carewe and Owein Glyndour; and we do wish you to know that the night before the battle Owain was on purpose to have avoided him and to find out whether the way was clear to pass, if he had need of it. He sent 700 of his many to search the ways and there they met with the baron's men who slew everybody so there was none on that scene alive ... he (Owain) sent for Hopkyn ap Thomas of Gower to come and speak with him on truce and Hopkyn came. Owain prayed him, in as much as he held him to be a Master of Brut,

to tell him how and in what manner it should fall out for him; and he told him that he should be captured in a short time between Carmarthen and Gower, and the taking would be under a black banner ... be glad and merry, and dread you nought for you have no need ...

Llansteffan Castle fell at this time. John de Penres (Penrees, Penrhys) was the owner, but was captured in 1403 by Glyndŵr and was not released until 1408. David Howel, Sheriff of Pembroke, was made keeper. When the castle was surrendered 'to Glyndŵr and the Welsh rebels by Thomas Rede, who held it in his demesne as of fee of the Prince Henry,' the lordship was deemed forfeited to the Crown. On its recovery from the rebels, Henry IV granted it back to 'Sir John Penrees', 'for his service in capturing Llanstephan Castle from the Welsh rebels', and Penres was made constable for life. After his death in 1410, in 1411 it reverted to and remained in the hands of the Crown. Henry V granted it to his brother Humphrey, Duke of Gloucester, in 1416, calling it the 'castle and lordship of Llanstephan in Wales, in the king's hands on account of the rebellion and forfeiture of William Gwyn, Welshman, and the forfeiture of Henry Gwyn, his son, who was killed ...'

On 10 July Hotspur was welcomed at Chester, whose citizens were always loyal to Richard II. Unfortunately for him, Glyndŵr had been delayed in meeting him, being held up by the seer Hopcyn ap Thomas, which turned his forces south-west to face Carew's Flemish army, rather than east and north towards Chester. On 12 July Henry IV received news at Nottingham (or at Lichfield on 11 July) of the plot by Hotspur, his father the Earl of Northumberland, and his uncle, the Earl of Worcester to overthrow him. Guessing correctly that the Percies would make for Shrewsbury to battle Prince Henry, the King marched there with his army. Glyndŵr, after the hold-up with Lord Carew, marched east along the Roman road, probably intending to sack Glamorgan and then head north from Monmouthshire to Shrewsbury. Owain attacked Glamorgan and Gwent, taking Cardiff and Newport, and Abergavenny and Usk Castles were attacked and burnt. It seems that Glyndŵr was meant to join up with Hotspur's forces to fight the Usurper King.

To arrive at the crucial battle of Shrewsbury on 22 July, we need to return to the Percies in Northumberland. Five Scottish Earls, those of Douglas, Fife, Angus, Moray and Orkney had been taken prisoner on 13 September 1402 at the Battle of Homildon Hill. Henry IV issued an edict strictly forbidding that any of the prisoners taken should be ransomed or exchanged. This was against the 'rules' of chivalric warfare in this day. Rich captives wanted their liberty back, and their captors wanted their ransoms. Henry then ordered that all the prisoners be taken to him in London. Hotspur absolutely refused to comply in sending the Earl of Douglas and other nobles whom he had personally captured. Many Scots and French lords were taken to London, but the Scottish leader, the great Earl Douglas, was missing, infuriating the King. Couriers were sent to Warkworth Castle demanding that Hotspur came to the King's court, with the Earl of Douglas. Hotspur did so, but left Douglas back at Warkworth in Northumberland.

En route to London, Hotspur heard Edmund Mortimer had been captured by Glyndŵr at Pilleth. Hotspur had recently married the Earl's sister, Lady Elizabeth Mortimer. When he met Henry IV, Hotspur applied to have his brother-in-law Mortimer ransomed, but

Henry refused, on the grounds that Douglas had not been handed over to him. Edmund Mortimer was also uncle to that young Earl of March, another Edmund Mortimer who was the rightful heir to the Crown, but whom Henry kept in custody. The Lancastrian King was not favourably disposed to Mortimer, fearing the prior claim of the House of York to his crown. Henry had no wish for either Mortimer, each with a better claim to the English throne than his, to be released. In March 1403, Henry granted Henry Percy, Earl of Northumberland, all the lands of Earl Douglas, wishing the Percies, who were popular, would leave London. However, to take Douglas' lands, Hotspur and his father the Earl of Northumberland would need to raise an army, and campaign for months. Hotspur and Northumberland asked for payment to conquer part of Scotland, as Hotspur had not been paid for all his activities in Wales. In the meantime, Hotspur and Elizabeth Mortimer had a son, Lord Henry Percy, who through Hotspur's mothers Plantagenet blood and the Mortimer's royal line, had right over that of Henry Bolingbroke. Thus both the Percies and the Mortimers had legitimate claims to the throne of England.

The Percies had been the main supporters who had placed Henry Bolingbroke on the throne, and thought themselves ungratefully treated. Henry IV neglected to pay for their soldiers who formed the main defensive force on the Scottish and Welsh borders. Hotspur had complained of being nearly ruined by his financial outlay for the Government. The Earls of Northumberland and Worcester, his father and uncle, took up the quarrel, and Archbishop Scrope of York advised then to dethrone Henry, and put the boy Edmund Mortimer in his place. They thus collaborated with Glyndŵr, now a kinsman of the Mortimers, who it is said promised to assist the Percies with 12,000 men. Hotspur set the Earl of Douglas at liberty without ransom, on condition that he should join the Percy army with his vassals. Douglas brought a large force from Scotland to join with Hotspur. The Earl of Northumberland was very ill, and Hotspur took command of part of his forces. The Earl was to follow with the other part. Hotspur and Douglas marched towards North Wales, and Thomas Percy, Earl of Worcester joined them with a large body of the renowned Cheshire archers, and most of the knights and squires of that county.

The King had seemingly forced Hotspur into rebellion by not releasing his brother-in-law Mortimer, trying to take Douglas from him, and not paying him for campaigning, and assembled an army to defeat the Percies. One chronicler wrote: 'The King began to think that now Hotspurs' son had nearer right to the crown than his own offspring. It was not to be borne with'. On arriving at Chester Hotspur sent couriers to Wales to meet Glyndŵr and Mortimer. He then drew up a manifesto declaring that the King had obtained his crown by fraud and perjury. On about 17 July, Worcester declared his manifesto, and he and Hotspur issued a proclamation that the Earl of March was the rightful King of England and that Henry of Bolingbroke was to be deposed. They had assumed the 'style and title of joint protectors of the Commonwealth'. They also sent out letters of defiance accusing Henry of breaking the oath that he made at Doncaster that he would not claim the Crown and further stating that he arranged Richard's murder.

THE BATTLE OF SHREWSBURY (HAYTELEY FIELD) 21 JULY 1403

On the advice of the Scottish Earl of March, George Dunbar, the King raced north-west to intercept Hotspur before he could join forces with Glyndŵr, or the Earl of Northumberland could bring his army from Berwick. He covered sixty miles in just three days, amazingly fast for a grand army to travel. Percy was joined at Chester by a number of Welshmen, including men from the lordships of Denbigh and Dyffryn Clwyd and the county of Flint. John Kynaston, a Glyndŵr ally, steward to the lordship of Ellesmere, had taken men to support Hotspur, telling them that Richard II would be leading the army. Hardyng, Hotspur's librarian, noted that many great nobles had pledged support for Hotspur, but few came to meet him. Learning from Carmarthen that Glyndŵr was marching to meet him, Hotspur and his uncle the Earl of Worcester had left Chester, and on the morning of 21 July his army marched down the Oswestry road towards the Castle Foregate of Shrewsbury. However, the race for Shrewsbury was won by the King, who reached the town shortly before Hotspur. On the walls of Shrewsbury Castle the banners and flags of Henry IV and the House of Lancaster hung. By taking Shrewsbury, the King effectively prevented the armies of Hotspur and Glyndŵr linking up.

The sides were evenly matched, with the Percies having around 10,000 men and the King perhaps 14,000. Henry was aware that the armies of both Northumberland and Glyndŵr were on their way. He offered Henry 'Hotspur' easy terms to abandon the rebellion, but Percy refused them, telling Henry that he was not the rightful heir, and was not to be trusted. Hotspur withdrew and spent the night 3 miles north-west of Shrewsbury at the village of Berwick. The following morning, there was no sign of Glyndŵr or Northumberland, and Henry IV's army advanced out of Shrewsbury. One source states that Glyndŵr had arrived on the other side of Severn, and attempted to cross, but heavy rains had fallen, the Severn was flooded, and the fords were impassable. Some of his men managed to join Percy, however. The only bridge was join Hotspur was too strongly guarded by the King's troops.

Hotspur quickly mobilised, abandoning Berwick, heading away from the River Severn towards Harlescott. Hotspur chose a position of considerable strength on the slope of the Hayteley Field, where three small ponds protected his front. On Friday 20 July, the King's army crossed the Severn to encamp, and lined up for battle on Haughmond Hill, west of Haughmond Abbey. The King then next took up a position at the foot of Hayteley Field, and sent messengers to Hotspur asking Hotspur and Worcester to come forward and discuss terms to avert bloodshed. His proven duplicity led the Percies to refuse his offer. A battle was now inevitable. Saturday 21 July had started with negotiations, but later in the day the talks broke down, and the battle started near where Battlefield Church stands today. Hostilities began with the bowmen, possibly the first battle where both sides made great use of longbows in tactical formations. Initially Hotspur held the upper hand with many of his Cheshire archers killing most of the royal vanguard, which fell back.

Hotspur and Douglas led the first charge, and parts of the King's guard were broken. The Earl of Stafford, Sir Walter Blount and two other knights, who wore the royal dress, were slain by Douglas. Henry IV had dressed several of his knights in armour exactly resembling his own, as Adam of Usk informs us:

> 1403 Battle of Shrewsbury. In the next year, on behalf of the crown of England claimed for the Earl of March, as is said, a deadly quarrel arose between the king and house of Percy of Northumberland, as kin to the same earl, to the great agitation of the realm as it took part with one side or the other; and a field being pitched for the morrow of Saint Mary Magdalene (July 23rd), the king, by advice of the said Earl of Dunbar of Scotland, because the father of the lord Henry Percy and Owen Glendower were then about to come against the said lord Henry and the lord Thomas Percy, then earl of Worcester. And, after that there had fallen on either side in most bloody slaughter to the number of sixteen thousand men, in the field of Berwick (where the king afterwards founded a hospice for the souls of those who there fell) two miles from Shrewsbury, on the eve of the said feast, victory declared for the king who had thus made the onslaught. In this battle the said lord Percy, the flower and glory of chivalry of Christendom, fell, alas!, and with him his uncle. Whereby is the prophecy fulfilled: 'The cast-off beast shall carry away the two horns of the moon.' There fell also two noble knights in the king's armour, each made conspicuous as though a second king, having been placed for the king's safety in the rear line of battle. Whereat the earl of Douglas of Scotland, then being in the field with the said lord Henry, as his captive, when he heard victory shouted for king Henry, cried in wonder: 'Have I not slain two king Henries (meaning the said knights) with my own hand? Tis an evil hour for us that a third yet lives to be our victor.'

The Royal Standard was thrown down when its Standard Bearer Sir Walter Blount was killed by the war-axe of Douglas, and Prince Harry of Monmouth was gravely wounded in the face by an arrow. Different sources state that both Stafford and Blount were wearing the King's coat armour, as well as the two other disguised men. The charge of Hotspur and Douglas was not well supported, and the royal lines, through which they had broken, reformed and closed on the rear of them. When they turned to ride through the lines again, they found the royalists holding firm while arrows were fired at them from all sides. The bloody battle lasted for three hours, during which time some Welsh contingents arrived, 'but the main body of the confederates could not rescue their van.' Hotspur lifted his visor to gulp in air, and was killed by a chance arrow that pierced his brain. On seeing this, the King shouted out 'Harry Percy is slain!' and the tide of battle turned. Few of the insurgent army survived or left the field alive as the sun set on the cause of Mortimer. Douglas fled the field, but fell off his horse and was taken prisoner. The Baron of Kinderton and Sir Richard Vernon were also taken, and executed on the field of battle, and Worcester beheaded at Shrewsbury on 23 July, but Henry treated Douglas courteously as 'a foreign knight.' It is reported that the field was hidden by the bodies of the dead, with perhaps 10,000 slain. It seems that both sides lost equivalent numbers, so the arrival of either Northumberland or Glyndŵr would have meant the certain deaths of Henry IV and Prince Henry.

Henry was lenient to the Earl of Northumberland, grieving for his son and brother, who were killed at Shrewsbury, but the might of the Percy family was broken. Hotspur's corpse was displayed between two millstones outside the gates of Shrewsbury, before being beheaded and quartered. The parts were sent to across the land to dissuade others from taking up the fight.

Northumberland, who was with his army at Warkworth at the time of the battle, submitted to arrest at York, having suffered the indignity of entering the city past the impaled head of his son. He lost his title of Constable of England and was fined, but as he had not directly participated in the Battle of Shrewsbury, was not convicted of treason.

One source states that Glyndŵr was unable to reach the battle, and climbed a great oak (the oak of Chertsey), to view the battlefield, raging that the swollen Severn had prevented his joining the fighting. However, if he had been there, or at nearby Oswestry, surely Owain would have tried everything to give battle to the exhausted remnants of the royal army? 'An English Chronicle ... written before the year 1471' records the events leading up to the battle and its aftermath:

And this same year was the battle of Shrewsbury on Mary Magdalene eve, between king Harry and sir Henri Percy, the son of Northumberland: of which battle the cause and occasion was this. The earl of Northumberland prayed the king to pay him his war money, due unto him for keeping peace in the marches of Scotland, and said, 'My son and I have spent our goods in keeping of the said marches.' The king answered, 'I have no money, so none thou shalt have.' The earl said, 'When ye came in to this land ye made promise for to be rewarded by our counsel, and ye take yearly much goods of the realm and pay it, and so ye wreath your commons: God send you good counsel.'

Then came the earl's son sir Harry Percy, that had wed the aforesaid Edmund Mortimer's sister that was prisoner in Wales, praying the king that he would suffer that the said Edmund's ransom might be paid off on his own. The king said, that with the money of his realm he would not fortify his enemies against himself. Sir Henri Percy said, 'Shall a man spend his goods, and put himself in peril for you and your realm, and ye will not help him in his need?' The king was wroth and said to him, 'Thou art a traitor Henri Percy, wilt thou that I should succour mine enemies, and enemies of the realm?' Sir Henri Percy said, 'Traitor am I none, but a true man, and as a true man I speak.' The king drew to him his dagger: and sir Henri Percy said to the king, 'Not here, but in the fold'. And so he went his way.

And he and his uncle sir Thomas Percy, whom king Richard had made earl of Worcester, gathered a great host in the north country, and said they must fight against the Scots; and went in to Chestershire, and took with them many Cheshire men, and sent to Oweyn of Glendore for to come and help him, but Oweyne was afeared of treason and came not; but many of the Welshmen came to them and so they came to Lichfeld. And the said sir Henri Percy and all his men were arrayed in the livery of the harts, the which was king Richard's livery. And there the said sir Henri *('Hotspur')* cried openly, and said that he was one of the chief causers that king Richard was deposed, and the most helper to bring in king Harry, owning that he would have amended the rule of the realm; and now king Harry ruleth and governed the land worse than dead king Richard; wherefore, he said he would amend it if he might.

The king also gathered another host and met with him beside Shrewsbury, and asked of him the cause of his coming; to whom Percy answered and said: 'We brought thee in against king Richard, and now thou rulest worse than did he. Thou spoilest yearly the realm with taxes and tallage *(another type of tax)*, thou payest no man, thou holdeth no house, thou art not heir of the realm; and herefore, as I have hurt the realm by bringing thee in, I will help to reform it.' The king answered and said, 'I take tallage for the needs of the realm, and I am chosen king by common assent of the realm, wherefore I counsel thee to put thee in my grace.' Percy answered and said, 'I trust not in grace.' 'Now I pray God,' said the king, 'that thou most answer for all the blood that here shall be shed this day and not I.' And then said the king, 'Avant banner.' (Forward the flag.) Then was there a strong and an hard battle, and many were slain on both sides: and when sir Henri Percy saw his men fast slain he pressed in to the battle with 30 men, and made a lane in the middle of the host till he came to the king's banner, and there he slew the earl of Stafford and sir Thomas *(this should be Walter)* Blount and others; and at last he was beset about and slain, and anon his host was disheartened and fled. And sir Henri Percy's head was smitten and set up at York, lest his men would have said that he was alive. And sir Thomas Percy his uncle was taken and beheaded at Shrewsbury, and his head set on London bridge. And in this battle the prince, king Harry's son, was hurt in the face with an arrow. And this battle was done in the year of our Lord 1404 *(this should be 1403)*.

After this battle was done, the knights and squires of the north country that had been with sir Henri Percy, went home again to Northumberland, and kept themselves in strongholds and castles and would not trust in the king's grace. And afterward the king sent for the earl of Northumberland that was sir Henri Percy's father; and he said if the king would swear that he should come and go safe till he had excused him in the Parliament, he would gladly come; and so he came to the parliament, and excused him that he was not guilty of the battle of Shrewsbury, and swore upon the cross of Canterbury before the parliament, that he should ever be true to king Harry. To this parliament came letters as they had been sent from king Richard, seeming so evident and so true, that the king and all the parliament were thereof astonished, and had great marvel; and called him that was his keeper, and asked of him how he would answer to those letters; and he answered and said he would fight with any man that would say that he was alive.

John Kynaston had married the daughter of Llywelyn Ddu, and lost many tenants at the battle. His father Madoc also died here, who had married Isolda, Hotspur's sister.

According to Barnard, after the battle, Henry marched towards Wales, but lack of finances prevented his invasion. However, his losses had been severe, and he would have known that Glyndŵr had an extremely strong force. From July onwards, English power across Wales had crumbled – administrative records were no longer able to be kept. John Bodenham, Sheriff of Herefordshire, withdrew all his forces from Wales, and from Hereford appealed once more to Henry IV for assistance. From July through early August, Hywel Gwynedd, based on Halkyn Mountain, led Glyndŵr's followers into Flintshire, and was joined by the men of Flint in burning the towns of Flint, Rhuddlan, Overton, Hope and Howarden. The raiders even made ingress into Shrophire, although the King was here at this time. Support was rallied, not just in Flint, but along the Shropshire borders, near Chester, in the Wirral and Herefordshire. Glyndŵr himself is thought to have returned north to rally Flintshire following defeat of Hotspur at Shrewsbury, while Rhys Gethin returned with the bulk of the army to South Wales.

THE BATTLE OF STALLING DOWN (BRYN OWAIN) JULY/AUGUST 1403

The dates for this battle are variously given in any of the six years from 1400 to 1405. There could have been a separate Glamorgan rising in 1401 or 1405, but Glyndŵr was said to have been present. In 1404, Glyndŵr was leading the Franco-Welsh army past this site, but there seems to have been no resistance in the open field. The battle may have occurred in July, when Glyndŵr was on his way to meet Hotspur at Shrewsbury, causing his delay. However, it has been placed after the battle, on the Welsh army's return through South Wales. Stalling Down is next to Cowbridge, north of the main Roman road across South Wales, which leads from Newport to Cardiff, Neath and Carmarthen.

The general site is known locally as Bryn Owain, meaning Owain's Hill. There was said to be a French contingent assimilated into forces from Glamorgan led by Rhys Gethin and Cadwgan, Lord of Glyn Rhondda, commanding the contingent from the Rhondda Valleys. Cadwgan was from Aberochwy, near Treorchy, and fought using a battleaxe, being known as Cadwgan of the Bloody Axe.

> Cadogan of the Battle-Axe, lived at Glyn Rhontha, during the time of Owen Glyndŵr's war, and was one of that chieftain's captains over the men of that vale. When Cadogan went to battle, he used to perambulate Glyn Rhontha, whetting his battle-axe, as he proceeded along; from which circumstance, Owen would call out to Cadogan, 'Cadogan, whet thy battle-axe;' and the moment that Cadogan was heard to do so, all living persons, both male and female, in Glyn Rhontha, collected about him, in military order: and from that day to this, the battle-shout of the men of Glyn Rhontha has been, 'Cadogan! whet thy battle-axe,' and, at the word, they all assemble as an army.
> (Iolo Morganwg)

Glyndŵr was said to have been present, but it was possibly his almost-identical brother Tudur. The English force were said to be camped on nearby 'Kingshill'. This may be either St Hilary Down, or more likely Mynydd Gwyn where St Hilary TV transmitting station is today.

On old maps there is marked 'Site of Battle between the English and Welsh 1401', in the centre of Stalling Down, where the old Cowbridge race course used to be. Another site is simply marked 'Site of Battle' and seems to be the place of the 1403 fight. Iolo Morganwg quoted the Lan-y-Lai MS of the Rev. Thomas Bassett, against a date of 1400:

> In the year of Christ, 1400, Owen Glyndŵr came to Glamorgan, and won the castle of Cardiff, and many more: he also demolished the castles of Penlline, Llandough, Flemingston, Dunraven of the Butlers, Tal-y-Van, Llanblethian, Malefant, and that of Penmark; and he burnt many of the villages and churches about them. He burnt, also, the villages of Llanfyrnach and Aberthin; and many houses at Llantwit Major, and other places, the men of which would not join him. But many of the country people collected around him with one accord; and they demolished castles and houses innumerable; laid waste, and quite fenceless, the lands, and gave them, in common, to all.
>
> They took away from the powerful and rich, and distributed the plunder among the poor. Many of the higher order and chieftains were obliged to flee to England, under the protection and support of the king. A bloody battle took place on Bryn Owen mountain, near Cowbridge, between Owen and his men, and the king's men, but the latter were put to flight after eighteen hours' hard fighting; during which the blood was up to the horses fetterlocks, at Pant-y-Wennol, that separates both ends of the mountain.

The other end of the mountain is Mynydd Gwyn, where the St Hilary transmitting station is situated. Both are hills, rather than mountains, but in Glamorgan several large hills have the Welsh name of 'mynydd'. On a spur of Mynydd Gwyn is a large Iron Age fort ('y Gron' on old maps, from crwn/cron meaning round) in Llanquian Wood, which was probably not forested then. Llanquian Castle and Aberthin both adjoin Stalling Down. Llanbleddian (St Quintin's) Castle guarded the walled town of Cowbridge below it, where the Roman road crosses the River Thaw. Under the fort it is always very boggy in the valley between Stalling Down and Mynydd Gwyn. This valley is now called Pant-Wilkin. However, on an 1810 map Pant Wilkin is 'Pant Willan', a corruption of Pant-y-Wennol. (There is no word Gwillan in Welsh. Pant-y-Wennol is translated as Hollow of the Swallows – birds attracted because of flying insects above marshland.) Glyndŵr's army would have been on Mynydd Gwyn and its Iron Age fort, after heading west along the Roman road from Cardiff, and the King's men on Stalling Down. Both would have wanted to wait for the other to attack, trying to keep out of bowshot. In the summer, the horses and men would have been thirsty, and the only water was in the stream and a well between the hills. At some stage the armies met in the hollow, where blood and mud stained the horses' fetlocks.

The English army was then said in one account to have retreated through Cardiff pursued by the Welsh, in a thunderstorm and through floods. However, this may have been another battle as Cardiff had previously fallen to Glyndŵr. Regardless of the year and number of battles, there was certainly a major engagement here. Three miles away in Llanbleddian Church, 1896 renovations revealed a stone stairway leading to a crypt. Inside the crypt were piled 300 male skeletons, without coffins. The only known battle in this area was at Stalling Down. The crypt measured only 17 ft by 15 ft, and was 7 ft high at its apex. The bones were reburied in the churchyard. The clerk's pew contained an inscription that this church was the burial place of the Sweeting family 'before the war with Owen Glyndŵr'.

13 August saw a surprise attack on Cydweli by Henry Dwn, but floods hampered his progress. He took the town and the castle's corn supplies, but could not take the castle. Also in August Crughywel (Crickhowel) fell and its castle was partially castle. Abergafenni town was again burnt, with its castle just holding out. By the summer of 1403, many long-time supporters of the King, such as David Perrot, the Treasurer-Chancellor of Pembrokeshire, had gone over to Glyndŵr. Perrot was supposed to have helped organize the Welsh naval strategy against the English and was possibly involved in Glydwr's taking of Aberystwyth, Harlech and Cricieth, as supplies from the sea were prevented from reaching those castles. Dinas Powys Castle in the Vale of Glamorgan was taken.

Rhys Gethin began to move west from Glamorgan and with Morgan Gethin attacked the castles at Swansea and Neath, both of which submitted. Morgan Gethin was to reappear, fighting in Gower in 1406. Cilgerran Castle was known to be damaged at this time. On 3 September Richard Kingeston, Dean of Windsor and Archdeacon of Hereford, wrote to the King of raids into Hereford from a band of 400 rebels who took both men and livestock – Glyndŵr still needed men to fight for him and these were impressed into his service in a war band. Kingeston was severely alarmed by the threat not only to Wales but to Hereford:

There are come into our country more than four hundred of the rebels of Owen Glyn, Talgard and many other rebels besides, from the Marches of Wales, and they have captured and robbed within your county of Hereford many men and beasts in great numbers, our truce not withstanding, as Miles Walter the bearer of these presents will more fully tell you by mouth than I can write to you at present, to whom may it please you to give your faith and credence in that on which he shall inform you for the preservation of your said county and of all the country around. The said Miles Walter, moreover, is the most valiant man at arms in Herefordshire or the Marches as he has served his Majesty well and lost all that he hath.

He begs for a hundred lances and six hundred archers at once until your most gracious arrival for the salvation of us all; for the preservation of your said county *(Hereford)*, and all the March to send me this night or tomorrow morning at the latest my most honoured Master Beaufort *(the Duke of Somerset)* or some person who is willing to labour with 100 lances and 600 archers, until your most gracious arrival to the salvation of allfor otherwise my most dread Lord, I hold all your country to be destroyed. For all the hearts of your faithful lieges in our country, with the commons, are utterly lost; and for this, that they hear you are not coming to this place in your own person (which God Avert). You will find for certain that if you do not come in your own person to await your rebels in Wales you will not find a single gentleman that will stop in your said county. Wherefore, for God's sake, think on your best friend, God, and thank him as he hath deserved of you; and leave naught that you do not come, for no man that may counsel you to the contrary, for, by the truth that I shall be to you yet, this day the Welshmen suppose and trust that you will not come there and therefore, for God's love, make them false men. And it please you of your high Lordship to have me excused of my coming to you, for in good faith I have naught here left with me over two men for to withstand the malice of the rebels this day ... for salvation of your shire and Marches trust you naught to any lieutenant. Written at Hereford in very great haste, our humble creature and continual orator.

Local communities in England along the border were known to be making truces with the Welsh, which in the case in the letter above, was ignored. In September 1403, Swansea Castle was still in hands of the King, as orders were given in Somerset to provision the castle and town. However, at some time between 1403 and 1405 Swansea Castle was taken, and Swansea and Gower were controlled by Glyndŵr. From 1403-1408 no income was taken from the Duchy of Lancaster territories adjoining Gower, and it was probably a similar situation in the Gower lordship also. North-east Wales and Cheshire were also a focus of war, as records from *The Wapentake of Wirral – The Hundred of Wirral 1403-1509* reveal:

The revolt of Owen Glendower was naturally a most disturbing influence throughout Cheshire, and for some years the men of the county were constantly engaged in repelling the invasions of the Welsh. The records are full of writs commanding every one holding possessions on the marches to hasten home and make defence. Among the duties thrown upon the officers of the Hundreds on the marches was that of preventing the Welsh getting supplies. In June of 1403 the Prince of Wales ordered the bailiffs of the Hundred of Wirral to prohibit the sale of grain or provisions by the men of Wirral to Welshmen of the county of Flint or other parts of Wales. The reason for this was that the Prince had heard that many men of the Hundred were in the habit of furnishing the men of Flint and of the townships of Denbigh, Denfrencluyt (Dyffryn-clwyd), Hawarden, and Hopedale with supplies, and they in their turn sold them to the Welsh rebels.

Commissioners were also appointed to seize all the grain, &c., in the Hundred which had been sold to the Welsh, who, the Prince had heard, entered the Hundred by night and day by certain fords 'ultra aquam de Dee' and carried thence a great quantity of grain for the support of the rebels, contrary to proclamation ... in the autumn of 1403, it again became necessary, in view of the near approach of Owen Glendower, who was reported in the marches of the county, to appoint special conservators and guardians for the Hundred of Wirral. The names of John de Pulle, William de Stanley, John Lytherland, and John de Meoles appear in the writ. They were instructed to appoint watches, and to make hedges, ditches, and other impediments on the sea coast of Flint to repel the invaders. Another step taken was to appoint Hamo de Mascy of Puddington and others as keepers of the passes between the city of Chester and 'Hazelwa' to prevent traffic with the rebels.

So far as we can gather, the bedells (beadles) never had much difficulty in paying their rents, but from the constant recognisances entered into by the bailiffs, it would seem that they found great difficulty in collecting that part of the revenue for which they were responsible, and no doubt the disturbed and deteriorating state of this part of the county had much to do with their troubles ... early in 1404, a jury of the Hundred was ordered to be empanelled for an unusual object. False rumours (probably relating to the Welsh rebellion) were being spread about in Cheshire, and malicious letters circulated by messengers and runners, which the Earl of Chester considered constituted a national danger and caused great disquiet in the county. He therefore issued a commission to each Hundred to inquire into the matter ... John le Barker of Wallasey, beadle in 1408, was perhaps originally a Wrexham man. We find him coming in from thence to Chester in 1404, with one Matthew le Cornifer, because they were unwilling to join the rebels. Their loyalty was cruelly doubted, and both had formally to do fealty to the Earl and find a surety ...

In North Wales, Glyndŵr's men were still regularly crossing the Dee to sack English settlements. Rhuddlan, Coleshill and Prestatyn were on high alert to halt shipping raids. In Chester, defensive stockaded ditches were built outside the city on the approaches from Wales. Welshmen were forbidden to live there, and if found after dusk could be beheaded without trial. Anyone entering Chester was searched, and stripped of all weapons except a small knife for eating. 25 August saw Prince Henry order William de Stanley, William de Poole, John Litherland and John of Moels, to 'appoint watches and make ditches, hedges and other impediments on the sea coast of the County of Flint against the coming of Glyndowrdy now in the Marches of the County of Chester.' Glyndŵr obviously knew that the King was raising forces to meet in Hereford to attack the south, so was making the best of his limited resources with guerilla attacks far away from royal strength.

Guy de Mona was not only Bishop of St David's but also the King's 'surveyor of castles' in South Wales and the Marches, and in September 1403, Henry IV ordered him, on pain of losing Llawhaden Castle, his lordships, manors and lands, to ensure that castles were furnished 'with fencible men, victuals, armour, artillery and all the things needful for the purpose, that no damage or peril shall arise by his default or negligence or by careless guard thereof.' The bishop was ordered to ensure that castle owners across South Wales and the borders received the same writ. The King's castles of Cardiff, Builth, Carreg Cennen and Brecon, and those of the Prince of Wales at Carmarthen,

Aberystwyth and Cardigan were also resupplied and subject to the same command. On 8 September, 1403, Henry committed Clyro and Painscastle to the Earl of Warwick, Huntington Castle to Countess Ann of Stafford, Crickhowell to John Pauncefoot and Tretower to James Berkeley. A partial list of castles and their owners subject to this strict order are: New Radnor and Cefnllys (the Earl of March); Newport (Gwent, the Earl of Stafford); Snodhill (also called Snowdoun, in Golden Valley, John Chandos); Brampton Bryan (Brian Harley); Stapleton (Richard Cornewall, Lord Burford); Lyonshall and Dorstone (Walter fitz Walter); Llawhaden (Guy de Mona); Llandovery (John Touchet, Lord Audley); Abergafenni and Ewyas Harold (William Beauchamp, brother of Richard, Earl of Warwick); Laugharne (Henry Scrope); Crickhowell (John Pauncefoot); Tretower (James Berkeley); Goodrich (John Neville, Lord Furnival – his son by Angharad was Gilbert Talbot); Usk and Caerleon (Edward Charleton); Caerffili and Ewyas Lacey (Lady Despenser); Manorbier (John Cornwall, husband of Elizabeth of Lancaster); Painscastle and Clyro (Earl of Warwick); and Huntington and Eardisley (Nicholas Montgomery was custodian of Eardisley, but both were owned by Anne, widow of the Earl of Stafford killed fighting for Henry at Shrewsbury). The list did not mention Hay-on-Wye Castle, which had been described as ruinous after a 1403 attack by the Welsh, but which had a garrison attached to it again in 1404. Henry wanted South and Mid-Wales on full war alert to prepare for his new invasion.

THE FOURTH ROYAL EXPEDITION INTO WALES SEPTEMBER 1403

On 8 September, a new royal order was sent to the Mayor of Bristol, which was an instruction to send food and stores to the ports of Cardiff, Newport, Carmarthen and Haverfordwest for the use of the King's army in South Wales. Instructions were also issued to Constance, the widow of Thomas le Despenser, to take immediate steps, on pain of forfeiture of Caerffili Castle, 'so that no danger or peril might arise from the Welsh by default or negligence or by careless guard.'

The difficulty of taking Caerffili, where the eastern gatehouse appears to have been destroyed in the Llywelyn Bren revolt, is summarised by a partial list of its supplies when it surrendered in 1327. It was held by the Despensers and had been besieged by the army of Queen Isabella and her lover Roger Mortimer. There were almost 800 lance shafts, 14 Danish axes, 1,130 crossbow bolts fitted with hedgehog quills, 118 quarters of wheat, 78 carcasses of oxen, 280 mutton carcases, seventy-two hams, 1,856 stockfish (usually dried cod), 6 tuns of red wine and one of white. Fourteen thousand pounds in cash was taken, with 600 silver vessels and the personal belongings of Edward II. (Edward II had stayed at the castle, then went to Neath Abbey, and was trying to return to the safety of Caerffili when captured near Llantrisant with Hugh Despenser. Despenser was hung, drawn and quartered at Hereford, and King Edward murdered at Berkeley Castle.) Caerffili passed to Lady Despenser, and Bradley counts the other nobles holding Welsh castles at this time:

Lord Audley was at Llandovery, Sir Henry Scrope at Langhame, John Pauncefote held Crickhowl, and James Berkeley, Tretower. At Abergavenny was a Beauchamp, at Goodrich a Neville. The splendid pile of Caerphilly, whose ruins are the largest in Britain, was in the charge of a Chatelaine, Lady Despenser. The noble castle of Manorbier, where Giraldus was born, is that of Sir John Cornwall, while the Earl of Warwick was at Paines, and a Charlton, of course, at Welshpool.

Glyndŵr was said to have Caerffili Castle in 1403, but the occupation lasted only 100 days. One source states that Glyndŵr returned with additional French forces in 1405 and retook the castle, holding it for a year.

There is no absolute evidence that Glyndŵr was in the region of Shrewsbury when that battle was fought, but the encounter may have served to divert his forces eastwards. There were serious fears of a Welsh attack on Shrewsbury and an invasion of Shropshire (where several manors had been destroyed in 1403). The Southern March was also under threat. A royal expedition was planned, to set out from Worcester in mid-September. Kingeston and others had pleaded with the King to come to Wales in person as so many had defected to Glyndŵr. King Henry IV once again invaded South Wales – Prince Henry was recovering from his wound at Shrewsbury. He called on men from no less than thirty-five shires, and ordered the repair of twenty-two castles. His army moved to Hereford and then to Brecon. On 13 September we have noted that John Pers was pardoned on the supplication of the King's kinswoman, Lady Joan of Abergafenni, and other rebels were pardoned at the same time, including Harry Ddu ap Gruffydd of Ewyas Lacey in Hereford. The area of Ewyas Lacey (later named Longtown) was devastated during the war, and Longtown Castle was continually heavily garrisoned from 1402-1408.

From Hereford the King had marched through Hay-on-Wye and Talgarth to Brecon and Defynnog, killing suspected traitors and rewarding their lands to loyalists. On 15 September, the King headed to Defynnog Castle, just west of Brecon, where he gave nobles including Sir John Oldcastle of Herefordshire commissions to offer peace to the rebels of Breconshire, Builth, Cantref Selyf, Hay-on-Wye, Glynbough and Bwlch-y-Dinas, if they gave up their arms and swore loyalty. The royal presence in central Wales, north of Brecon, had been reduced to one safe refuge, Builth Wells Castle. From Brecon the royal expedition lumbered down the Tywi Valley, reaching Carmarthen on 24 September. The castle was regarrisoned and rebuilding commissioned. Its constable John Beaufort pleaded to be replaced as Commander, such had been the intensity of Welsh attacks over the previous year. Also in September, William Beauchamp at Abergafenni Castle pleaded that his men were being killed and that he needed support from the King. Earl Richard Beauchamp of Warwick was given command of royal forces, based in Brecon, when Henry returned to England.

As soon as Henry IV had returned to England in late September, normal warfare resumed across Wales – it had never stopped in the north. From late September through to October, Gwent rebelled, and from 29 September to 3 October Henry Dwn once more attacked Cydweli, this time with support from French and Breton troops. They burned the town but the castle barely held out. This took place when Henry was only seven miles away in

Carmarthen, showing that the Welsh had no real fear of his army. They could escape more quickly than he could follow, and they knew that he did not have the leadership skills of his son Prince Hal. Henry took punitive measures on his march to and from Carmarthen, but once again retreated to England without truly stamping his authority on the Welsh. It is recorded that Glyndŵr, after each royal invasion, attending the funerals of civilians killed by English forces.

The appearance of French and Breton ships off Cydweli on 3 October, and off Caernarfon in the following month, and the assaults made on both castles and towns gave fresh heart to Glyndŵr in his alliance with France. In October huge reinforcements had to be sent from England to safeguard Beaumaris, which had been subject to attacks all year. A relief mission was sent from Devon and Somerset to beleaguered Cardiff Castle, which instead plundered Llandaff Cathedral, which had been spared by Glyndŵr. The Welsh drove them off, the English suffering heavy losses. November and December saw more attacks on Beaumaris, Caernarfon, Harlech and Aberystwyth. Harlech could not be relieved by land, as North Wales was all Glyndŵr's except for a few royal castles. Robin Holland of Eglwys Fach had already captured its constable, John Hennore, when Hennore led a raiding party out of the castle. His successor William Hunt wanted to leave the castle to the Welsh, and his own men placed him under armed guard in a dungeon.

More relief columns had to be sent over the winter of 1403-1404 to Radnor, Montgomery, Builth and other Welsh castles. In December, ships were sent to try and save Beaumaris and Cardiff castles. In December Glyndŵr himself was said to have led the burning of Cardiff and its castle, but spared the Llandaff Cathedral. Llandaff's Bishop's Castle was sacked by Owain, whether now or at another time in the war is unknown. Cardiff had 24 men-at-arms and 479 archers when it surrendered – it had only twenty-four stone cannonballs remaining, with just four pounds of gunpowder. There were three barrels of salted meat, a pipe of salmon (a wine barrel full of this fish, abundant in the fifteenth century), a few beans and the ale had almost run out. Caerleon, Newport, Usk and Caerffili castles all fell in 1403. The Earl of Arundel again fortified Clun Castle and the castle saw service against the Welsh. Near the town is a single entrenchment said to have been raised by Glyndŵr to shelter his troops while attacking Clun Castle. French pirates attacked Plymouth and Salcombe, despite Henry's peace with France. The end of 1403 and the beginning of 1404 saw the further advancement of Owain's cause. In the late autumn, French troops had arrived to support Glyndŵr, and from November the French blockaded the Celtic and Irish Seas. Glyndŵr had failed to storm the massive Harlech Castle, so he decided to starve out the occupiers. Aberystwyth Castle was subject to repeated attack. Glyndŵr's power was at its height, with the greatest royal castles under constant siege, and French ships along the coast adding support.

THE FRENCH INVASION & THE SIEGE OF CAERNARFON

In November 1403, Jean d'Espagne landed near Caernarfon, beat off an English attack, and began to construct siege engines, supported by offshore warships. It was a new development for the Welsh to construct such machines, but now they had access to French expertise. Carpenters may have constructed 'belfries', mobile wooden siege towers for attacking fortifications. Other 'engines' would include the 'penthouse and ram'. The penthouse was a mobile shed protecting the men operating a battering ram. The ram was usually a large heavy object like a tree trunk, swung against the gate from within the protective structure, and suspended on ropes or chains. Also, bores and pointed picks could be used to weaken and demolish stonework. Glyndŵr had no real access to cannon.

William Venables, Deputy Warden of the Marches (whose brother Richard had been beheaded by Henry IV after the Battle of Shrewsbury) wrote to the King:

> Robert Parys, the Deputy Constable of Caernarvon (*the constable had been captured*), has apprised us through a woman, because there was no man who dared come, for neither man nor woman dare carry letters on account of the rebels of Wales, that Owen Glyndŵr with the French and all his other power is preparing to assault the town and castle of Caernarvon and to begin this enterprise with engines, sowes and ladders of great length; and in the town there are not more than 28 fighting men, which is all too small a force, for 11 of the more able men who were there at the last siege of the place are dead; some of the wounds they received at the assault and others of the plague; so the said castle and town are in imminent danger.

'Sows' were mobile hide-covered huts, underneath which miners would excavate castle walls. They were needed to gain access to the base of a wall or a moat, to allow mining operations. A tunnel would be dug under the moat and walls, supported by timber props. The end of the tunnel would be packed with combustible material, e.g. pig carcasses for their high fat content. The bonfire was then set alight, causing the tunnel to collapse and the walls fall in. Fire was also used to reduce a castle – the building's surrounding the fortifications would be set alight before any siege engines were brought forward. Almost every castle would have enough combustible material inside its walls to make an incendiary attack attractive. Wooden accommodation, store-rooms, stables, huts etc. were erected against the interior walls. Various recipes for Greek Fire are documented, and this was often catapulted into the castle in earthenware pots. The defenders would also drop Greek Fire onto the protective sow used by the attackers. Greek Fire was a liquid mix of petroleum and naphtha, used as an incendiary weapon and very difficult to extinguish. Water only spread its destruction. Defenders would also use boiling oil against attackers. One long siege records defenders running out of Greek Fire and oil, and pouring a mixture of boiling water and ale through murder-holes and onto men climbing ladders, such that the attackers' 'skin peeled off'.

Conwy Castle also was threatened again, and its constable Henry of Scarisbrooke wrote to Henry: 'I durst lay my head that 200 men in Conway and 200 in Caernarvon would be sufficient to protect the two counties with ease and the inhabitants, with the exception of 4 or 5 gentlemen and a few vagabonds would gladly pay dues to the English for protection rather than suffer from the rebels.'

However, a letter sent to William Venables shows an even wider concern: 'Owain has been to Harlech Castle and is in accord with all the men who are there, save only 7, for to have deliverance of the castle as a certain day for a certain sum of gold if it be right ordained it is lost and so is all the country thereabout.' The rumour that Harlech would succumb to a payment of gold would resurface later in the campaign. At the end of 1403, all of the major castles outside north-east Wales were under siege – Aberystwyth, Harlech, Conwy, Cricieth, Caernarfon and Beaumaris. A message reached Conwy, pleading in vain for help for Harlech and Cricieth. Carmarthen was being rebuilt and Cardiff and Caerffili had been sacked. Newport, Usk and many others across Wales never recovered from their slighting. Glyndŵr virtually controlled all of Wales except for a few castles and the south of Pembroke, which, like many border towns was paying him not to invade. The last royal expedition had stayed less than a month in Wales, with the sole end-result of regarrisoning Carmarthen. Independence was almost tangible for Owain's supporters.

As Abbot Walter Bower commented in 1447: 'It is a fact that, by the providence of God himself, within three years the Welsh had expelled all their enemies, and had further extended their Marches to the final boundaries of the same kingdom established by Brutus, who had first divided Britain with his brothers.' (Brutus was said to be a descendant of Aeneas of Troy, who settled in Britain and on his death the land was divided between his sons – Kamber had Wales, Locrinus had England and Albanactus had Scotland. The legend can be found in Nennius and Geoffrey of Monmouth.)

CHAPTER 8

The Zenith 1404

The years between 1404 and 1406 were the high-water mark of the war, but the movements of Glyndŵr are elusive, as ever. Because there was less campaigning across Wales, and Owain now controlled most of the nation, there are fewer records from keepers of garrisons to consult. Senior Churchmen and members of society from all of Wales had joined Owain, and probably old allies of Richard II were sending money and arms to the Welsh. It is almost certain that Cistercian and Franciscan communities in England were channeling funds to support the Welsh. English towns in Shropshire, Herefordshire and Montgomeryshire had stopped resistance and made their own treaties with Owain's local warbands. Parliament even sanctioned the people of Shropshire and Montgomeryshire to pay Glyndŵr funds to save further destruction. However, raiding parties seem seldom to have attacked Cheshire, as its people had been consistently faithful to Richard II. French ships were said to have brought cannon to a siege at Conwy Castle. Beaumaris, Caernarfon, Harlech and Aberystwyth were also besieged, and could only be supported from the sea, not overland.

Hotspur, and his uncle the Earl of Worcester, great warriors who had enforced order across Wales, had rebelled against Henry and were now dead. The English Prince of Wales had been badly injured, almost dying from his wound at Shrewsbury. A far better leader than his father, he was still not able to lead the English fight back against Owain. English resistance was limited to a defensive role in a few isolated castles, walled towns, and fortified manors. No less than four Royal Expeditions into Wales had been forced back, and Henry IV also now had major problems in France and Scotland. The anti-English Louis, Duc de Orleans, with the approval of the French Council, began a campaign of conquest in Guyenne, taking several castles. Henry IV was only able to respond by sending Lord Berkeley, with a small force. There was conflict all year across Wales as the last vestiges of English power were constantly attacked.

The kingdom was in a desperate state. The Royal Exchequer was so bare that Henry was obliged to accept parliamentary control of spending, and over his own council. This was a breakthrough in English constitutional history. In January at Beaumaris, Anglesey, a French and Welsh force was victorious. Maredudd ap Cynwrig, Deputy Sheriff of Anglesey, had left the castle and taken many of the garrison to escort him collecting the King's dues. His train of 200 men was ambushed, and most were killed. Maredudd was taken for ransom. The town of Beaumaris was later retaken by the English, but the Welsh gained the castle in the winter of 1404. The French continued their assistance to the Welsh in the siege of Caernarfon Castle, with Jean d'Espagne ably commanding the siege engines and artillery.

Caernarfon Castle was commanded by William of Tranmere, and by the end of 1403 the castle had lost three of its ablest commanders, including Ieuan ap Maredudd, whose brother Robert was in Glyndŵr's army. Ieuan's body was smuggled out of the castle and buried in secret at Penmorfa, for fear that the Welsh would desecrate the traitor's grave. In *Wynn's Families of Wales* we read:

> Ieuan ap Maredudd, the father, held steadfastly Henry IV and the House of Lancaster, when Owain
> Glyndŵr rebelled; so that in the time of that war Ieuan and Hwlkyn Llwyd of Glynllifon had the
> charge of Caernarfon town, and an English captain was in the castle; in revenge whereof Owain
> burned his two houses, Cefn y fan or Ystumcegid, and Cesail Gyfarch. In the continuance of this
> war, Ieuan ap Maredudd died at Caernarfon, and was brought by sea (for the passage by land was
> shut up by Owain's forces) to Penmorfa, his parish church, to be buried. Robert ap Maredudd,
> the brother of Ieuan ap Maredudd, taking the contrary side, was out with Owain, as may be gathered by
> a pardon granted him by Henry the Fourth, and Henry his son, then Prince of Wales.

On 24 January, a relief force was sent to Radnor Castle, near the border. Prince Henry was still recovering from his injuries, so Arundel had taken charge of English garrisons as Royal Lieutenant in North Wales, and the Duke of York had the southern command. Armies traditionally ceased to campaign through the winter, but the Welsh did not stop their attacks. In January in Parliament, the King officially transferred overall command of the Welsh effort to Prince Henry. The King was ill, and had suffered five years of war to no avail except to empty his coffers and make Parliament more powerful. The French and Bretons were constantly raiding the South Coast. There were rumours that the Earl of Northumberland was plotting the revenge of his son and brother. There were still rumours that Richard II was alive. The Scottish situation was not resolved. There were several claimants to the crown whose claim was better than his – the Mortimers, and Hotspur's son – and Glyndŵr was still undefeated. Apart from the mighty Pembroke Castle in southern Pembrokeshire, only five castles in the other twelve counties were thought absolutely secure in English hands – Brecon, Beaumaris, Conwy, Harlech and Aberystwyth. Before the end of the year three of these incredibly powerful castles were to fall.

In February, the men of upland Breconshire were called upon to submit to the King's authority and pay taxes. They answered with the offer that if the King defeated the rebels in Glamorgan they would submit, but that if he failed to do so, they could not be expected to submit. The King told his commanders that he would have to suppress the revolt in Glamorgan and Gwent before May, otherwise the men of Brecon would not be allowed to reside 'in the King's peace'. Along with Pembroke, Glamorgan, Gwent and Brecon were the areas of Wales that had had English domination for the longest period, so represented a real groundswell of support. Welsh attacks were continuous into the English border towns and counties and the King was powerless to help. The best he could do was to put larger garrisons in Welshpool and Bishops Castle in the Marches.

CRICIETH CASTLE FALLS 1404

The garrison at Cricieth had been strengthened. The Constable, Roger Acton, had six men-at-arms and fifty archers at an annual cost of £416 14s 2d. A French fleet in the Irish Sea supported Glyndŵr and had stopped provisions reaching the main West Coast castles (Cricieth, Aberystwyth and Harlech). In the spring of 1404, Cricieth fell to Glyndŵr and the castle and the borough were burned. One of Glyndŵr's men fighting here was Ieuan ab Einion, the nephew of the famed Hywel y Fwyall (Hywel the Battleaxe, knighted at Crecy by the Black Prince). The Castle was never rebuilt, so its noble remains are substantially as Glyndŵr left it. The borough slowly recovered, but was no longer a garrison borough and became wholly Welsh once more. In February 1404, the Earl of Warwick received at Brecon Castle six cannon, 20lbs of gunpowder, 10lbs of sulphur, 20lbs of saltpetre, forty-two breastplates and twelve basinets. With new forces, he forced some Welsh west of Brecon to agree a peace with them offering to pay 100 marks, in 10 weekly instalments.

The French made several attacks upon maritime towns, William du Chatel burning and plundering Teignmouth, Plymouth and others. In 1404, John Hawley was ordered by the King to organise the defence of Dartmouth from attack by Bretons who had landed at Slapton in April 1404. The Bretons lost The Battle of Blackpool Sands. Henry ordered a Te Deum in Westminster Abbey in celebration. Henry was not only ill, but financially impoverished. In North Wales, only the castles of Rhuddlan, Denbigh, Powys and Flint in the north-east, and Beaumaris, Conwy and Caernarfon in the north-west were still in royal hands. On the Western Coast, only Aberystwyth and Harlech remained, both having been besieged for months. The bishops of St Asaf and Bangor Cathedrals, John (Ieuan) Trefor and Lewis Byford (Lewis ap Ieuan) officially joined Glyndŵr's cause in April 1404. They had probably been sympathisers for a long time. In two of Iolo Goch's surviving poems, to Ieuan Trefor, we can see the relative luxury they gave up to join Glyndŵr. Iolo Goch praises the court of Ieuan at St Asaph, with its doorman, butler, beerman, baker, chamberlain, cooks, stabler and his own vineyard. There are guest rooms, a mead-cellar, kitchen, pantry, buttery and log fires, not made up of 'dumb sea-coal'. Iolo, as his guest, could have anything – 'cardamom seeds, rice, raisins, herbs, mead, a fine feast and wine' and 'free-flowing liquor'. The major ecclesiastics joining Glyndŵr's force were Gruffydd Yonge (Chancellor and Archdeacon of Merioneth), Ieaun or John Trefor (Bishop of St Asaf), Hywel Cyffin (Dean of St Asaf), Ifan ap Bleddyn ap Gronw (Archdeacon of Anglesey), Dafydd ap Ifan ap Dafydd ap Gruffydd (Dean of Bangor), Llewelyn ap Ieuan (called Lewis Byford, Bishop of Bangor) and John ap Hywel (Bishop of Llantarnam).

Later that month, letters were again sent from Caernarfon imploring for help against the French force's siege engines and warships. Jean, Duc d'Orleans, sent correspondence to Henry several times asking to meet him in single combat to settle English claims to France.

THE WELSH TAKE HARLECH CASTLE APRIL 1404
(some sources state January 1404)

In 1404, the castle fell after a long siege when starvation had reduced the determined garrison to just twenty-one men. There had been twelve men-at-arms and forty-five archers in this grim coastal castle with walls up to 12 ft thick, which cost the equivalent of £10 million to build. It had been defended by Richard Massey of Sale and Vivian Collier of Harlech throughout 1402 until June 1403. However, Massey was replaced in June by John Hennore, who was captured by Robin Holland of Eglwys Fach soon after. Another guardian replaced him, William Hunt, who had managed to access the castle by a small sea-gate. He arrived to find the garrison starving. French ships blockaded any supplies from landing. Hunt was locked up by his troops as he wanted to surrender; such was the plight of its defences. Two men known as 'Favian Collier' and 'Sir Vivian' then took over, but this may be a single reference to the aforesaid Vivian Collier of Harlech. With sickness, injuries and malnourishment, only sixteen Welsh and five English soldiers were fit to defend it by the spring of 1404, with no possibility of a relief column from England or fresh supplies from the sea.

Its imprisoned constable, William Hunt, in desperation, was allowed to leave the castle with two yeomen, Jack Mercer and Harry Baker, possibly to parley. He was taken by the same Robin Holland who captured John Hennore, in January 1404. Hunt may have wanted to be captured and ransomed – it is difficult to know. The defenders may have succumbed to bribery – it is still unknown how the great castle fell. (Robin Holland was from Plas Berw, Llanfihangel-Ysceifiog, and died in 1410.)

Harlech became Owain's residence, court, family home and military headquarters for four years, and he held his second Parliament in Harlech in August 1405 (and probably a third in August 1406). Cadwgan of Aberorci, Robert ap Jevan (Ieuan) of Ystymcegid, Rhys Ddu, Rhys Gethin, the Tudurs, the Scudamores, the Hanmers, Bishop Trefor and Lewis Byford all assembled here to discuss strategy. Owain and Marged had their quarters in the constable's home in the massive gatehouse. Edmund Mortimer, Catrin and their children resided in what is now known as Mortimer's Tower. Holding court at Harlech, Glyndŵr appointed Gruffydd Yonge as his chancellor, and soon afterwards called his first Parliament or Cynulliad (gathering) of all Wales at Machynlleth.

There were constant Welsh attacks into England, into Cheshire, Hereford, Archenfield and Shropshire, and the English settlement at Abergafenni was again taken and destroyed. Deals were made along the border for protection from attack, with the proceeds going to swell Glyndŵr's treasury. In May and June, Bretons, Frenchmen and Welshmen were serving on each others' ships and destroying English shipping in the English Channel. The Bretons beat an English fleet in early June off Brittany, and once more attacked the area around Dartmouth.

THE FIRST SENEDD AT DOLGELLAU AND THE MISSION TO FRANCE 10 MAY 1404

The first Parliament was held at Machynlleth, but there was a meeting of nobles, a Senedd, preceding it at Dolgellau:

The years that followed up to 1404 saw Glyndŵr's Power extending, and no doubt prisoners like Edmund Mortimer and David Gam passed through Dolgelley. Harlech fell to his arms in January 1404, and in May, Glyndŵr held a council in Dolgelley of some of the chiefs adherent to his cause. Popular tradition used to designate an old house, which formerly stood in Dolgelley, his Parliament house, a quaint and rather handsome house made of undressed stone and wood, with some very fine carving in the interior. It was never a 'parliament' house; for nothing, which could be called a parliament, ever sat in Dolgelley, but it is quite possible that Glyndŵr's council of chiefs assembled there. The house was built, so some accounts say, some 40 or 50 years earlier; but others assert it did not come into existence until some 150 years after Glyndŵr died. It was generally known as Cwrt Plas yn Dre, and it was a kind of townhouse of the family to which Baron Owen belonged. However, it was a charming old building; but the good folk of Dolgelley destroyed it ruthlessly in 1881 or 1882, and its place has been taken since by an up-to-date ironmongery stores. It was, probably enough, at this demolished house that Glyndŵr wrote his despatch on the 10th day of May, 1404, to the King of France, recommending to that King, Dr. Griffith Yonge, who was Archdeacon of Merioneth, and John Hanmer, his own son-in-law, as his ambassadors to enter into negotiations and a treaty with France. These two, together with a priest named Benedict Cornme of St. Asaph, journeyed to Paris from Dolgelley, and on the 14th July concluded a treaty with the French King's representatives to wage war together against Henry of Lancaster. They returned home, bearing with them a suit of armour for Glyndŵr from the King, with a message that the latter knew that 'Owain loved arms above all things', and the treaty which they brought with them was ratified by Glyndŵr at Llanbadarn in the following January. This was the hey-day of Glyndŵr's success, and thereafter, little by little, his cause declined. (T.P. Ellis, 1923)

Part of the building known as the Old Parliament House in Dolgellau was still standing in the nineteenth century, among a group of old houses near the Ship Inn, and was called Cwrt Plas yn y dre'v, 'the town-hall court'. The Roman Via Occidentalis seems to have taken its course from Menavia (St. David's) to Segontium (Carnarvon) via Dolgellau and Machynlleth, so it was part of an important communications system in medieval Wales. (Academics have believed for many years that the main Roman road through South Wales terminated at Carmarthen, but other stretches have been found heading towards St David's. The same historians stated that the Romans never went to Ireland, but a huge Roman fort has been found at Drumanagh fifteen miles north of Dublin, and the Romans probably sailed and traded from around St David's.)

The exact number of parliamentary and senedd meetings held by Glyndŵr is unknown, but there were events at Machynlleth, Harlech, Dolgellau, Llanbadarn (Aberystwyth) and at Cefn Caer (Pennal). Glyndŵr sent letters from Dolgellau to the Kings of Scotland and France, asking for help and pleading the justice of his fight against the English:

To Our Cousin the King of France

To all who examine these letters, greeting. Know ye that on account of the affection and sincere regard which the illustrious prince, the Lord Charles, by the same grace, King of the French, has up to the present time borne towards us and our subjects and of his grace bearing daily, we desire to cleave to him and to his subjects as by merit we are held to this purpose. Wherefore we make, ordain and consecrate by these presents Master Griffith Yonge, Doctor of Canon Law, Chancellor and John de Hanmer, our well beloved kinsman, our true and legal ambassadors proctors, factors, negotiators and special nuncios, giving and conceding to our same ambassadors, and to both of them ... general power ... (to) consider and complete for us.. a perpetual league with the aforesaid most illustrious prince ...

Owain, by the grace of God prince of Wales dated at Dolgellau 10th May 1404

Perhaps by serendipity, 10 May was the date in 1372 when the Treaty of Paris had been signed between Owain Lawgoch and Charles V of France. Glyndŵr's request for armed aid was carried to the French court by John Hanmer, Owain's son-in-law, and the cleric Gruffydd Yonge (Young), described as his chancellor, in this document sealed with Glyndŵr's privy seal and dated in the fourth year of his principate. Around 20 May, the Welsh ambassadors were received by Charles VI of France. The widower Richard II had married the six-year-old Isabella de Valois of France in 1396 as part of the peace process. She was the daughter of Charles VI of France, and on Richard's murder, Henry IV wanted her to marry his son, Prince Henry.

She absolutely refused, and in 1402, the Constable of England, Thomas Percy, escorted her back to her family in France. However, Henry IV had refused to return Isabella's massive dowry, causing bitter enmity with Charles VI. Charles 'the Mad' always refused to accept Bolingbroke's kingship as Henry IV. He referred to him in correspondence as 'the successor to the late King of England', 'Our adversary of England' or simply as 'Henry of Lancaster'. Charles' brother, the Duc d'Orleans, was infuriated at the loss of the dowry, and had challenged Henry several times to a duel. Correspondence between the Duke and the King was bitter, Henry once replying disdainfully that 'we are not bound to answer any such demands unless made by persons of equal rank to ourselves.' As a result, Gruffydd Yonge and John Hanmer, the Welsh envoys to the French court, were always made most welcome, especially by Orleans, the leader of the party that wanted all-out war with England.

In June, Prince Henry was based in Worcester after raids into Archenfield near Monmouth, and warned Henry IV that the Welsh were planning to attack Herefordshire again. Welsh raiding parties were active all along the border. He again wrote to Parliament, telling them that he needed more money, or Wales would have to be left to its own devices. Henry levied troops from four counties to meet at Hereford to be ready to fend off any attack on Abergafenni. The young Earl of Warwick, Richard Beauchamp, was put in charge of the Hereford army and moved towards Abergafenni. In late June and July urgent reinforcements were sent to Welshpool, Oswestry, Bishops Castle, Radnor, Abergafenni, Hay, Brecon and Carmarthen. Cardiff Castle and town also fell to Glyndŵr again in June, and was garrisoned in Welsh hands. Llantrisant Castle, Peterston Castle and St Ffagan's Castle were destroyed some time in Glyndŵr's War. Llangynydr was probably taken, and the bastide of Cowbridge (Y Bontfaen) overwhelmed. Cowbridge has a notable defensive Norman church. On the crossing of the River Thaw (Afon Ddawen) on the Roman road from Cardiff to Carmarthen, it was formerly known as Y Dref Hir yn y Waun - the long town in the marsh - and still has a gatehouse and some thirteenth century town walls remaining. Penllyn Castle was taken at the same time as its town of Llanfrynach near Cowbridge, as well as St Quintin's Castle at Llanblethian (guarding Cowbridge), Boverton Castle and Castell Cynffig (Kenfig).

In the fourteenth century, Tretower passed to the Bluets, who, like most castellar owners, saw it sacked and burned by Owen Glendower in the early fifteenth century... so proudly posed and the bridge between the eastern and western Marches, it is not surprising that Leland's "faire waulled towne, meately well inhabited" *(Abergafenni)* was for centuries a bone of contention between Welsh and English, a hornets' nest of the Marcher Lords, a racial cockpit, a mart of vale and mountain produce, a trade-route, a node and focal point between Gwent and Siluria and a palimpsest of history. Glendower, of course, tediously and tirelessly strumming on his only and discordant string, sacked it in 1404 ... by 1376 the degeneration *(at Llanthony Priory)* had reached such an abyss of horror and barbarity that the Prior had both his eyes torn out by his own canons. The postman at Llanthony claims once to have seen the devil and he would certainly have been likely to have seen him in the ruins of the Priory. Glendower put the finishing touch to this macabre parallel with King Lear by burning the Priory a quarter of a century later, and by 1481 only a Prior and four canons were left.

(Massingham, who also mentions that Glyndŵr burnt Leominster, but this is unlikely).

THE FIRST PARLIAMENT - MACHYNLLETH & THE CROWNING OF OWAIN IV 21 JUNE 1404

Many sources, including Pennant, believe that the first Parliament was at Machynlleth in 1402, upon 2 September. However, in 1402 Harlech and Aberystwyth, on either side ot Machynlleth, were still in English possession, making it too dangerous. It must have been in 1404, probably after the fall of Harlech and with Aberystwyth safely besieged, and was on 21 June. Summoning four men from every 'commote' (Welsh Administrative District), Owain convened his Parliament. Before a vast assembly that included envoys from Scotland, France, and Castile, Glyndŵr was formally proclaimed and crowned 'Owain IV, Prince of Wales - Owynus Dei Gratia Princeps Wallia.' The coronation was attended by all the major nobles in Wales, and his Great Seal shows Glyndŵr as an armed warrior on one side, and a seated prince with a sceptre, orb and crown on the other.

The Welsh State was instituted with a legal system, administration and treasury. After the Parliament, Glyndŵr appointed clerics to help administer the independent state of Wales. The Senedd (Welsh Parliament) agreed funds to hire sixty French ships - the 'de Bourbon mission'. Owain stated his vision of an independent Welsh state with a regular Senedd and a separate Welsh church. He wanted two national universities (one in the South and one in the North), and a return to the traditional and more equitable laws of Hywel Dda. Adam of

Usk wrote later from the safety of England, 'Owain and his hill men, even in their misery, usurping the right of conquest and other marks of royalty, albeit to his own confusion, held, or counterfeited or made pretences of holding parliaments.'

Legend tells us that Davy Gam tried to assassinate Glyndŵr as he walked to the Machynlleth Parliament, but the story may be mixed up with that of Hywel Sele. The legend goes on that Glyndŵr allowed Gam to be freed, but in retaliation burned Gam's manor at Cyrnigwern in Brecon, telling one of Gam's squires:

Shouldst thou a little man descry
Asking about his dwelling fair,
Tell him it under a bank doth lie
And its brow the mark of coal doth bear.

The still standing medieval Royal House is where Dafydd Gam was said to be imprisoned when the attempt failed. (It is called the Royal House because Charles I allegedly stayed there.) Some stories state that in a generous gesture, Owain let Gam go soon after the Parliament, despite Gam's refusal to submit. The Medieval Senedd building is open to the public in Maesgwyn Street, Machynlleth. The paths of Glyndŵr and Gam were to cross again, in 1412.

THE TREATY OF ALLIANCE WITH FRANCE 14 JULY 1404

It appears that Wales has the oldest peace treaty with France - Owain was not regarded as a rebel, but as the legitimate ruler of Wales. Charles VI gave the Welsh envoys a golden helmet (a sign of sovereignty), breastplate and sword for Owain, and on 14 June, appointed the Bishop of Chartres and the Bourbon Earl of March to make an agreement with 'the magnificent and mighty Owen Prince of Wales'. The formal treaty of alliance against 'Henry of Lancaster' between Wales and France was signed on 14 July, in the Paris mansion of the Chancellor of France. It was signed by John Hanmer and Gruffydd Yonge for Glyndŵr. The French signatories included the bishops of Arras, Meaux and Noyon, the Chancellor of France (Arnaud de Corbie), le Compte de la Marche (the Earl of March, Jacques II de Bourbon) and his brother Louis, Compte de Vendome. Glyndŵr wasted no time in announcing the treaty to his new Parliament:

In the first place that the said lords, the king and the prince shall be mutually joined, confederated, united and leagued by the bond of a true covenant and real friendship and of a sure, good and most powerful union against Henry of Lancaster - adversary and enemy of both parties - and his adherents and supporters. Again that one of the said Lords shall desire, follow and will ever procure the advantage of the other and should any damage or injury intended against the one by the said Henry, his accomplices, adherents, supporters or others whatsoever come to the notice of one, he shall prevent that in good faith ... again, that none of the lords, the king or prince aforesaid will make or take truce, nor make peace with the aforesaid Henry of Lancaster.

The ensuing treaty was dated 14 July 1404, and ratified on 12 January 1405, 'in the sixth year of our principate' at the castle of Aberystwyth. Sealed with Owain's new 'great seal', it bound Charles VI and Owain in a covenant against 'Henry of Lancaster', both parties promising that neither would enter into a separate peace with Henry, and that disputes arising between their subjects on land or sea should be amicably settled. No formal promise of military assistance was given or received, although a French chronicler recorded that a list of ports and seaways had been provided by the Welsh Prince to the French.

The envoys had asked for more aid, and Charles was sympathetic, being the father-in-law of the murdered Richard II. They were given weapons to bring back to Wales, and Charles VI ordered Jacques de Bourbon to assemble a French fleet at Harfleur and a Breton fleet at Brest.

Bourbon joined the fleet late, being delayed at court. Twenty warships from Castile joined, and Plymouth was sacked by a land force in mid-August. Fearing a counter-attack, the French withdrew to St Malo, losing twelve vessels in a storm. Then Bourbon wandered along the English Channel looking for easy plunder, to the dismay of his Breton and Castilian contingents. He again attacked Plymouth, but his forces failed there and at Falmouth. The fleet dispersed – he had won no real booty nor followed his mission to land in Wales with a force of 800 knights and squires. August saw a fleet of sixty French ships with 700 men sail from Brittany and Normandy. However, they returned to France in November without actually landing in Wales. By the end of 1404, French ships were regularly raiding the coast of England, some with Welsh troops on board, setting fire to Dartmouth and devastating the coasts of Devon.

> The rebellion under Glendour had now grown to a dangerous pitch. He had lately reduced the castles of Harlegh and Aberystwyth, defeated a strong body of English near Monmouth, and ravaged the country as far as the Severn. The king, who well knew the objects that demanded, at that moment, his sole attention, was averse to an expedition into Wales, and was restrained from prosecuting that war by a trivial incident. The report of Richard's being alive was now revived, and gained more credit than ever. One Serle ... wrote letters to different persons ... assuring them that the king ... was in good health.
> (Barnard 1783.)

Sir William Searle was supposed to have been the knight who murdered Thomas, Duke of Gloucester, in Calais in 1397. He had served Richard II and on his dethroning escaped to Scotland and pretended to be the dead King, having had a copy of Richard's royal seal made. He was backed by the Scottish nobles and the Countess of Oxford, who was briefly imprisoned, and had sent letters with the royal seal to nobles across England, hoping for a rebellion. He surrendered to Sir William Clifford, who sent him to Henry IV in June 1404, and was executed. A priest who said that Serle was Richard II was hung, drawn and quartered:

> The 5 year of king Harri ... Johan Serle, sometime yeoman of king Richard's robes, that was one of the principal slayers of the duke of Gloucester, came out of Scotland in to England, and said to

divers persons that king Richard was alive in Scotland; wherefore he brought many people in great error and grouching against king Harri, for the people wanted faithfully it had been so. But at last he was taken in the north country, and was drawn thorough every city and burgh town in England, and then he was brought to London, and there at Guildhall he was judged to be drawn from the tower of London through London unto Tyburne; and there he was hanged and beheaded and quartered, and his head set on London bridge, and his quarters were sent to the 4 good towns of England.

This Serle confessed that when king Richard was taken in Walis, he stole his signet and fled in to Scotland, and therewith he sold many letters, and showed them to such men as were king Richarde's friends, and said he was alive; and so he was cause of many men's deaths: and he said also that there was a man in Scotland much like to king Richard, but it was not he.

(An English Chronicle)

In the early summer a third of Shropshire was devastated, and on 10 June Archdeacon Kingeston was once more pleading with the Prince Henry, fearing that Hereford would be over-run:

> The Welsh rebels in great numbers have entered Archenfield and there they have burned houses, killed the inhabitants, taken prisoners and ravaged the countryside to the great dishonour of our king and the unsupportable damage of the country. We have often advertised to the king that such mischief would befall us, we have also certain information that the rebels are resolved to make a attack on the March of Wales, to its utter ruin, if speedy succour be not sent. It is indeed true that we have no power to shelter us except that of Richard of York and his men, which is far too little to defend us; we implore you to consider this very perilous and pitiable case and to pray to our sovereign that he will come in his royal person or send some person with sufficient power to rescue us from the invasion of the said rebels. Otherwise we shall be utterly destroyed, which God forbid. Whoever comes will, as we are led to believe, have to engage in battle or will have a very severe struggle with the raiders. And for God's sake remember that honourable and valiant man the lord of Abergavenny who is on the very point of destruction if he be not rescued.

On 19 July 1404 there was a major skirmish in Flintshire. Prince Henry wrote to his father – he had pawned jewels and gold plate to pay his men, and he had no money to pay for any further action. By the end of June, Prince Henry had withdrawn all his forces to the safety of Worcester, and North Wales was totally in Glyndŵr's control. There were constant raids on the Marches, especially upon Shropshire. The Montgomeryshire Collections tell us that the men around Welshpool had flocked to join Glyndŵr, after his forces attacked Powys Castle and the town:

> Chiefest among them being Sir Griffith Vaughan of Garth (a descendant of Brochwel and likewise of Gwenwynwyn), and his brother Ieuan neither of them being more than mere youths at the time, but both entering into the national cause with all the enthusiasm of their young manhood. It was in 1402 that the Welsh leader and his followers marched through Powys-land to the mountains of Plynlumon, from whence they made plundering excursions, and were the terror of all who declined to espouse their cause. The territory of John de Cherleton suffered terribly, and it was on this

occasion, probably, that the suburbs of Welsh Pool were burnt by Glyndŵr, who, it is said, at the same time, made an attack upon the castle, but was compelled to retire without effecting an entrance into its impregnable walls.

On August 5th of that year Lord Powys wrote a letter to the Council, dated from the 'Castell de la Pole', deploring the state to which the neighbourhood had been reduced by the rebellion then raging, and praying 'that the garrisons might be furnished with men-at-arms and archers'. Whether this letter received the attention of the Council or no, we are not informed. In 1404, on August 30th, the Council gave permission to the county of Salop to make a truce for the country of Wales until the end of November, and the King also assented to the Lord of Powys making the like truce for his castle of La Pole.

Griffith Vaughan was Gruffydd Fychan, who with his brother Ieuan joined his father Gruffydd ap Ieuan ap Madoc ap Gwenwys on the side of Glyndŵr. His father was appointed Seneschal of Caus Castle by Sir Hugh Stafford, Lord of Caus, to defend it against Glyndŵr. Following pleas from Welsh lawyers and students from Oxford, the family changed sides and supported Glyndŵr. As a result the family lands were forfeited in 1404. However, by summer 1406, Griffith Vaughan/Gruffydd Fychan was supporting Edward Charleton, Lord of Powys, once more.

Prince Henry had returned to the Marches in June 1404. At Lichfield on 29 and 30 August the Herefordshire gentry requested that the Prince might be thanked for the good protection of the county, and at the same time money was granted to pay his troops. In late August, Haverfordwest was taken in south-west Wales, with its important port. (Repairs to the castle stable cost 18 s and a new castle gate cost £3.3s 6d. The janitor's fee was increased to 2d per day, and the wages for the armourer were £13.4s per annum.) Henry Dwn and William Gwyn ap Rhys Llwyd burned Cydweli in the mid-south-west. William Gwyn had been a loyal servant of the King, but like many other gentry had been dispossessed in the anti-Welsh laws. These able men nearly all came over to Glyndŵr's cause. The Welsh were forbidden to inhabit such 'boroughs' or to carry arms within their boundaries (even today, there are laws remaining on the statute books of Chester, a border town, that proscribe the activities of the Welsh within the city walls). Abergafenni was attacked in 1404 and St. Mary's Priory burnt.

On 2 August, Richard Yonge, Bishop of Bangor from 1399/1400-1405 wrote to Henry IV, warning him that the Count of the Marche was preparing to invade Wales.

BATTLES OF CAMPSTONE HILL AND CRAIG-Y-DORTH 20 AUGUST 1404

In charge of the southern forces, Rhys Gethin swept through Glamorgan. Cardiff and Newport had already been taken. He sacked Caerleon and Usk, Tretower Castle was attacked and the Welsh were looting and burning Grosmont when the forces of Richard Beauchamp, Earl of Warwick caught up with them. The Welsh fell back to Campstone Hill (Mynydd Cwmdu, near Tretower Castle) and regrouped, but had little time. Ellis ap Richard ap Hywel ap Morgan Llwyd, their standard bearer, was killed, and Owain's standard was captured. It was said that Owain was nearly taken, but again this may have been his brother Tudur. The Welsh were said to have lost 1,000 on the hill but regrouped and moved down the Usk Valley and fought back. At Trelog Common between Tintern and Monmouth, the English baggage train was captured. There was a major skirmish at Craig-y-Dorth, between Trellech and Mitchell Troy in the Trothy Valley, where the large fields are still referred to as Upper and Lower Battlefield. The fighting was carried on up to the gates of Monmouth Castle.

The details of the engagement(s) are extremely sketchy. Other sources state that in the spring of 1404, Glyndŵr's army diverted around Abergavenny and attacked the English army's base at Grosmont. Because Owain did not have siege engines, he could not make a direct attack on Grosmont Castle. Thus Owain sent lightly armoured groups to attack and burn the town and draw Henry's army out of the castle. Meanwhile Owain's main army occupied a nearby Iron Age Hillfort, 'Campstone Hill' (Mynydd Cwmdu or Bryn Du), and had the advantage when his lightly armoured troops led Henry's army from the castle into the full force of Owain's army. Both times (1404 and 1405) Glyndŵr's tactic failed, because the slope up to the hill fort was not steep enough. However, would Glyndŵr use the same failed tactic twice?:

> 1404 Owain won the castles, namely Harlech and Aberystwyth. In the same year was the slaughter of the Welsh on Campstone Hill and another of the English at Craig y Dorth, between Penclawdd and Monmouth town. Here most of the English were slain and the remainder were chased up to the gate *(of Monmouth)*. (Peniarth MS 135)

August 1404 saw sixty French ships in the English Channel, unfortunately for the Welsh returning to France. Also in August, the people of Shropshire and around Welshpool signed a truce with Glyndŵr, paying protection money to prevent an attack. Glyndŵr moved down to Cardiff, in anticipation of the French fleet, which had returned to France. John Trefor, Bishop of St Asaf, had joined Glyndŵr, making nonsense of the later claim that the Welsh had ransacked St Asaf cathedral. Iolo Goch wrote a poem to celebrate Trefor's change of heart, as he had earlier supported Henry. Border counties were still paying protection to Glyndŵr's men at the end of 1404.

THE PARDON OF SIR JOHN KYNASTON 27 SEPTEMBER 1404

Among the small group of relatives and supporters which met in 1400 at Glyndŵr's manor at Glyndyfrdwy was John Kynaston of the Stocks (near Ellesmere), brother-in-law to Sir David Hanmer of Bettisfield. Hanmer's daughter Margaret had married Owain Glyndŵr in Hanmer Church. Kynaston was also the kinsman of Northumberland and Hotspur, as his son, Madoc had married Hotspur's sister and had been killed at Shrewsbury. When Glyndŵr's force first raided along the border from Chester, reaching Oswestry on 22 September 1400, he was joined by John Kynaston; 'arrayed in horse and armour for war', and a companion, William Hunte, also 'arrayed with a shield, sword, bow and arrows'.

The Welsh set fire to Oswestry, and the event is preserved in the name 'Pentre Poeth', the Burnt Hamlet. The estates of both Owain and the Hanmers of Bettisfield were quickly confiscated and given to the King's relatives. The whole community of Maelor Saesneg was reported to have become 'rebels before the feast of St. Peter' (1 August 1403). This detached portion of Flintshire included the seat of the Hanmers at Bettisfield and also Welshampton and Ellesmere, which were under the stewardship of John Kynaston of the Stocks. It was probably the last area to submit during the war.

Forty marks owed to John Kynaston, by one Henry Savage, were forfeited to the King on 28 January 1404, 'on account of his insurrection'. A few weeks later 'the lands of John Kynaston within the Hundred of Ellesmere and Hamptonswoode, worth twenty marks yearly, in the King's hands on account of the rebellion of the said John', were confiscated. They were granted to Richard Laken, 'because he was prepared to ride to resist the Welsh rebels without any reward and they in their last ride burned and destroyed forty marks of his rent and took beasts and goods to the value of £100'. Thus, sometime in the summer of 1404, John Kynaston decided to make his peace with the King. On 27 September 1404, Henry IV met with his Council at Tutbury Castle and considered the case of John Kynaston. Kynaston had been indicted in the Court of the King's Bench with aiding and abetting the rebellion of Owain Glyndŵr. He had been seen in 'war-like guise' at a number of places including Oswestry, which was at that time outside the jurisdiction of English law; Kynaston's plea to this effect was upheld. However, Kynaston had been imprisoned in Windsor Castle until a number of his supporters, including the Lord of the Manor, raised £100 bail.

The indictment against Kynaston was then changed to include Oteley, which was subject to English law. However, although Kynaston had met Glyndŵr there, this was not breaking the law. Kynaston's defence plea was again upheld. (A manuscript in the Shropshire Archive states that the boundary of Wales was at that time marked with a stone, on the Oswestry road 3 miles out of Ellesmere.) Thus, on 27 September, the King issued a pardon 'for all treasons, insurrections, felonies and misdeeds committed by him'. By 1408 Kynaston's land had been restored to him and he had resumed his earlier office as Steward of Maelor Saesneg and Ellesmere. The Kymastons were 'armigers', squires entitled to heraldic devices. The loss of men like Kynaston meant that Glyndŵr's power was waning.

THE WELSH TAKE ABERYSTWYTH AND BEAUMARIS CASTLES – THE NEW FLAG

The fall of Aberystwyth and Harlech castles, long under threat, into Welsh hands during 1404 (the castle of Aberystwyth was garrisoned by the English from March to November 1404) confirmed Glyndŵr's influence over western Wales, giving him two key coastal fortresses and a refuge after the destruction of Sycharth and Carrog. Aberystwyth now became his administrative centre. This was possibly the zenith of Glyndŵr's campaigning. Glyndŵr kept his personal banner of the golden dragon on a white background, but now not only adopted but adapted the flag of the House of Gwynedd as the new flag of Wales.

The quartered flag of four lions passant, alternately red on gold and gold on red, was altered. The lions passant became lions rampant, to symbolise that Wales was once again showing its strength after so much passivity. The huge Beaumaris Castle had finally fallen sometime after August 1404, before the winter of 1404-5.

FIFTH ROYAL EXPEDITION INTO WALES NOVEMBER 1404

By October Prince Henry was ready to fight again, and in November, accompanied by his brother Prince Thomas, rode to relieve Coity Castle. In the south-east, Newport had been subject to raids since 1403, Cardiff Castle and town had been burned in 1404 (one of whose residents, John Sperhauke, had earlier been executed for his support for Glyndŵr). Coety Castle was the only castle in the region left in English hands. Its lord, Sir Lawrence Berkerolles (d. 1411) had been besieged for months. The Princes arrived just in time to save Coity, and then reached Cardiff to find it burning and the Welsh forces gone, in December. Over 450 men had been urgently sent to Cardiff, with supplies from Bristol and Monmouth, but were too late. The royal force returned to Hereford, but arranged fresh supplies for the castles at Cydweli, Carmarthen and Llansteffan. The winter, as usual, was bitterly cold, and unusually, Glyndŵr stopped campaigning and returned to Harlech. He had a secure base at last, in his fifth year of campaigning.

CHAPTER 9

The Turning-Point 1405

January 1405 saw the formal ratification of the treaty with France, signed by Glyndŵr in Llanbadarn (Aberystwyth). It was sent to France with Morris Kerry and Hugh Eddouyer, where Charles VI also endorsed it.

THE PLOT TO RESCUE THE HEIRS TO THE CROWN

Over the winter a plan was hatched for Constance Despenser, Countess of Oxford, to bring the legitimate heirs to the crown into Wales. From Glamorgan, the young Mortimers could be taken to Glyndŵr and serve as a focal point for rebellion across England. The nation was sick of heavy taxation to pay for Henry IV's continual warring. Lady Despenser's husband, the Earl of Gloucester, had been beheaded by Bristol in 1400 after the Epiphany Rising, so although a kinswoman, she hated Henry IV. In February, Lady Despenser asked the court locksmith for a duplicate set of keys, and abducted the thirteen-year-old claimant to the throne, Edmund Mortimer, and his brother Roger, from Windsor Castle. They left at midnight, and at Abingdon the Countess sent her Welsh squire, Morgan, to tell the French King of the successful plot to restore the real King of England. However, she was arrested at Cheltenham near the Welsh border on 15 February, just a few miles from safety. The infant Mortimers were to be included in the negotiations held later that month by Glyndŵr, with the object of supporting their bid for the kingship.

Called before the Privy Council on 17 February, the Countess implicated her brother, the Duke of York (a cousin of Richard II), as the instigator of the plot. The Duke denied the charge, and Lady Despenser called for a champion to do battle in her name. Her squire volunteered to fight the Duke, and Lady Despenser said that she would burn in flames for treason if the Duke of York defeated him. Too fat to fight, the Duke was taken to the Tower of London and a few days later confessed that he knew of the plot but had helped foil it. His estates were temporarily confiscated, as were those of the Countess, but soon both were restored. The locksmith responsible for the doors to the brothers' quarters had his hands cut off before execution. Henry seemed grateful that he still held the Mortimers – it is difficult otherwise to understand his extreme leniency in the affair. Lady Despenser's son Richard, the last in the line of Despensers, was taken from her into royal wardship and then placed into the wardship of the Duke of York. Richard Despenser died suddenly (possibly murdered) in 1413, and the Duke illegally kept his immense property rights, but York died at Agincourt in 1415, falling off his horse and being suffocated in the crush.

THE TRIPARTITE INDENTURE 28 FEBRUARY 1405

Henry Percy, the Earl of Northumberland, had not been punished for the revolt of his son Henry (Hotspur), and his brother Thomas Percy, the Earl of Worcester, although he had raised an Anglo-Scottish force to try to join them at Shrewsbury. Henry had been lenient as he needed the Percies to safeguard the Scottish border, but Henry Percy wanted vengeance for the death of his son and brother. After discreet negotiations, probably led by the Welsh bishops Trefor and Byford, the Tripartite Indenture was signed in Bangor. It was said to have been signed in the house of David of Aberdaron, a Dean of Bangor, who had come over to Glyndŵr's cause. (In 1406 the Privy Council discovered his defection, and outlawed 'David Daron'.) The agreement was between Owain Glyndŵr, Henry Percy the Earl of Northumberland and Edmund Mortimer, who undertook to divide Britain into three parts. Glyndŵr would take Wales and the West of England as far as the rivers Severn and Mersey, including most of Cheshire, Herefordshire, and Shropshire. The Mortimers would take all of Southern and Western England. Thomas Percy, the Earl of Northumberland, would take the North of England and as far south as Leicester, Northampton, Warwick and Norfolk. Lord Thomas Bardolf, 5th Baron Bardolf, signed the document on behalf of Henry Percy. The young Earl of March, Edmund Mortimer, and his brother Roger, were still held by the King, and the signatories had no reason to believe that Henry would allow them to gain the throne. If the young Mortimers were killed by Henry, Edmund Mortimer, Glyndŵr's son-in-law and Henry Percy's kinsman, was the true heir to the throne. Another claimant would be the son of the dead Hotspur by his marriage to a Mortimer. Thus all the three parties had a share of a legitimate claim to the throne of England.

THE BATTLE OF GROSMONT CASTLE 11 MARCH 1405

Rhys Gethin was in charge of Glyndŵr's southern forces, and was responsible for the real first hammer-blow against Owain's cause. On 11 March 1405 Prince Henry wrote from Hereford that the rebels had burned Grosmont Castle in Monmouthshire, so he had sent Lord Talbot against them, who had defeated the Welsh with heavy loss, but he does not seem to have been present in person. Some accounts combine this with the battle at Campstone Hill, and others say that there were engagements at Campstone Hill in 1404 and 1405:

> On the 11th March 1405 an attack was made on Grosmont by 8000 of Owen Glyndŵr's men, who burnt part of the town. Assistance was sent for from Hereford, and Prince Henry (after Henry V), who was there with a small army, immediately sent Lord Talbot, and with him Sir William

Newport and Sir John Grendour, to the assistance of the garrison at Grosmont. The English were victorious, and slew 800 to 1000 of the Welsh, victory being, as Prince Henry said in a letter to his father reporting this event, 'not in a multitude of people, but in the power of God, and this was well proved here'.
(J.A. Bradney 'A History of Monmouthshire' 1907.)

Glyndŵr was in South Wales, and had sent Rhys Gethin, with the main army, towards Abergavenny, to harry Herefordshire again. In Grosmont Castle an unexpectedly strong English forces was waiting. After the battle, Prince Henry excitedly wrote to his father of this first major English victory in the war:

> On Wednesday, the 11th of the present month of March, your rebels of Overwent to the number of 8,000 burnt your town of Grosmont. Presently went out from the Castle my well-beloved cousin the Lord Talbot, and the small body of my household, and by the aid of the blessed Trinity vanquished all the said rebels, and slew of them some say 800, others 1,000. Of prisoners none were taken except one, a great chief among them, whom I would have sent to you, but he cannot yet ride at ease. Written at Hereford the said Wednesday at night.

Because the Prince and the Earl of Warwick and their retinues were present, the royal force must have been large, despite the Prince writing that he had 'but a small force'. Lord Talbot, Sir William Newport and Sir John Greyndour were also present with their men. Greyndour had been in charge of Radnor from 1402 to 1404, seeing constant action, before he was sent to try and halt the capture of Aberystwyth by Glyndŵr in 1404. Greyndour may himself have been captured and ransomed at this time. Prince Henry claimed that the Welsh were made up 'from the districts of Glamorgan, Morgannwg, Usk, lower and upper Gwent assembled to the number of 8000 men, by their own account.' However, it seems to have been a minor skirmish with a few hundred in a Welsh warband, who expected to find Grosmont not as heavily defended. Whatever happened here, there is no real record on either side, and it may have been propaganda to try and finally start a record of success in the record of English armies in Wales since 1400. Thus the Battle of Grosmont may have been confused with that of Campstone Hill, or there were two skirmishes around Grosmont in 1404 and 1405. It certainly does not seem to be a great battle, unlike the one which followed.

THE BATTLE OF PWLL MELYN, OR USK, 16 MARCH 1405
(12 March, 15 March and 5 May are also given as dates)

Grosmont had probably been the first serious defeat which Glyndŵr's forces had received, and sources state that it was followed within a week by another defeat at Usk, in which 1,500 Welshmen were killed or taken. We are still unsure of the date, but this was the key battle of the war, the defeat of the Welsh devastating and disheartening the men of Glamorgan and Gwent, who suffered the most casualties. 5 May is given in one source, but others say

12 March (which seems too soon after Grosmont) and others say five days after Grosmont and a week after Grosmont.

Following the defeat at Grosmont it seems that the Welsh wished to quickly obliterate the memory. At the time of battle, Prince Henry was probably still based in Hereford. The battle began with an assault by Welsh forces, led by Owain's eldest son, Gruffydd, against Usk Castle. The Welsh retreated pursued by unexpected numbers of garrison troops inside the castle. These forces were led by Sir John Oldcastle of Herefordshire, Sir John Greyndour, Dafydd Gam and Richard Grey, 1st Baron Grey of Codnor. It seems that Gruffydd had no idea of the strength of the forces he faced inside Usk castle – there were four major warriors and their forces, when he might have expected only 100 or so defenders. Only two years earlier in 1403, Glyndŵr had burnt the town of Usk, with loss of life and property, so local people may not have favoured his cause. John Leland wrote that the 'praty townlet upon Usk' was 'deflored by Glindore'.

The Welsh retreated across the fordable River Usk and into the forest of Monkswood towards 'Mynydd Pwll Melynthe' – 'Hill of the Yellow Pool'. Adam of Usk recounted 'they slew with fire and the edge of the sword many of them, and above all the Abbot of Llanthony (this should be Llantarnam), and they crushed them without ceasing, driving them through the monk's wood, where the said Griffin (Owain's son) was taken.' Hopcyn ap Tomos, one of Glyndŵr's greatest warriors, was killed. Checking the bodies of the slain and gathering weapons, there was great excitement as the English thought that Glyndŵr had been killed. However, it was his almost identical brother Tudur, who did not have Glyndŵr's wart above the eyebrow. Perhaps the traitor Dafydd Gam made the correct identification. According to the Scottish chronicler Walter Bower, Dafydd Gam of Brecon, who held land at Llantilio Crosenni in Monmouthshire, played a major part in the victory with his local knowledge and reputation. He possibly won over local Welshmen to fight against Glyndŵr, or may have gained warning of the attack in advance. According to Adam of Usk, Usk Castle 'had been put into some condition for defence' prior to the attack.

1405 Battle of Pwll Melyn. On the feast of Saint Gregory (March 12th), Griffith, eldest son of Owen, with a great following made assault, in an evil hour for himself, on the castle of Usk, which had been put into some condition for defence, and wherein at the that time were the lord Grey of Codnor, Sir John Greyndour, and many other soldiers of the king. For those same lords, sallying forth manfully, took him captive, and pursuing his men even to the hill-country of Higher Gwent, through the river Usk, there slew with fire and the edge of the sword many of them, and above all the abbot of Llanthony, and they crushed them without ceasing, driving them through the monk's wood (1.5 miles north-west of Usk), where the said Griffin was taken. And their captives, to the number of three hundred, they beheaded in front of the same castle near Ponfald; and certain prisoners of more noble birth they brought, along with the same Griffith, prisoners to the king. The which Griffith, being held in captivity for six years, at last in Tower of London was cut off by a pestilence *(Griffith died c.1411.)* And from that time forth in those parts the fortunes of Owen waned.

(Adam of Usk.)

The 300 prisoners beheaded in front of Usk Castle might have been the actual death toll – no mass graves are recorded in the area. Gruffydd ab Owain Glyndŵr was imprisoned in Nottingham Castle, to die later in the Tower of London, probably starved to death. Another major blow was the death of John ap Hywel, Abbot of the Cistercian Llantarnam Abbey north of Newport (not Llantony as Adam of Usk states). The abbot was killed during the battle, as he ministered to the dying and wounded of both sides. He may have been killed in a stand on the riverbank to cover the retreat of the main body of the Welsh, and was recorded as promising he would join them 'that very evening, to supper at Christ's table in your company, where the toast will be to you men.'

The Welsh Annals (Peniarth MS 135) state that:

1405 – A slaughter of the Welsh on Pwll Melyn Mountain, near Usk, where Gruffydd ab Owain was taken prisoner. It was now the tide began to turn against Owain and his men. At this time Glamorgan made its submission to the English, except a few who went to Gwynedd to their master.

It seems the battle saw more or less the end of the rebellion in south-east Wales. One historian says that the defeat 'suggest that the rashness of local initiatives was endangering the revolt as a whole,' as fixed battles like Grosmont and Pwll Melyn were not suited to the guerrilla way of fighting. Defeat in the battle and the loss of many men and commanders undermined the support offered by the French troops, which arrived later that year to support Glyndŵr. In March 1405, either at Grosmont or Usk, John Hanmer was captured, along with Glyndŵr's secretary Owain ap Gruffydd ap Rhisiart. They were imprisoned in the Tower of London, but Hanmer survived. (Another source claims Hanmer was captured 3 months later).

Of the English participants, Richard, Lord Grey of Codnor, was admiral of the King's fleet, and in 1403-1404 made justice of South Wales. Sir John Greyndour was Lord of Abenhall in the Forest of Dean, Sheriff of Gloucestershire 1405 and 1411, and was present at both Grosmont and Usk. Ponfald, where 300 men were beheaded, was probably a bridge over the Usk – were their bodies tipped into the river? Pont-ffald means the bridge of the enclosure, or sheepfold. The battles at last gave the English hope across Wales that Prince Henry's men could turn the tide. On 29 March, Greyndour was rewarded by being appointed Steward of Usk and 'Caerlleon' during the minority of the Earl of March.

THE THREAT OF ANOTHER INVASION

The King, in April, raised 3,500 men, and sent another 2,000 to reinforce the remaining garrisons across Wales and the borders. He wanted to finish off Glyndŵr's defeated forces. Henry IV had a personal retinue of 144 permanent men-at-arms and 720 archers, to which he indented an additional 400 lances and 120 archers from 26 April to 22 June, preparing for another Welsh invasion. He appointed the following lords to accompany him into Wales: the Duke of York, to head for Newport with 50 indentured lances and 260 archers; the Earl of Warwick (20 and 100); Mowbray, Earl Marshall (20 and 120); the Earl of Dunbar

(14 and 28) and Lord Lovell (30 and 60). Thus the King's personal army was to be 678 lances, 1,408 archers, and probably at least another 1500 armed men to support his lances, to make up an army of at least 3,500 men. Upon 27 April, his 3,500 men were reinforced by other royalist forces from along the borders, and moved to Usk, waiting to begin the 6th Royal Expedition from Hereford into South Wales. Brecon and Radnor (Lord Grey of Codnor) had garrisons of 40 lances and 200 archers, and 30 and 200 archers respectively. In Hay (the young Earl of Arundel) there were sixteen lances and eighty archers, and other garrison were Abergafenni (Lord Abergavenny) eighty and 400; and Aberystwyth (Prince Henry) forty and 200. Sir Thomas Beaufort commanded Carmarthen, Newcastle Emlyn and Cardigan, where the defenders were 120 and 600, 10 and 50 and 60 and 300 respectively. As well as these 2,376 men there would have been at least another 1,000 armed men supporting the lances (men-at-arms). These large garrisons could now be used as flying columns by Prince Henry rather than as purely defensively, as had been seen in the case of the attacks on Grosmont and Usk in March 1405.

On 13 April 1405, there was a skirmish in Flintshire, where Llywelyn's wife's uncle, Maredudd ap Llywelyn Ddu of Maelor Saesneg, was killed. In Chester, Prince Henry tried to stop the incessant smuggling between Wales and England. Markets and fairs were being held across Wales with English goods, horses and cattle being sold. Lawlessness was not confined to the Welsh along the March. Caus Castle in Shropshire guarded an important trading route to Shrewsbury, and was garrisoned for the King by its seneschal, Gruffydd ap Ieuan ap Madoc ap Gwenwys, during the Glyndŵr War. Following calls from students at Oxford, Gruffydd changed sides in 1404, and his lands and castle taken from him. In 1405, 100 men from Baschurch and surrounding districts raided the town around Caus Castle, killing Gruffydd ap Gruffydd (not Gruffydd Fychan) and Iorwerth ap Gwyn, and taking women and children as captives. The new Keeper of the castle, William Bromshall, wrote that 'they imprisoned them at ransom and wrongfully and violently chased out of the said lordship 100 other tenants.' Caus Castle is on one of the best defensive sites in the Marches, near Westbury in Shropshire, and guarded an important trade route between the English settlements around Shrewsbury and Mortgomery castles. The Medieval borough around the castle has vanished.

Caus Castle's keeping, and his full estates, were returned to Gruffydd ap Ieuan in 1419 after his sons Ieuan ap Gruffydd and Sir Gruffydd Fychan captured John Oldcastle for Lord Charleton. He and his sons deserted the Glyndŵr side in 1406 and served Edward Charleton for the remainder of the war. As an interesting aside on the nature of the Grey family, which triggered the Glyndŵr War, Sir Gruffydd Fychan probably fought at Agincourt in 1415, being traditionally credited with saving Henry IV's life, and fought valiantly at the Battle of Bauge in 1421. Lord John Grey fell next to him, and Gruffydd retrieved Grey's body and brought it back for burial. In 1443, Gruffydd Fychan pierced with a lance Sir Christopher Talbot at Caus Castle, possibly by accident in a joust. Talbot was the son of the Earl of Shrewsbury and the 'champion tilter' of England. Gruffydd's lands were confiscated and he was outlawed with a massive reward for his capture of 500 marks (worth c. £79,000 according to the Retail Price Index and £780,000 using Average Earnings). In 1447 Henry Grey, Lord Powys, summoned Sir Gruffydd to Powys Castle, but Gruffydd Fychan was suspicious, until Grey issued a safe conduct for him. On 9 July, upon entering the courtyard, he was taken and 'beheaded on the spot without judge or jury', in the presence of Lord Grey, whose father's body Gruffydd had brought back from France. The Greys had not changed in their treachery over a period of 50 years.

THE SCROPE REBELLION & THE 'BATTLE' OF SKIPTON MOOR 29 MAY 1405

Upon 14 May 1405, Henry IV arrived to join his forces at Hereford for yet another invasion, hoping to build on the battle at Usk and finally subdue Wales. However, he had to abandon his plans on 28 May, and headed north as the Scrope Rebellion broke out in the North of England. It seems that Archbishop Scrope of York had thought that Glyndŵr would invade England at the same time as his rising, or that he wanted to rebel when Henry was invading Wales. Lewis Byford, Bishop Trefor and Dean David of Aberdaron had wanted immediate action, however. Scrope promised in pamphlets that the Welsh would stop warring with the English, as the Welsh bishops wished it to be so. He promised peace at last for England. The Welsh bishops possibly knew of the recent defeats of the Welsh and wished to stave off Henry marching through Wales, as the battles of Grosmont and Pwll Melyn had demoralised the previously victorious Welsh army. Scrope's service to Richard II had been rewarded with the Archbishopric of York in 1398. The Earl of Northumberland was bitter about the loss of his son and brother at Shrewsbury, and persuaded Archbishop Scrope to join him in rebellion. In the spring of 1405 Scrope composed a manifesto indicting the King on several charges of willful misrule. Having raised three knights and an armed mob of 8,000 men, Scrope set out with Earl Mowbray to join forces with Henry Percy and Lord Bardolf. Before they could meet, however, Percy found himself hopelessly outmaneuvered and delayed. As a result, Percy decided to abandon the expedition led by Scrope and Mowbray, leaving his inexperienced allies to face a large royalist army led by Westmoreland and Lancaster. After a three-day stalemate on Shipton Moor, Scrope agreed to parley with Westmorland, but as soon as the Archbishop disbanded his followers in accordance with the terms of the truce, he was arrested and imprisoned at Pontefract. (It is no wonder that Glyndŵr showed no trust for the King's forces in his long war.) The King travelled to the Archbishop's Palace near York for the treason trial. English histories record the betrayal as a 'battle' won by Henry IV – he was not present and there was no battle.

The Earl Marshall (Thomas Mowbray), then Sir William Plumpton and then Scrope were executed by beheading in a nearby field. It took five blows of the axe to take off the Archbishop's head. Sir John Griffiths, a Welsh knight, was also executed. Archbishop Scrope's tomb in York Minster became a shrine, and some medieval writers saw Henry's poor health as punishment for killing an Archbishop. Henry would have probably been excommunicated, but for the Roman Pope's fear of his switching his allegiance to the Pope at Avignon, as Glyndŵr had done. The rebellion had orchestrated by the Henry Percy, Earl of Northumberland and Lord Bardolf, but they escaped to Scotland in June, along with Glyndŵr's bishops, Byford of Bangor and Trefor of St Asaf.

BEAUMARIS CASTLE FALLS JUNE 1405

There were mixed fortunes for Owain in June 1405. English ships sailed from Dublin and attacked Anglesey. There was some kind of battle at Rhos-y-Meirch. Stephen Scrope, Deputy-Lieutenant of Ireland, had landed and Beaumaris Castle fell back into English hands. It had fallen to the Welsh some time after August 1404, and the Anglesey landowner Gwilym ap Gruffudd ap Tudur Llwyd, 'The Green Squire', was killed defending the castle. Welsh church relics were looted and taken to Ireland. The Welsh abandoned Anglesey and fled to Snowdonia. Also in this month, John Hanmer was captured, a grave blow to Glyndŵr. (He may have been captured at Usk in March, however). His brother-in-law was one of his closest advisors, and such was his importance that his captor was rewarded with 40 marks, over £26, worth over £130,000 today on the average earning index. John Hanmer eventually ransomed himself and survived the war. However, Radnor Castle was surrendered by Sir John Greyndour – it had only nine men-at-arms and twenty-two archers left defending it – Cefnllys Castle on the Ithon was taken and burned, and the areas of Cnwclas and Knighton and Ogmore laid waste.

As Edmund Mortimer was a minor, the Crown assumed control of his territories. On 24 November 1401 Hugh Burnell was appointed keeper of the Mortimer-owned Cefnllys Castle near Llandrindod Wells. Burnell was empowered to accept the unconditional surrender of rebels, but not to issue pardons without the King's permission. The garrison at Cefnllys under Sir William Heron, Lord Say, about 1402-3, was stated to be twelve spearmen and thirty archers. On 12 September 1403, the Bishop and Sheriff of Worcester and John Ryall were given a commission to supply Cefnllys with eight quarters of wheat, one tun of wine, three tuns of ale, 200 fish and sixty quarters of oats. There is a record of 27 January 1406 of the grant of the castle to Richard, Lord Grey, which says it was 'burned and wasted by the Welsh rebels' (along with the lordships of Knighton and Knucklas), probably in June 1405.

GLYNDŴR'S SECOND PARLIAMENT, HARLECH JULY 1405

The Parliament at Harlech had ambassadors from France, Castile, Brittany and Scotland, and a tourney for entertainment. A possible truce with England was discussed, on the lines of the Treaty of Shrewsbury in 1267, whereby Llywelyn ap Gruffydd was recognized as Prince of Wales. By the treaty, Llywelyn's gains of former Welsh estates off Marcher Lords were accepted, and the status quo had been restored. An agreement was made to hire 2,000 men from France, who soon came to support the Welsh war effort. Another agreement was made to hire 10,000 troops from Scotland or the North of England, which was to be effected at a later date. Perhaps Henry IV might have accommodated a peace, but he was suffering from a skin illness and increasingly his affairs were passing to his dynamic son, Prince Hal of Monmouth. Prince Henry had been brought up a warrior, and saw glory in finally defeating Wales. After his men's victories at Grosmont and Pwll Melyn, he was now feeling confident of overall victory. There is a story that two men of Flint infiltrated the Harlech Parliament, and reported to Sir John Stanley in Cheshire. If Prince Henry knew of the deal to hire Scottish and French troops, it would have further strengthened his resolve to fight Glyndŵr rather than parley. However, Stanley was told by these agents, David Whitmore and Ieuan or Jevan ap Maredudd (Meredith) that Glyndŵr had called the most important men from every commote in Wales, and that his purpose was to seek a treaty with Henry IV. (There was probably another Parliament in Harlech in August 1406.)

THE FRENCH ARRIVE AUGUST 1405

Glyndŵr made a treaty with France in 1404 and an expedition under the Comte de Marche was planned for that year but came to nothing except for a raid on Falmouth. A stronger expeditionary force landed in August 1405 with 140 ships but had lost almost all their horses through lack of fresh water. Lord Berkeley and Henry Pay burnt 15 of their ships in the same harbour. The French took Carmarthen, allowing defenders to leave with their goods and chattels. At the same time 15 ships were captured by Lord Berkeley, Henry Pay and Sir Thomas Swinburne when they were sailing from France to help Owain. With these ships the seneschal of France and 8 other captains were taken. (Walsingham's Historia Anglicana.)

On the continent, the French army invaded English Aquitaine. Simultaneously, a French fleet assembled in Brest and landed in force at Milford Haven. The Duc d'Orleans wanted to abide by the 1404 treaty with Owain after the ignoble behaviour of de Bourbon. He wanted the English fighting on another front. Part of the funds for the expedition had been raised by the Harlech Parliament, and it left Brest in July with 800 men-at-arms (each with a squire, a page and three archers), 600 crossbowmen and 1,200 light infantry, led by Jean de Rieux, the Marshall of France. Jean of Hengest led the 600 crossbowmen. The army commander was Robert 'One-Eye' of La Heuze. The admiral of the fleet was Renaud de Trie, Lord of Fontenay.

Unfortunately, the fleet was becalmed and the fleet had not been provided with sufficient fresh water. All of the heavy cavalry horses died of thirst. Instead of turning back and re-supplying, the fleet landed in the 'Englishry' of Pembroke, at Angle Bay near Milford Haven. They also brought modern siege equipment. However their knights had no 'great horses', destriers, and the smaller Welsh horses used by Glyndŵr's warbands were not strong enough to take them in full armour. Also, their crossbows were of little use compared to the rapid-firing longbow favoured by the Welsh. It may be that the tower house at Angle was taken. Tower houses are rare across Wales, but in Pembrokeshire there are examples at Carswell, Eastington, Haroldston, Lydstep, West Tarr, Carew and Caldey Island, built probably because of coastal raids by the Welsh on the Flemish and English settlers. Joined by some of Owain's forces, the French force slowly marched inland and burned the town of Haverfordwest on 10 August, but failed to take the castle. The French admiral's brother, Patrouillard de Treyes, was said to have died at Haverfordwest. A French contingent also took the small Picton Castle.

The army then moved and laid siege to Tenby, where the Welsh main army was waiting. French siege engines were set up, but the French appear to have fled, fearing an English fleet was about to attack. It appears that Lord Berkeley and Henry Pay, Warden of the Cinque Ports, with a fleet of thirty warships destroyed a convoy of fourteen French munitions ships, either lying at anchor or making for the Welsh coast. It then destroyed fifteen of the French transport ships lying in the Haven at Milford. French historians seem to believe that the sinking of these ships helped Glyndŵr by keeping the French in Wales. They had intended to return to France quickly after a token effort of solidarity. Tenby was not taken, but a French force negotiated with the garrison at St Clears Castle to take it, and it was agreed that St Clears would surrender if Carmarthen did so first.

Carmarthen Castle had been refortified and regarrisoned, but the French siege engines were useful at last. The walls were undermined and breached, and the defenders surrendered to the French rather than to Glyndŵr. Glyndŵr agreed and allowed the defenders to return freely to any English-held towns, on condition they left behind their arms and goods. The town was then sacked. Cardigan Castle was taken around this time, whether by Glyndŵr or a local warband is unsure. The taking of Cardigan (Aberteifi) ensured that Glyndŵr had an exit route up the western coastline, if the English came down the Tywi Valley or through South Wales to face him.

Henry IV had ordered the strengthening of castles at Llawhaden, Laugharne, Manorbier and possibly Newport (in Pembroke), and stronger garrisons at Haverfordwest, Pembroke, Narberth, Cilgerran and Tenby, to try and hold Pembroke for England. He had also given additional lands and St Clears Castle to Carew, and made Francis de Court Lord of Pembroke. Some time in 1405 the constable of Pembroke Castle, Thomas Roche, was captured. The King had given the lordship of Haverfordwest to Prince Henry, as Thomas Percy had been killed at Shrewsbury. However, now with control of Cardigan Castle and Ceredigion, and the valleys of the Teifi and Tywi, Glyndŵr felt secure enough to march east. The expedition lumbered into Glamorgan and Gwent. There could have been sacking of Glamorgan and Monmouth castles at this time – it is difficult to assess whether they had been regarrisoned.

In August John Oke accused John Scudamore of having been a secret supporter of Glyndŵr as early as 1400 and having received £6,870 in gold and silver from twenty-seven disaffected persons for the support of the Welsh uprising. He said that support was strong, especially in East Anglia, and stated that high-ranking clergymen were also involved. Oke said he had been an agent of Glyndŵr, collecting funds from English religious houses for the war. Another prisoner, John Veyse, supported the claims. The criminals turned informer to escape the death penalty, but named abbots and priors across the country. Oke and Voysey were hung, but the King ordered six separate inquiries into their testimonies. They implicated Sir John Scudamore, who had been captured by Glyndŵr when Carreg Cennen fell in 1403, and had illegally married Alys ferch Owain Glyndŵr after his wife died in the siege. Clerics were arrested and released, and Scudamore escaped punishment but fell from royal favour. However, his lands were not forfeited.

There were problems for Glyndŵr in his north-east homelands however. In August 1405, the most powerful man in Flintshire, Gwilym ap Gruffydd ap Gwilym, with his brothers Robin and Rhys, and four other Flintshire gentry, surrendered, going to Chester prison. They had joined him in 1403.

THE FRANCO-WELSH INVASION OF ENGLAND

The Franco-Welsh army marched through Herefordshire and into the Midlands of England. Henry had heard of the invasion when in Pontefract on 7 August. Two English spies in the Welsh camp, who had also been at the Harlech Parliament, Ieuan ap Maredudd (the Steward of Hope) and his neighbour David Whitmore of Whitmore Llan, had ridden to Chester. There they passed the news of the French invasion to Sir John Stanley. When the news reached the King at Pontefract, he sent out for musters from eighteen counties to meet at Hereford. The King, although ill, headed south for Leicester from Pontefract to begin to organize the nation's defences.

Worcester was possibly sacked by the French and Welsh, and baggage carts filled with loot. Hearing of the approach of the English, the army moved to the old Iron Age camp on Woodbury Hill, a few miles north of Worcester, waiting for Henry. According to Camden, in the seventeenth century Woodbury Hill was known as Owain Glyndŵr's Camp. Henry arrived at Worcester upon 19 August with his army, with more contingents of seasoned, well-paid veterans arriving until 22 August. The royalist army took a position on Abberley Hill on 22 August, facing Owain across a mile-wide valley. Why Glyndŵr encamped there is unknown – perhaps the French wished for a pitched battle in the valley between the armies. It was strongly defensible, but had no water supply, and a huge army would need feeding. Had Glyndŵr stopped there as a symbolic gesture that it would represent the old Welsh border? He possibly did not continue his advance for fear of a surprise attack on a slow-moving army, much as he had attacked the last five royal expeditions into Wales. Glyndŵr possibly feared that he had overextended his army logistically. Again, if he had a Welsh army instead of a combined army, he might have headed for London, hoping for support along the way. He must have known that there was no chance that the English would come to the support of a French army.

There were a few skirmishes between raiding parties, but an impasse between the two main armies – both had strong, defensive positions and neither would want to attack uphill. Equally, a battle in the valley would not assure victory because both armies were relatively well-matched, both being between 5,000 and 8,000 strong. Eight days of 'chivalric combat' were fought, with around 400 men killed, including the French knights Sieur de la Valle and Sieur de Martelonnes, the Bastard of Bourbon, and possibly Patrouillard de Tries, the brother of the French admiral. (He was also supposed to have died in Pembroke.)

After these eight days of combat, however, overnight Henry secretly retreated back into the stronghold of Worcester. The Welsh were too late to do anything but attack his rearguard, and eighteen carts were taken from Henry's baggage-train, but Owain dared not attack Worcester. There was little point in dispersing and sacking the countryside, as a sortie from Worcester could severely damage Owain's divided forces. Equally, to lay siege could mean that greater English forces could arrive and trap Glyndŵr. An attack on the heavily defended Worcester, against a strong army, would be madness.

Thus the Welsh and French withdrew back through Wales towards Cardigan. More French were to arrive as the year went on but the high point of French involvement had passed. Money was taken from Pembroke in exchange for not attacking it, and on

1 November, nearly all the French knights left Wales, leaving most of their troops in Wales. The only minor noble to remain over the winter was Le Borgue de Bellay. It may be that the French invasion was to 'test the waters' for a full-scale invasion of England. Charles VI's advisors were possibly hoping for a spontaneous rising against Henry IV in England.

> In July a French force of some five thousand men landed at Tenby, and they were joined by Owen with ten thousand Welsh. It is almost wearisome to tell the tale of their march through Herefordshire, burning and destroying what little was left unburnt and undestroyed in the unhappy county. The King, hastening back from the North, met the combined force at Woodbury Hill, but did not dare to venture a battle. Glyndŵr and his allies, with an immense amount of booty, retired across the border, and Henry came once more to Hereford to prepare for his fifth invasion *(this should be sixth)* of Wales. This, however, proved little more than an idle promenade, through a country by this time practically a desert, to Glamorgan and back. In this year the Court of Exchequer *(Trinity Term, 6 Henry II.)* called upon William Beauchamp to prove how many Knights fees he owed to the King for the castle and manor of Ewias Harold, and to offer the King 'rational aid' for the same *(ad respondendum regi de rationali auxilio pro eisdem Feodis)*. Does this mean, perhaps, that William Beauchamp had grown tired of his long and all but hopeless fight, and had made some sort of terms with Owen? (Bannister, 1902.)

SIXTH ROYAL EXPEDITION INTO WALES SEPTEMBER 1405

This intended invasion had been delayed because of Scrope's conspiracy. Caernarfon Castle was still in real danger of falling, but Beaumaris had been recaptured and the King was confident of defeating Glyndŵr, persuading Parliament to grant him more funding. He left Hereford with around 40,000 men and heavy artillery. Glyndŵr refused to give fixed battle against overwhelming odds, and concentrated on hit and run tactics with his lightly armed horsemen and archers. Coity was relieved once again, but instead of heading west and relieving other besieged castles, Henry IV headed almost immediately back to England. There were constant guerrilla attacks with English losses, and extremely bad weather made the retreat to Hereford miserable. The King's baggage train was lost in flash floods and forty valuable wagons laden with jewellery, arms and supplies fell into Welsh hands. This is the time of 'Cadwgan of the Axe', from near Treorchy, who led a warband from the Rhondda to harass the English.

French troops began to return to France in November, and there is evidence that the revolt began to subside in Glamorgan, with submissions being made. Perhaps having seen Glyndŵr and the French pass through and achieve nothing except yet another invasion by the English, the county was war-weary after five years of sporadic warfare. In November, Parliament complained of taxes for the never-ending war in Wales, not realising that Welsh resistance was waning in the south, and also accused the King of not doing enough to end it. His loyal subjects were struggling to prosecute the war. New Radnor Castle was a crucial element of the border defences, as Sir John Greyndour had informed a royal commission in September 1402. In 1405 he complained that he had received £462 in revenues from the lordship since 1402, and spent £877 on the garrison alone. The £415 difference would today represent £2,200,000 using the Average Earnings Index. By 1405 the great lordships of Abergafenni and Newport in Gwent were producing no revenues whatsoever for their Marcher Lords.

Stephen Perrot of Eastington and John Castlemartin are named in Sir Francis de Court's commission in 1403 to be receivers of money raised for Glyndŵr's 'benefit'. Also known as Francis a'Court, he had been appointed Governor of Pembroke as long ago as 1391, and a commission granted to him as 'Dominus de Pembroke', allowing him to treat with Glyndŵr, is still extant. De Court was later at the fall of Aberystwyth Castle, and had received monies from the estates of the dead Thomas Percy. He was a Lombard Knight, not granted 'denization' (English citizenship) until 1406. In November 1405 Sir Francis de Court offered Glyndŵr £2000 for a year's truce with Pembroke, at this time against the King's specific orders. Stephen Perrot remained loyal to the Crown during the war, and negotiated a truce on behalf of the people of Pembrokeshire in 1405, whereby de Court gave Owain money. Along with the proceeds of the King's baggage train, this money from de Court brought welcome financial help to Glyndŵr. However, Owain was receiving little support from France or Scotland, and the Percies had been defeated forever. Ireland was quiet. Glyndŵr's hopes of any peaceful ending to the war were disappearing, and the chances of a military victory were also receding. His people were tired and war-weary after six years of constant fighting all over the small country of Wales, and six royal invasions raping, murdering and looting their way across the land.

The country had been stripped bare. No landlords, Welsh or English, could collect taxes. People were starving as crops were despoiled and farm animals slaughtered. Six royal chevauchées had desolated Wales and it's people were starving. The hope of independence was dying. In a small population, everyone knew people who had been imprisoned, raped, killed, maimed or starved to death.

CHAPTER 10

The Beginning of the
End 1406-1407

RETREAT FROM ANGLESEY

Henry was having problems throughout 1406 and 1407 sourcing taxes for his constant campaigning in Wales. The Commons formally demanded the public audit of Government accounts for the first time, and the principle that Parliament was to be the source of all money grants was legally established. Parliament did not understand at this time how weak Glyndŵr's power was. Throughout 1405 to 1407, Glyndŵr had been withdrawing men from Anglesey, along with cattle and grain stores. The English were attacking with ships from Chester, and he did not want his men cut off on an island, which would be difficult to retake. The flatter terrain of Anglesey was not suited to the guerrilla attacks that gave Glyndŵr a military edge. Possibly Glyndŵr had knowledge, from agents in the English forces, of Henry's intention to take Anglesey. As the traditional 'bread-basket' of North Wales, Henry knew that Glyndŵr could not support large numbers of followers with few food supplies. Throughout 1405 the English had attacked the dwindling number of Glyndŵr's men in Anglesey.

In February there was more fighting in Anglesey and Caernarfon, and naval warfare on the Menai Straits. English reinforcements were sent to Caernarfon to back up the campaigning on Anglesey. That month, the Commons granted Prince Henry another 5,000 troops, as it was summoned to deal with the Welsh problem.

On 6 March, Hywel Gwynedd of Llys Edwin was killed in a night attack on his stockade on Halkyn Mountain near Flint. Many died on both sides. He was the focus for many attacks over the English border, so had been specifically targeted to the raid:

This valiant gentleman, who had sided with Prince Owain Glyndyfrdwy against Henry IV, was surprised by his enemies from the town of Flint, about the year 1410, and beheaded in the enclosure of the Camp of Caer Alhwch, on the summit of Moel y Gaer, in Llaneurgain, and his lands were forfeited and given to Bryan Saxton.

(This is the version of J.Y.W. Lloyd, in his History of Powys Fadog, but it is thought that 1406 is the proper date of death.) Upon 8 March, Glyndŵr's ambassadors arrived back with a message from Charles VI. He promised more military support if Glyndŵr supported the French Pope in Avignon, in preference to the Pope in Rome. The French nobles had already returned home, and in March the French had withdrew their remaining forces in 28 troopships.

The French and the Welsh had different priorities. The Welsh wanted to secure an independent Wales, but the French were more interested in invading England. The Welsh were involved in guerrilla warfare between castles in Wales. The French wanted a full-scale invasion of England, but it was not Glyndŵr's priority to take the crown of England. Besides, the French were still fighting the English in Picardy and Gascony, but by the autumn had retreated on both fronts. There was little help to be hoped for from France, but Glyndŵr now had unexpected guests.

NORTHUMBERLAND & BARDOLF ARRIVE

In March, the Earl of Northumberland and Lord Bardolf with some supporters landed in Wales, having left their Scottish refuge to join Glyndŵr. They were no longer safe in Scotland, because events there happened that hurt Glyndŵr's cause:

A.D. 1406 The earl of Northumberland and the lord of Bardolf, after many misfortunes, first fleeing from before the face of king Henry into Scotland, (the son of the lord Henry Percy, and grandson and heir of the same earl, having been surrendered as hostage,) thence passed under a safe-conduct into Wales to Owen, seeking aid, and there they tarried for a season; and at length they were overthrown in stricken field by the English under my lord of Fowls. Then they came into France also, under safe-conduct, seeking aid against the same king, but labouring in vain, for that the duke of Orleans withstood them. And, because I too often held converse with them, I thereby drew down on me the greater wrath of king Henry, when he knew thereof. At last the earl was traitorously enticed again into Scotland and thence into England by certain who promised under false seals that he should have the kingdom. And he held out to me great advancement, if I should pass over along with him; but God visited mine heart, and I bethought me: 'Adam, thus beset in a maze, place thyself in the hand of the Lord!' And God sent an evil spirit, and according to their deserts, between the king and the same earl, after the way of Abimelech, as it is read in the book of Judges. And therefore I turned my cloak, and I inclined my footsteps to my lord of Powis, abiding the favour of the king and his kingdom, if God should grant it; and so it came to pass.
(Adam of Usk.)

THE PENNAL LETTER 31 MARCH 1406

Leaving the safety of Harlech Castle, Glyndŵr called the nobles and princes to Pennal near Machynlleth, to hold a 'House of Lords' or *Senedd*. This assembly was also a synod of the

Welsh church, because the leading churchmen of the day had to decide to change their religious allegiance from the Pope in Rome, to the French Pope Benedict XIII in Avignon. The Pennal Policy was written in Latin and on goatskin parchment, and is still housed in the Archives Nationales in Paris. It was almost definitely drafted at Cefn Caer, the Medieval hall-house in Pennal that still stands today, and prayers offered in the church of St Peter ad Vincula. Cefn Caer is on the site of a Roman fort, overlooking a Roman road, and most of the materials used in the fort were taken to rebuild the church. At Cefn Caer is 'Coron Glyndŵr', a full-size gold-plated silver crown, similar to that made for the Coronation of Prince Owain IV on 21 June 1404. Replica bolts encircle the crown, to indicate the fact that medieval crowns were bolted to helmets in time of war. The crown was created by the late master silversmith and jeweller Tony Lewis, known for the making of over thirty Eisteddfod Crowns, two of those being for the National Eisteddfod. At Cefn Caer is also a replica of the sword given to Owain by Charles VI of France. Nearby is the small motte known as Domen Las, which also has associations with Owain.

> One would have liked to associate Dolgelley with the famous outline of policy which Glyndŵr drafted in 1406, and sent to the King of France; but the evidence is overwhelming that Pennal, on the other side of Cader, can claim that honour. Nevertheless, we are probably right in assuming that the cardinal points of it had been cogitated upon in Dolgelley itself, and that it was there that Glyndŵr determined on an alliance with Charles of France, adhesion to the cause of the French-supported Avignon Pope, a severance of the Welsh Church from Canterbury, the creation of an archbishopric at St. David's, and the foundation of two universities in Wales, one for the North, and one for the South, so that Wales might be spiritually and intellectually empowered to work out her own salvation. From his love towards Dolgelley, it is quite possible that the great Welsh hero contemplated that the northern University should be located here, and that he hoped to see arising, at the foot of Cader, 3 spires and pinnacles like those which grace his own beloved University of Oxford. What a charming setting it would have been to realise the dream in; and had just this one part of his objects alone been brought to fruition, what a change there might have been in the future of the land he loved.
> (T.P. Ellis)

The Pennal Policy, outlined in the letter, was dated 'in the sixth year of our rule', and tells of an assembly that included the 'proctors of the nobles and prelates of our principality and others'. Proposals included the restoration of St David's church to its original position as a metropolitan church, and the institution not only of the Welsh dioceses, but also those of Exeter, Bath, Hereford, Worcester, and Lichfield as its suffragans. Only clergy who knew the Welsh language would be given ecclesiastical offices in Wales. An agreement was reached that all Welsh monetary grants to English monasteries and colleges would end. Two universities, one in North Wales and the other in South Wales, were to be instituted in places to be determined by Owain's ambassadors. In it we see references to letters patent, a council, chancellor, secretary, notaries, and proctors, as well as to the Prince's privy seal (a quartered shield charged with the four lions rampant of the Princes of Gwynedd). Along with Owain's Great Seal, previously mentioned, we can see all the devices of a trained and experienced administration of state.

The 'Pennal Letter' is in two parts. A brief letter declares the Welsh intention to give allegiance to the Charles VI's Pope Benedict XIII at Avignon, and accompanies a formal document sealed with the Great Seal. In March 1406, Glyndŵr appealed to the French King for additional forces against the 'barbarous Saxons', who were trying to take over Wales. His request, known as the Pennal Letter (after the village of Pennal in Meirionnydd), set out in Latin his plan for Welsh greatness. The brief letter reads:

To the most serene and most illustrious prince, lord Charles, by the grace of God, King of France. Most serene prince, you have deemed it worthy on the humble recommendation sent, to learn how my nation, for many years now elapsed, has been oppressed by the fury of the barbarous Saxons; whence because they had the government over us, and indeed, on account of the fact itself, it seemed reasonable with them to trample upon us. But now, most serene prince, you have in many ways, from your innate goodness, informed me and my subjects very clearly and graciously concerning the recognition of the true Vicar of Christ. I, in truth, rejoice with a full heart on account of that information of your excellency, and because, inasmuch from this information, I understood that the Lord Benedict, the supreme pontifex intends to work for the promotion of an union in the Church of God with all his possible strength.

Confident indeed in his right, and intending to agree with you as indeed as far as it is possible for me, I recognize him as the true Vicar of Christ, on my own behalf, and on behalf of my subjects by these letters patent, foreseeing them by the bearer of their communications in your majesty's presence. And because, most excellent prince, the metropolitan church of St. David was, as it appears, violently compelled by the barbarous fury of those reigning in this country, to obey the church of Canterbury, ad de facto still remains in the subject of this subjection.

Many other disabilities are known to have been suffered by the Church of Wales through these barbarians, which for the greater part are set forth full in the letter patent accompanying. I pray and sincerely beseech your majesty to have these letters sent to my lord, the supreme pontifex, that as you deemed worthy to raise us out of darkness into light, similarly you will wish to extirpate and remove violence and oppression from the church and from my subjects, as you are well able to. And may the Son of the Glorious Virgin long preserve your majesty in the promised prosperity.

Dated at Pennal the last day of March (1406), Yours avowedly, Owain, Prince of Wales.

This 'letter patent' was carried and presented by Dr Gruffydd Yonge, Morris Kerry and the Dominican priest Hugh Eddouyer, decrying 'the usurper, Henry of Lancaster' and 'the madness of the Saxon barbarian'. It committed the Welsh, a nation 'oppressed by the fury of the barbarous Saxons' to the Avignon Pope and asked him to brand Henry IV and his adherents as heretics, and to give full remissions for sins for whoever fought the English. ('The Great Schism' lasted from 1378 to 1417 across Europe, with the French and Rome having separate Popes – it was basically a battle for finances and power rather than any religious debate.) In 1397, Glyndŵr had asked the Roman Pope Boniface IX for plenary remission in the hour of his death. In 1403, he wrote again to Boniface to alter the terms of his heavenly remission to happen 'at any time', which the Pope signed. Obviously Glyndŵr thought he would no longer have time to prepare for death and summon a priest to pardon him – he could die at an instant by a spear, sword, arrow or cannon ball. Boniface died in

1404, succeeded by Innocent VII. In 1406, at the time of the Pennal Letter changing Welsh papal allegiance, the Italian Pope was Gregory XII. With the Pennal Letter, Wales altered its allegiance to the French Pope at Avignon, Benedict XIII.

In his letter to Charles VI, Owain reminded him that Wales was France's oldest ally, when in 1212 Llywelyn the Great and Philip VII agreed their common enemy was England. He also spoke of Yvain de Galles, Owain Lawgoch, who led Welsh companies across Europe in the service of the French crown, dying in their service against England in 1378, just 28 years earlier. The French King wished to ally with the Scots and Welsh against England, and sent the famous Welsh crusader Dafydd ab Ieuan Goch to discuss the alliance. Adam of Usk recorded:

> ... a certain knight, called Sir David ap Jevan Goz, of the county of Cardigan, who for full twenty years had fought against the Saracens with the King of Cyprus and other Christians, being sent by the King of France to the King of Scotland on Owen's behalf, was taken captive by English sailors and imprisoned in the Tower of London.

Unfortunately Dafydd's ship was captured, and this 'killer of Saracens' vanished from history. (Dafydd ap Ieuan Goch ap Dafydd Goch ap Trahaearn was born about 1344 Penllech, Cymydmaen near Pwllheli in Caernarfonshire, and it seems that red hair ran in the family. Dafydd's brother Madog was known as Madog Goch.) Apart from the failed mission of Dafydd, Glyndŵr's request for aid to France went unanswered. With dwindling support and with Henry IV regaining territory, Owain's hopes began to fall.

On 3 April, the Commons prayed the King to thank Prince Henry for his services in 'chastening' the Welsh rebels, and begged that the command on the Welsh Marches should be entrusted to him. The King was severely suffering from a painful and disfiguring skin condition, and may have had scrofula (tuberculosis affecting the skin of the neck), leprosy, venereal disease or any combination of these and other ailments. Many said it was vengeance for executing the Archbishop of York, Richard Scrope. Prince Henry's appointment as Lieutenant in Wales was renewed two days later.

THE LOSS OF SCOTTISH SUPPORT 4 APRIL 1406

In Scotland, after the Battle of Homildon Hill, Robert III's brother Robert of Fife had captured and starved the heir to the throne, David, to death in 1402. (Confusingly, Robert III was born John, but altered his name to that of his brother Robert, as John was considered an unlucky name). King Robert now feared for the life of his other son James, and sent his eleven-year-old heir to France. Prince James of Scotland was marooned on Bass Rock in the Firth of Forth for a month, before a ship arrived trying to take him off to France. (Accompanying the prince was a Welsh bishop.) His uncle Robert of Fife informed Henry IV, who arranged for the ship's interception off Flamborough Head in March. Thus Prince James became a prisoner in England for eighteen years. When Robert III heard of his son's capture, he became depressed and supposedly died from grief on 4 April 1406 over the capture of James.

King Robert asked to be buried under a dunghill with the epitaph: 'Here lies the worst of Kings and the most miserable of men'. Robert of Fife, Duke of Albany, was now in control of Scotland, and would not ransom the new King, James I of Scotland. As a result, the Scots were no longer in a position to ally with Glyndŵr, or to attack England and draw off Henry's forces. Henry and his son could now concentrate all their resources upon extinguishing the war with Wales. Robert Stewart, Robert of Fife, was installed as the 'client-ruler' of Scotland, ensuring no interference in the plans for the conquest of Wales. Early in 1406, negotiations were opened without result for a marriage between Prince Henry and one of the French King's daughters, to try and also stop hostilities with France. From henceforth, Glyndŵr's alliance with Scotland was virtually worthless, and Henry could concentrate all his forces upon Wales

On 23 April, St George's Day, there was a single report of an English victory with 1,000 Welshmen killed, including one of Glyndŵr's sons, but there is no record of who took part or where it occurred. The same skirmish seems to have been also recorded for 11 January 1406, with Edward Charleton claimed to have killed 1,000 of Glyndŵr's men with his Shropshire and Cheshire levies, with one of Owain's sons dying. Nothing else is known of this event – its whereabouts or the name of Glyndŵr's son. It may have been propaganda surrounding a skirmish to beef up Henry's pleas for more money to Parliament. Alternatively, there may have been two skirmishes and Owain lost two sons. Only one of his six legitimate sons is known to have survived the war.

In April 1406, Parliament repeated its congratulations of 1405 to Prince Henry, for his work in Wales. In 1405, his commission as King's Lieutenant in Wales had been renewed. Later in the month, the Speaker of the Commons asked that the Prince should reside 'continuously' in Wales, because of the unrest there. In June, Parliament noted its concern that the Prince had still not gone to Wales. From May to August 1406, there were reports of Welsh raids in Herefordshire, Worcestershire, Powys and Shropshire. This led to the Commons House once more petitioning on 7 June, that the Prince might be sent into Wales with all haste. Prince Hal went into Wales shortly after, and offered pardons in Ceredigion and Gower. Both areas seem to have reverted to English rule, and in December the Prince was back in London. In June, the retinues of Lord Bardolf and Northumberland were defeated in north-west Powys by Sir Edward Charleton, but little is known of the clash. It may be confused with the skirmishes recorded in January and April. The English lords escaped back to Glyndŵr in Harlech, and later left for Scotland.

On 16 June in the English Channel, a French fleet was alarmed by a solar eclipse There is a record in Walsingham's 'Historia Anglicana': 'AD 1406 While the French were hastening to help Glyndŵr, with 38 ships, 8 of them, full of armed men, were captured, and the rest fled in fear from Wales. Not long after, another 15 ships, carrying wine and corn were captured.' This is more likely to have happened in 1405, however.

MORE DEFECTIONS

Sir John Kynaston had left Glyndŵr's forces in 1404, and now we see another notable warrior deserting him. From the Montgomeryshire Collections Vol XXIX, we find that

Gruffydd Vaughan of Welshpool had left Glyndŵr to join the English. In the Welshpool charter of 29 June 1406, 'EDWARD DE CHEULETON' (Charleton):

> ... extended the privileges of the burgesses, enlarged the boundaries of the Borough to its present great area, and granted the burgesses certain immunities. In the text of the charter the Lord of Powys states his reasons for thus conferring these fresh favours: the keynote to the whole transaction being contained in these significant words: 'Because they (the burgesses) ... in the time of the Rebellion of Owen ab Griffith, were always faithful to our Sovereign Lord the King, and to us.' Perhaps it was their fidelity to the English crown that caused Glyndŵr to burn the suburbs of the town; and because of the sufferings they endured by this wanton act, Edward de Cherleton was prompted to recompense them after this fashion. Among the names of assenting burgesses who appear as co-signatories of this important document are the following: viz., Hugh Say (Captain of Pool garrison, a cadet of the family of De Say, Barons of Clun), Sir Griffith Vaughan of Garth (an ancestor of the Myttons of Garth, and of the Lloyds of Harrington: Glyndŵr's quondam ally), Evan Blayney of Tregynon (of the Tribe of Brochwel: an ancestor of the Blayneys of Gregynog), Owen ap Meredith of Neuadd Wen (of the Royal Tribe of Griffith ap Cynan), and Howel, David, and Madoc ap David Aber (Grandsons of Ieuan Caereinion, the ancestor of the Owens of Llynlloedd, Woodhouse and Bettws).
>
> The extension of the boundaries of the Borough was made for the 'enlargement of the liberty of the town', and to benefit the burgesses 'for their great fidelity'. The Borough being clearly in the main an English garrison, it was surrounded by the rebellious followers of Owen Glyndŵr; it is probable the enlargement of the liberties was really to extend the area over which the garrison of Pool had the charge, and, perhaps, for defensive and strategical purposes the river Helygy (Lugg) on one side, the Belee on another, and the Severn on a third side, may have been regarded as boundaries of defence from the incursions of the rebels; but it was not easy to see the reason for extending the boundary beyond the Severn, unless it were to impose on the burgesses the duty of defending the lord's possessions on the English side of Severn. Doubtless the lord relied mainly upon the burgesses for furnishing him with men as well for defensive as offensive purposes. In addition to the motive of defence above alluded to, the extension of the boundary may have been to include the possessions of the Abbey of Ystrad Marchell, viz., the abbey itself, the land and manor of Tir-y-mynach adjoining, and partly in the parish of Guilsfield, and also the grange at Moydog and land at Trehelig, which are situate in the parish of Castle Caereinion, and the lands called Monksfield.

On 1 August 1406, Henry Dwn yet again attacked Cydweli castle and town, and Glyndŵr personally raided Clwyd, north-east Wales. Some sources record a Fourth Parliament at Harlech in July or August. In September to October, Peniarth MS 135 records that 'Gower and Ystrad Twyi and most of Ceredigion yielded and took the English side.' This must have been as a direct result of Prince Henry's offers of pardons, and the loss of Ystrad Tywil would have been a hammer blow to Glyndŵr. Even worse, Aberystwyth Castle in Ceredigion could now be more safely besieged by the English. August saw seven leading Welshmen being given safe conduct to go to Chester to make their submission. October 1406 saw official inquiries at Caerwys, St Asaf, Rhuddlan and Holywell to gather information upon rebels in order to confiscate their lands. Inquisitions in that month in Flintshire revealed that of almost 150 followers of Glyndŵr, ninety-four died during the war, another eleven when fighting at Shrewsbury, ten had died since making their submissions but before paying their fines, twenty-nine were still fighting and two had gone to Scotland with the Bishop of St Asaf – almost eighty per cent of Owain's men were dead. In November, the rebel of 1403, Morgan Gethin and Rhys Gethin (not the more famous Rhys Gethin) led a fresh insurrection in Gower, trying to re-establish support for Glyndŵr, but there were more problems for Glyndŵr.

Owain had been withdrawing his forces in Anglesey to consolidate his army and because of incessant English attacks by sea. On 9 November, some 2,000 'rebels' were named, and pardoned upon submitting and paying a fine. To try and whip up support after this setback, on 18 November Glyndŵr led a massive raid around his homelands in north-east Wales, including attacking Rhuddlan. It seems his actions were to try and capture an English spy, Maredudd Ieuan Gwyn, who had been passing on information on Glyndŵr's movements. Maredudd had a farm west of the Conwy River, and was in the pay of his landlord, Sir Henry Conway of Rhuddlan Castle. Alerted, the agent emptied his house of his contents and made for the safety of the castle. Glyndŵr's men found Maredudd's son tending cattle outside the castle and killed him. Maredudd Ieuan Gwyn was killed inside the castle, probably murdered by Glyndŵr sympathisers. His daughter recorded the story.

In 1406, Northumberland and Bardolf left their uncomfortable refuge in Scotland, being unable to raise any support, and arrived on the continent. Here they still tried to drum up support for an invasion of England from Northumbria and Scotland. Adam of Usk recalls:

> While I was in Bruges, the above-named earl of Northumberland and lord of Bardolf were lodged, the one in the monastery of Eeckhout, and the other in a hospice in the midst of the city. And on the eve of Saint Brice (12th November), in the twilight of the evening, there came from the side of England in the air a ball of fire, greater than a large barrel, lighting up, as it were, the whole world. And, as it drew near, all men were astounded and stood in fear lest the city should be destroyed. But it passed on.

Prince Henry, back in London, took part in the presentation of the great petition against the Lollards. In December 1406, Bishop Mascall of Hereford listed the damage that had occurred in a 10-mile strip of land along the Shropshire and Hereford borders, where by the end of 1406, fifty-two churches had been destroyed by Welsh raiders. Archenfield, Clun, Pontesbury, Leominster, Weobley, Old and New Radnor, Presteigne, Kington, Lyonshall and Titley all suffered, even up to the outskirts of the great garrison towns of Hereford, Chester and Shrewsbury. They were probably all gutted by fire after being looted, as their medieval cores still stand. Castles like New Radnor were never really properly dismantled by Welsh raiders, who lacked the necessary tools in their fast war-parties. Often we simply do not know what happened to many castles. For instance, Leland stated that Montgomery was destroyed by Glyndŵr, but this may have meant the town rather than the castle on the hill overlooking the town. Animals were taken back into Wales, but the buildings generally survived. In February 1407 Gruffydd Yonge was appointed Bishop of Bangor.

A NEW ENGLISH STRATEGY

At the same time, the English were adopting a different strategy. Rather than focusing on the punitive expeditions favoured by Henry IV, the young Henry of Monmouth had adopted a strategy of economic blockade. Using the castles that remained in English control he gradually began to retake Wales while cutting off food from Anglesey, plus trade and the supply of weapons. By 1407 this strategy was working. It seems that Monmouthshire was lost by now. Sir John Greyndour was now steward of Usk and Caerleon in the minority of Edmund, 5th Earl of March, and on 10 February 1407, pardon was granted to the tenants and residents of Usk, Caerleon, Trelech, Tregrug and Edlogan for 'felonies and insurrections', so some of those pardoned had assisted Gruffydd ab Owain in his fatal attacks on Grosmont and Usk. In March, 1,000 men from all over Flintshire appeared before the county's Chief Justice and agreed to pay a communal fine for their adherence to Glyndŵr. Gradually the same pattern was repeated throughout the country. English forces, with their dominance of the sea now the French had left, and numerical superiority, inevitably overpowered the Welsh.

Over the winter of 1406-07 Glyndŵr was reported to be in various places across Wales – local groups were still active, and he may have been trying to stop the war faltering to a halt, as it started its eighth year. He was said to have hidden in a cave at the mouth of the Dysynni near Tywyn, and at Valle Crucis Abbey near Llangollen. At East Orchard Castle near St Athan in the Vale of Glamorgan, he is said to have stayed with his enemy Lawrence Berkerolles in the guise of a French nobleman.

May saw battles around the Menai Straits and fighting in Gwynedd – especially again around Caernarfon. Meirionnydd and Ceredigion also saw skirmishes. In June, Lord Powys issued Welshpool with a charter – the Welsh were forbidden to enter the town, gather in groups or bear arms near the town, and only French and English were to be used in official proceedings there. In July the Earl of Arundel's north-east lordship submitted. One by one the lordships such as Oswestry, Chirk, Oswestry and Yale began to surrender. In late March-early April 1407 over 1,000 men from Flintshire submitted, appearing at Flint before Gilbert Talbot and agreeing to pay fines.

THE SIEGE OF ABERYSTWYTH 1407-1408

From May 1407 Prince Henry was again in Wales, supervising the siege of Aberystwyth. He was supported by thousands of troops led by Sir John Oldcastle, Sir John Greyndour, Lord Audley, Lord Carew and the Earl of Warwick. The baggage train brought 538 pounds of gunpowder, 971 pounds of saltpetre and 303 pounds of sulphur. Glyndŵr's men fended off this siege of Aberystwyth, but for most of 1407-1408 it was battered by English cannon, explaining the sorry remains there today of one of the greatest castles in Wales.

> 1407 – The English prince came with a great host to lay siege to Aberystwyth castle, nor did he retire
> until he had received a promise of the surrender of the castle after a short interval, with four of the

most puissant (powerful) men in the castle as pledges of the bargain. Before the day Rhys the Black went to Gwynedd to ask Owain's leave to surrender the castle to the English. Owain kept Rhys with him until he had gathered his power around him and then went with Rhys to Aberystwyth, where he threatened to cut off Rhys's head, unless he might have the castle; whereupon the castle was given to Owain.

(Peniarth MS 135.)

With Aberystwyth cut off, around August a second army came into Wales led by Edward Charleton, Lord Furnival, Sir Edward Gilbert and his brother Richard, to besiege Harlech. Prince Henry's containment strategy was working well. On 22 September, the King wrote from York that he had left his first-born son in Wales for the chastisement of the rebels. The powerful Aberystwyth Castle desperately held out throughout that winter under Rhys Ddu (Rhys ap Gruffydd ap Llywelyn ap Ieuan). Timber was cut in the Forest of Dean for carpenters to construct siege engines. It was the first occasion when heavy guns were used on a castle in Britain. Six cannon were shipped from Pontefract Castle to Bristol and then dragged overland to Aberystwyth. The besiegers also had the 'messager', a huge cannon for the time, weighing over 5,000 pounds, but fortunately for the defenders, it exploded, killing its gun crew. In September, Rhys Ddu parleyed under a flag of truce with Richard Courtenay, the Chancellor of Oxford University. A six-week truce was agreed until 24 October, and the beleaguered Welsh were to surrender by All Saints Day, 1 November. Rhys Ddu travelled to inform Glyndŵr under a flag of truce.

Prince Hal thought that the deal was sealed, and took his main force back to Hereford, leaving a token force of 120 men-at-arms and 360 archers at Ystrad Fflur (Strata Florida). Glyndŵr was furious with the proposed surrender, threatening to cut off Rhys Ddu's head if he accepted a pardon, and took his own bodyguard with him to Aberystwyth. He reinstalled Rhys Ddu as commander, telling him never to surrender – only Glyndŵr, as Commander-in-Chief, was allowed to come to terms with the English. When Glyndŵr was known to have arrived and strengthened the defenders' resolve, Prince Henry and some nobles returned to England from the siege, not wishing to stay there in a bitterly cold winter. Somehow Glyndŵr left Aberystwyth Castle that winter – probably protected by the foul weather – and returned north to Harlech. The winter was the worst on record.

Later in 1407 King Henry attended the Parliament at Gloucester, where he was thanked for his services, and bore witness in favour of his cousin Edward, Duke of York, who was still under suspicion for the plot to take the young Mortimers to Glyndŵr. In September 1407, an official royal pardon was offered to the tenantry of Ogwr (Ogmore). Heavy arrears, until new rents were agreed in 1428, show the decline of the area. By 1416, none of the vacant lands of the area had been let. In 1422, revenue from such leases was only a quarter of the amount that had been received in rent before the Glyndŵr War. There was the same situation with rents in Llantrisant, Cowbridge, Caerffili, Cardiff, Swansea and Gower- all had been in Glyndŵr's hands in 1404 and took decades to recover their prosperity.

THE DEATH OF THE DUC D'ORLEANS 23 NOVEMBER 1407

Louis I, Duc d'Orleans, the brother of Charles VI, was ambushed and assassinated on the rue Vieille-du-Temple in central Paris. His left hand was chopped off, for fear he would raise the devil with it, and his brains were knocked out onto the road. Louis had been the power behind the throne, as Charles VI was mentally unstable, and a powerful proponent of the Welsh cause and of war with England. The perpetrator and English ally, Jean de Bourgogne, pretended to be distraught, weeping at the funeral. Allegedly, Henry IV's agents were involved in the murder. On 25 November, Jean de Bourgogne, realizing that his assassins were about to be discovered, admitted to one of his uncles that he had ordered the murder of Louis d'Orleans. He confessed, 'I did it; the Devil tempted me'. Bourgogne fled from Paris to Flanders, fearing the wrath of Charles VI. France was now divided into two camps, the Burgundians and the Armagnacs. In late November, Northumberland and Bardolf returned to Scotland from their fruitless mission to France, after the death of their major source of hope, Louis of Orleans. They spent the winter trying to organise an army to invade England.

Glyndŵr had already seen his Scottish allies made ineffective by the capture of their King. Now France was divided and all assistance from that quarter disappeared. Charles VI sought a peace treaty with England, to try and bring stability. Henry IV agreed, upon condition that the French 1404 Treaty of Alliance with Wales was rescinded. The Anglo-French treaty was agreed on 7 December, and soon after Henry IV made a similar agreement with the Bretons. Now Owain was alone against a country which possessed over thirteen times his resources. The population of Wales at this time was around 150,000 and that of England over 2,000,000. The English could also call on French allies such as Gascon crossbowmen. In 1407-08 there was yet another uncommonly severe winter, with Glyndŵr having problems feeding his men and horses, and with support slipping away.

CHAPTER 11

The Fall of the Castles 1408-1409

ADAM OF USK JOINS GLYNDŴR

The winter had been terrible, with animals across Europe dying from the cold. Adam of Usk returned from exile, landing at Barmouth, but was uncertain of his reception with the King's men, and said that he hid in woods and caves before being discovered by Glyndŵr's men. According to Adam, he was kept prisoner under Owain's orders, and while there he wrote the following:

AD 1408 The aforesaid Lancaster king of arms, returning back from England, made known to me, the writer of this history, at Paris, that he had spoken with the king to make my peace, but that both by reason of my commerce with the said earl of Northumberland and of disparagements written of me by my rivals from Rome, there was no means of reconciliation with him, for that his indignation waxed stronger day by day. Wherefore, I, Adam, the writer of this history, made a declaration before the same king of arms that I would feign myself Owen's man, and with my following would cross over into Wales unto him; and thence, taking my chance, I would steal away from him to my lord of Powis, to await under his care the king's favour. And so it came to pass. And this declaration saved me my life. Snares were laid for me by sea; and eight ships of Devon chased me for two livelong days, and again and again I was hunted like a hare by so many hounds.

But at last, through the prayers of Saint Thomas of India, whom I beheld in a vision praying to God that he would bless me, I escaped to the port of St. Pol de Leon in Brittany; and there in the chapel of Saint Theliau, where too he slew a dragon one hundred and twenty feet in length, committing myself to his care, I daily celebrated mass. At length, taking my chance, I landed in Wales at the port of Barmouth, and there I hid in the hills and caves and thickets, before that I could come unto my said lord of Powis, because at that time he had taken to wife, in the parts of Devon, the daughter of the earl of the same, sorely tormented with many and great perils of death and capture and false brethren, and of hunger and thirst, and passing many nights without sleep for fear of the attacks of foes. Moreover, on behalf of the same Owen, when it was found out that I had sent to my said lord for a safe-conduct, I was laid under the close restraint of pledges. But at last, when my lord had come again to his own country, and when I had gotten from him letters of leave to come unto him and to rest safe with him, I got me by night and in secret unto him at his castle of Pool; and there and in the parish church of the same, not daring to pass outside his domain, like a poor chaplain only getting victuals for saying mass, shunned by thankless kin and those who were once my friends, I led a life sorry enough and how sorry God in His heart doth know.

In February 1408, the burgesses and bailiffs of Shrewsbury were excused from paying royal taxes of £47 'in consideration of the great losses which they have sustained by the malice and invasion of the Welsh rebels.' Later in the year, in September, an esquire of the King named Robert Middleton was allowed to forego his annual rent of 6 marks as his land in Montgomeryshire had been plundered by the Welsh. In 1408, Jean, Duc de Bourgogne, with a Sorbonne theologian to justify his assassinating Louis d'Orleans on the grounds that Louis had been a tyrant, returned to Paris and extracted a pardon from Charles VI. With Bourgogne in favour, Owain's last chance of French aid was lost.

THE BATTLE OF BRAMHAM MOOR 19 FEBRUARY 1408

Northumberland and Bardolf had returned to the North of England. It was the last throw of the dice of the 66-year-old Earl of Northumberland to try and stop Henry IV sequestrating the profitable estates of the Percies. They had ruled the north-east of England as almost an independent kingdom for decades, and Henry Percy gathered an army of lowland Scots and loyal Northumbrians and marched south towards York. The winter of 1407-8 was the worst in living memory, with heavy snow, so many of Northumberland's tenants failed to arrive for battle. The Scots were possibly hired with the money raised at Glyndŵr's 1405 Parliament. Chroniclers scoffed at Percy's makeshift army, made up of 'mostly smiths, tailors, falconers, countrymen, mercers and artisans'.

South of Wetherby, at Bramham Moor, the army met a force of local Yorkshire levies, led by Sir Thomas Rokeby, High Sheriff of Yorkshire. He had decided not to wait for Henry IV's army to arrive, and had been pursuing Percy's force. The outcome was largely decided by use of the longbow to thin the enemy ranks before charging into their main body. Bardolf was mortally wounded early in the action, and the Earl himself either died fighting a furious rearguard action as his army was routed, or was executed on the battlefield, along with sixteen others who were beheaded. The Bardolf estates were forfeited, and the power of the Percy family was broken. Glyndŵr had lost his last remaining allies. The former Bishop of Bangor, Lewis Byford (Lewis ap Ieuan), had gone under Glyndŵr's instructions to accompany the army, and was captured. As he was unarmed and wearing his robes as a bishop, Byford was spared but imprisoned. Bardolf's body was quartered, and his head and one quarter of his body were set up over one of the gates of Lincoln. The Earl's head was cut off, fixed on a hedge stake, and carried with mock procession to London where it was put on display. The four parts of his torso were exposed at Newcastle, Berwick, York and Lincoln. After several months, the Earl's remains were buried at the right side of the high altar in York Minster beside the grave of his son, Hotspur, on 2 July 1408. Rokeby was given one of Percy's largest manors at Spofforth, and with the North of England secured, rode with a large force to Wales to take part in the siege of Harlech Castle. The outcome of this minor battle at Bramham Moor secured the Lancastrian claim until the bloody Battle of Towton in 1461.

> A.D. 1408. The aforesaid lords passed over into Scotland and thence with an armed band into England, trusting to have the kingdom for themselves. But the sheriff of York, being well ware of their coming, crushed them in battle and beheaded them, and sent their heads to king Henry; which were afterwards set up beyond London bridge. And when I heard these things, I, the writer of this history, gave thanks unto Him who foreseeth what is to come, for that I had stayed behind.
> (Adam of Usk.)

The Lords of Abergafenni, Glamorgan, Pembroke, Maelienydd, Rhuthun, Gower, Powys, Ewyas Lacey and Oswestry were ordered to return to their castles on 16 May 1409, as Glyndŵr and Bishop Trefor were reported to be raiding across the nation. Owain was aided by Scottish and French mercenaries, according to some accounts, and Lord Talbot was ordered to kill him.

ABERYSTWYTH CASTLE FALLS 23 SEPTEMBER 1408

Throughout the summer, the English attacks on Harlech and Aberystwyth mounted, with some English reinforcements landing by sea and others marching across Wales. In May 1408, ambassadors were once again sent to France pleading for help. Welsh troops had been able to evacuate in safety as long as Harlech and Aberystwyth held out and they had control of the sea, but that was no longer the case. (Harlech was then situated by the sea, but the coastline has altered so it is now inland.) After being bombarded and attacked since May 1407, Aberystwyth finally fell sixteen months later. Towards the end, Rhys Ddu offered the English terms to surrender, but the offer was unacceptable and the fighting grimly carried on, with the Welsh starving and running out of weaponry. William Gwyn ap Rhys Llwyd, who had served the crown at Cydweli but joined Glyndŵr's men, was killed by a cannonball. The Welsh could not respond to the continuous bombardment and attacks on the walls. In the few nights before it surrendered, many men escaped from the beach at night, heading north to try and join Glyndŵr, who was thought to be under siege in Harlech.

There was still unrest in 1408. In Clun on 17 October Symkin Marter was detained for selling arms and food to the rebels. The Mayor of Chester was replaced by a military governor 'for want of loyalty'. John Talbot, Lord Furnival, the 1st Earl of Shrewsbury, had been one of the signatories to the surrender of Aberystwyth in September 1407, and had stewarded Montgomeryshire during the Earl of March's minority. He was later present when Harlech fell. However, in 1408 Shrewsbury would not admit him through the town gates, when he went there on his way to join his brother Gilbert in searching for Glyndŵr. Like many other border towns, it had signed a truce, paying off Glyndŵr not to attack.

THE FALL OF HARLECH FEBRUARY 1409

From August 1407, Harlech had been under siege from Lord Edward Charleton of Powys and the Talbot brothers. The winter of 1408-09 had been exceptionally severe, with an abundance of snow from December to March, so cold that blackbirds and thrushes dropped dead from the trees. Wales had no sea power, since the French and Bretons had left. 1,500 crossbow bolts are known to have been fired in the sieges of Aberystwyth and Harlech. Llywelyn ap Madog ap Llywelyn, the commander of Harlech, was killed, and Lord Edmund Mortimer died sometime over that terrible winter after taking over command of the castle. The Irish Sea was filled with English, not Welsh or French ships supplying the starving defenders:

> 1408 – Now befell the second siege of the above castle and, without stirring from the spot, it was won; thence the host went to Harlech, where many gentlemen of Wales met their death; at last the castle was perforce given up to the English.
> (Peniarth MS 135)

Harlech fell to the forces of Gilbert, 5th Lord Talbot, and his brother John Talbot, Earl of Shrewsbury. We are unsure if Rhys Ddu and some of his men managed to break through the Aberystwyth blockade and join the Harlech defenders. Prince Henry had taken his army and cannon from Aberystwyth to help the army besieging Harlech. One 'great gun', The King's Daughter, blew up like the Messager had done at Aberystwyth. Apart from the great guns there were constant fusillades of arrows, and the starving and freezing defenders were taunted by the smell of meats cooking over English camp fires. Last minute envoys were sent in desperation to the French for help, as had happened at Aberystwyth. There was no response. Gruffydd Yonge was sent to Scotland to attempt to co-ordinate action, but no help arrived.

Marged Glyndŵr, Catrin Mortimer and her son Lionel and three daughters were captured by Gilbert Talbot of Goodrich Castle, and transported on a cold, difficult journey to London. The children were potential heirs to the throne, so Catrin knew that their future was bleak. Here she heard of the execution of Owain's bravest lieutenants. All were kept in solitary confinement, and they were all to die in the Tower of London before 1415. How Glyndŵr escaped is unknown, but folktales record that he disguised himself as an elderly peasant and passed through the English ranks.

> The wife of Owen (Margaret), together with his two daughters (one of them Catrin, Mortimer's widow) and three granddaughters, daughters of sir Edmund Mortimer, and all household goods, was taken captive, and sent to London unto the king; and Owen, with his only remaining son Meredith, miserably lay in hiding in the open country, and in caves, and in the thickets of the mountains.
>
> To make all safe, and to curb fresh rebellions by means of the king's soldiers and at his costs, the glades and passes of Snowdon and of other mountains and forests of North Wales were held guarded.

Mortimer's son, Lionel, was also taken. Owen's family fell into the hands of the English at the capture of Harlech, before February, 1409.

(Wylie, *Henry the Fourth*)

A sad footnote has been noted in John Lloyd's 1931 book *Owen Glendower* – he 'left behind him in the castle one little personal relic which has recently been unearthed in the course of excavations, viz. a gilt bronze boss from a set of horse harness, bearing the four lions rampant which he had assumed as Prince of Wales'. The four lions rampant, counter-changed in gold and red, were the ancient arms of the princes of Gwynedd.

Owain's power was waning, and Prince Henry now took little part in future campaigns in Wales. He had almost spent his entire fortune in Wales. In 1407-08 alone, his 2,400 soldiers had cost him £6,825 for only six months. There was nothing left across Wales to plunder and defray the expenses. Ceredigion, Gwent, the Gower, Pembroke, Anglesey and Caernarfon were virtually lost and men no longer flocked to Glyndŵr's banner. There was still some resistance in the northern hills of Glamorgan, but Cardiff and the Vale had been pacified. There was no longer the will to fight. Too many people had been killed, homes, towns, farms and churches destroyed. Welshmen were fined into poverty, disarmed and their lands taken. The Great War of Independence was ending.

THE LAST GREAT RAID 1409

However, not only the people had lost out in the war. Owain had lost his mansions, estates, his brother, brother-in-law, wife and had only one son of six still alive. Glyndŵr now determined on one last rampage, gathering what support he could. He may have been looking for death in battle, or simply for revenge upon the English who had destroyed his life and his country. Many remaining nobles came to his support, and a contingent of Scots and French who had fought for him in the past landed in North Wales in May. Glyndŵr's cousin Gwilym ap Tudur had been killed, but his brothers Rhys and Ednyfed ap Tudur of Penmynydd in Anglesey were still faithful, and had not taken any pardon. (Gwilym and Rhys ap Tudor had been captains of archers in Richard's campaigns in Ireland, and had been Glyndŵr supporters from the very beginning.) Rhys ap Gruffydd (Rhys Ddu of Aberteifi) still was at Glyndŵr's side, as was Owain's brother-in-law Philip Hanmer. All of his other best commanders had been killed. Glyndŵr started roaming his home estates, with a growing warband, causing panic once more in Oswestry (one of the 'burnt towns'), nearby Knockin Castle and Rhuthun. Out of nowhere, Glyndŵr had a major war party. They took no wagons for booty as they next headed into Shropshire – it was an attack of sheer bloody-mindedness, a final effort to make the English suffer.

There was fighting at Oswestry and Shrewsbury, but at Welshpool Rhys ap Tudur and Philip Scudamore were badly injured and captured, and they were then executed in Chester. The chronicler refers to Rhys Ddu, the defender of Aberystwyth, who was also tortured to death in London, stating that Rhys Ddu was: 'laid on a hurdle and so drawn forth to Tyburn through the city and was there hanged and let down again. His head was smitten off and his body quartered and sent to four towns and his head set on London Bridge.' He states that Philip Scudamore and Rhys ap Tudur were also beheaded and their heads displayed at Shrewsbury and Chester. Welshpool, Y Trallwng, was given to Lord Charleton, Constable of Welshpool for his services in killing Glyndŵr's only remaining commanders.

> 1409 – The men of Owain made an attack on the borders of Shropshire and there Rhys the Black and Philip Scudamore were captured. The one was sent to London and the other to Shrewsbury to be drawn and quartered. Thenceforth Owain made no great attack until he disappeared.
> (Peniarth MS 135.)

(Other sources tell us that Rhys Tudur was hung, drawn and quartered in 1410 or 1412.)

> The xij yeer of king Harri, a squire of Walis called Ris ap Die, that was supporter of Oweyn of Glendore, that did much destruction to the king's people in Walis, was taken and brought to London, and drawn and hanged and quartered.
> (*An English Chronicle*, ed. Davies.)

Adam of Usk seems to have a wrong dating:

> A.D. 1411. Meantime, while I there abode, among the other gentlemen of Owen's party, three men of fame, to wit Philip Scudamore of Troy, Rhys ap Griffith of Cardigan, and Rhys ap Tudor of Anglesey, being taken by the captain of the same castle, were drawn to the gallows and hanged; the first at Shrewsbury, whose head is still there set up beyond bridge, the second at London, and the third at Chester.

The Peniarth MS 135 tells us '1412 – Rhys ap Tudor of Anglesey and Ednyfed his brother were captured. They were executed in Chester.' Whatever the truth, Rhys Ddu, Philip Scudamore, Rhys and Ednyfed ap Tudur all were tortured to death between 1409 and 1412.

Henry IV was enraged that English officials were still seeking and making truces with, rather than exterminating, Glyndŵr's followers and on 3 November 1409 reprimanded his lords and knights in Wales and the Marches. He told the Earl of Arundel, Edward Charleton, Lord Grey of Rhuthun and Sir Richard Lestrange that he had heard that they, 'on their own authority, and without our warrant or knowledge, were making truces with Owin de Glendourdy and other rebels in those parts' that did not hold the rebels to 'abstain from war'.

In March 1410, violence erupted in Anglesey, possibly because of the deaths of the Tudurs. Ships were sent there and another 900 troops manned the island. Prince Henry was now de facto ruler, with his father in serious decline and the crown virtually bankrupt because of the wars from 1400 onwards. In 1410 it was claimed that the Welsh had ransacked and damaged St Asaf Cathedral and should pay reparations, but it had supported Glyndŵr from at least 1404. Even in 1410 Welsh ambassadors such as John Trefor were trying to get the French to honour their treaty with Wales. Owain was now a hunted man. The revolt continued to flicker, and there were still pockets of support around Glyndŵr's homelands of Carrog, Bala, Cymer Abbey, Strata Florida Abbey and Tregaron.

CHAPTER 12

Glyndŵr's Disappearance 1410-1415

THE DEATH OF BISHOP TREFOR 1410

This is the time of the legends of Glyndŵr hiding in several caves across Wales. Owain was also saddened by the death of John Trefor, Bishop of St Asaf, who had travelled to France twice to try to get French support. The Bishop was buried in the Chapelle de L'Abbaye de St Victor in Paris. Adam of Usk recounts:

> Master John Trevaur, doctor of laws and bishop of St. Asaph, casting off his special friendship for the English, threw in his lot with the fortunes of Owen, in peace and in war; and, having twice passed over into France seeking aid of armed men, he was translated to a see among the Indians; and the abbot of Llanegwast (*Valle Crucis, in Yale*) was chosen bishop of St. Asaph in his stead. But the same master John, thus fallen into ill fortune, betook himself to Rome, where, beyond Tiber, on the fifth day of October, in the year of our Lord 1412, he died.

1412 seems to be a clerical or copying error, for Trefor died in 1410. Trefor had been created bishop of St. Asaf in 1395, and went over to Owain in 1404, being immediately deprived of the bishopric. He had been involved in Northumberland's rebellion, fleeing with him into Scotland in 1405.

 Perhaps this story relates to the time when Glyndŵr was being pursued. Taliesin ap Iolo Morganwg wrote some time before his death in 1847:

> When Owen Glyndŵr travelled about the country, in the guise of a strange gentleman, attended by one faithful friend, in the habit of a servant, and both being unarmed, (for no armed person was secure at that time) and going about to ascertain the disposition of the inhabitants, he went to the castle of Sir Lawrence Berkrolles (*stated to be East Orchard Castle at St Athan rather than Coity Castle*), and requested, in French, a night's reception for himself and servant, which was readily granted, attended by a hearty welcome; the best of every thing in the castle being laid before him; and so pleased was Sir Lawrence with his friend, that he earnestly pressed him to remain with him for some days; observing, that he soon expected to see Owen Glyndŵr there; for that he had despatched all

his tenants and servants, with many other confidential persons, under an oath of fidelity, through all parts of the country to seize Owen, who, he was told, had come to that district of the principality; and that he was, himself, sworn to give honourable rewards to his men who should bring Owen Glyndŵr there, either alive or dead. 'It would be very well, indeed,' said Owen, 'to secure that man, were any persons able to do so.' Having remained at Sir Lawrence's castle for four days and three nights, Owen thought it would be wise to go his way; therefore, giving his hand to Sir Lawrence, he addressed him thus: 'Owen Glyndŵr, as a sincere friend, having neither hatred, treachery, nor deception in his heart, gives his hand to Sir Lawrence Berkrolles, and thanks him for the kindness and gentlemanly reception which he and his friend (in the guise of a servant) experienced from him at his castle; and desires to assure him, on oath, hand in hand, and hand on heart, that it will never enter his mind to avenge the intentions of Sir Lawrence towards him; and that he will not, as far as he may, allow such desires to exist in his own knowledge and memory, nor in the minds of any of his relations and adherents.' And then he and his servant departed; but Sir Lawrence Berkrolles was struck dumb with astonishment, and never afterwards recovered his speech; no word, thenceforth, having ever escaped his lips.

(From the MS. of Mr. Lleision, of Prisk (near Cowbridge); but then in the possession of Evan of the Farm, Llanblethian.)

The imprisonment of two Scottish merchants at Caernarfon in 1410, and the evidence contained in an undated letter referring to assemblies in desolate places, and expected landings of men from the outer isles of Scotland at Abermo (Barmouth) and Aberdyfi, suggest that the Welsh still hoped for external alliances. By 1411, after more than a decade of disruption, rents, heavy taxes and fines began to be systematically collected once again across Wales. Adam of Usk had 'escaped' to Lord Powys, Edward Charleton at Welshpool, in 1408-1409, where he said he was shunned by kinsmen and former friends. After two years, at the instance of David Holbache of Oswestry, he received the King's pardon dated 20 March 1411, on account that he had 'unwittingly' joined Glyndŵr. 1411 saw the death of Glyndŵr's son Gruffydd in the Tower of London. Negotiations were held in Ceredigion and Meirionnydd to stop Welsh attacks. Fighting in Meirionydd ceased in November, and more English soldiers were sent into Wales from 1412-1414 to enforce taxation collection. In 1412, Prince Henry twice entered London with armed troops, intending to take the crown from his dying father. He wanted war with France, while Henry IV, understanding the terrible state of the royal finances, did not want war.

THE CAPTURE OF DAFYDD GAM APRIL 1412

Dafydd ap Llywelyn ap Hywel Fychan ap Hywel ap Einion Sais was known as Dafydd or Davy Gam, being either squint-eyed or lame. 'Gam' can mean either, being one of the few Welsh words to pass into the English language as 'gammy', as in having a 'gammy' leg. (Gam is mutated from Cam, meaning crooked.) He may have been in service to Henry IV's father John of Gaunt, and was being paid the large annuity of 40 marks per annum from Bolingbroke's estate as early as 1399, before he became Henry IV. Later, Davy Gam and his brothers were described as 'the King's esquires', and from Penywaun near Brecon supported the King against Glyndŵr. His estates were attacked in 1402-1403, and he may have tried to kill Glyndŵr at Machynlleth. Bolingbroke was Lord of Brecon, and Davy Gam stayed loyal to him. He helped the English win at Grosmont, and tried to win over local Welshmen to fight against Glyndŵr. His family was rewarded with 'rebel estates' in Ceredigion.

In April 1412 Dafydd Gam was captured by Glyndŵr's men and estimates of the amount paid as his ransom range from 200 to 700 marks. It was paid quickly from King Henry's estates in Wales. 'Our chosen esquire Luellin ap Howel, father of our chosen esquire David Gamme, has told us that the said David was violently seized by our rebel and traitor Owen de Glendourdy, and kept in strict imprisonment...' Henry IV ordered John Tiptoft, Constable of Brecon, and its Receiver, William Butler, to pay Glyndŵr's men. Glyndŵr had made Gam swear an oath to never bear arms against him again or oppose him in any other way. The story is that on his release Gam told King Henry of Glyndŵr's whereabouts, and attacked Glyndŵr's men. Glyndŵr had Gam's Brecon estates attacked and burned in retaliation and his Brecon manor was razed. These latter events probably happened after the attack at Machynlleth however.

> Two kinsmen they of nearest blood,
> In steadfast friendship bred,
> Till gallant Glyndŵr took the field,
> And the dragon reared its head.
> Now David Gam was for the king,
> And for him drew his sword;
> But Owen Vaughan was for Glyndŵr,
> And owned him as his lord.

In this poem, *For Country or For King*, W. Llywelyn Davies wrote that Gam had tried to kill Glyndŵr at a Welsh Parliament but was stopped by Sir Owen Vaughan of Ystrad Lliw, his kinsman. Vaughan pleaded with Glyndŵr not to kill Gam, but to offer him for ransom, which the King is recorded as paying. Gam later fought at Agincourt for the King. The poem tells us that during Agincourt, Owen Vaughan tried to assassinate Henry V but was stopped by Gam. Gam was killed instead, and knighted as he lay dying, while Vaughan was shot by an archer and died also. Both men were said to be buried in the same grave, and the last verse of the ballad is:

> With his last breath, Vaughan cried out;
> His words through Wales yet ring –
> 'Tis nobler that a knight should die
> For country than for king.'

The only Vaughan this author can find who died at Agincourt was Roger Vaughan of Bredwardine (1377-1415), who married Gam's daughter Gwladus, however. Gruffydd Vaughan was also at Agincourt fighting for Henry – his father was Ieuan, as was his son

– and Gruffydd Vaughan (Fychan) had sided with Glyndŵr before going over to the King's side. After the taking and ransoming of Gam in 1412, Glyndŵr was never known to be seen again. At Agincourt, Adam of Usk noted that Sir John Scudamore also died. Another Glyndŵr supporter who died there was Henry Dwn's grandson Gruffydd.

> Sir David Gam, Kt., the most prominent member of this once prominent family, deserves more than a passing notice. The name by which he was known at the time he lived was Davydd ap Llewelyn, the dignity of knighthood being only conferred upon him as his last breath was escaping on the field of Agincourt. Of impulsive and violent temper, prompt in action without calculation of consequences, cruel, unscrupulous, and brave, he was a dangerous man to either friend or foe. To use Jones's words, he lived like a wolf, and died like a lion. He started in life by slaying a kinsman in the street of Brecon, and fleeing to England to escape the consequences. He was a strong partisan, after this, of the English kings, Henry IV and Henry V, under the former of which he undertook, in 1402, the assassination of the patriot insurrectionist, Owen Glyndŵr (Owen having just traversed Breconshire with fire and sword), at Machynlleth; and for his pains, though spared execution, got several years of imprisonment. This was the darkest blot on the stormy life of David Gam, for though the provocation was doubtless great, the mode of retaliation was base and atrocious.
>   He was no sooner released than he again devoted himself to the cause of the Henrys. In 1415 Henry V met the French at Agincourt, and there, in the crisis of a signal victory, when Henry himself was hemmed in and borne down by the enemy, 'Davydd ap Llewelyn' (with other of his countrymen) rushed to the rescue of the king, and effected his deliverance; but the brave deliverer fell mortally wounded. Henry, on the spot, as the last blood was ebbing, made him a knight, conferring the same honour on Gam's son-in-law, Roger Vaughan of Tre'rtwr (Tretower), who also fell. It has been held by many that Shakspere in his Henry V. has under the character of Fluellin portrayed Sir David Gam. Theophilus Jones gives his sanction to this opinion. It can scarcely be correct, for after the battle, Fluellin being in conversation with Henry, a list of the dead is handed to the king, who reads out the names of the principal men who had fallen, and amongst them is 'Davy Gam, Esquire.' Shakspere has frequent anachronisms and inconsistencies, but it is inconceivable that he should on the same spot represent the same person as two persons, the one living, the other dead.
> (Thomas Nicholas 1872.)

Davy Gam was ransomed by Henry IV personally, and this act was followed by a general pardon for all rebels except murderers, rapists, Thomas of Trumpington and Owain Glyndŵr. Thomas Warde (of Trumpington) was in Scotland, pretending to be Richard II. There is a royal letter of pardon dated 15 June 1412, to Thomas Arundel, Archbishop of Canterbury and Lord Chancellor, 'for his part in the rebellions of Owen Glendwr and Thomas of Trumpington'. It is not known if there were any contacts between Glyndŵr and Arundel. He would have known Glyndŵr, certainly, as his brother the executed Earl of Arundel was a neighbour of Glyndŵr's before the war began. Even in 1415, Thomas of Trumpington was considered for impersonating Richard II as part of the Southampton Plot of that year.

THE DEATH OF HENRY IV 20 MARCH 1413

By 1409 the King was gravely ill, and made the first royal will to be written in English. The new King began to adopt a conciliatory attitude to the Welsh. Pardons were offered to the major leaders of the revolt and other opponents of his father's regime. Fines had been imposed across Wales, but many went uncollected as Henry V now had his eyes on France. Henry IV was buried next to Thomas a'Beckett in Canterbury Cathedral. In a symbolic gesture, Henry V had the body of Richard II interred in Westminster Abbey.

> A.D. 1413. Henry the fourth, after that he had reigned with power for fourteen years, crushing those who rebelled against him, fell sick, having been poisoned; from which cause he had been tormented for five years by a rotting of the flesh, by a drying up of the eyes, and by a rupture of the intestines; and at Westminster, in the abbot's chamber, within the sanctuary, thereby fulfilling his horoscope that he should die in the Holy Land, in the year of our Lord 1412-13, and on the twentieth day of the month of March, he brought his days to a close. And he was carried away by water, and was buried at Canterbury. That same rotting did the anointing at his coronation portend; for there ensued such a growth of lice, especially on his head, that he neither grew hair, nor could he have his head uncovered for many months. One of the nobles *(gold coins)*, at the time of his making the offering in the coronation-mass, fell from his hand to the ground; which then I with others standing by sought for diligently, and, when found, it was offered by him. Henry the fifth, his first-born son by the daughter of the earl of Hereford, a youth upright and filled with virtues and wisdom, on the fourteenth day after his father's death, Passion Sunday, to wit, then falling (9th April), was crowned with great solemnity at Westminster.
> (Adam of Usk)

Rafael Holinshed explained Henry IV's unpopularity in his *Chronicles of England*: '... by punishing such as moved with disdain to see him usurp the crown, did at sundry times rebel against him, he won himself more hatred, than in all his life time ... had been possible for him to have weeded out and removed.' In the Issue Rolls of 1413 there is the following entry: 'To a certain Welshman, coming to London, and there continuing for a certain time to give information respecting the conduct and designs of Ewain Glendourdy. In money paid to his own hands for his expenses, and as a special reward for the cause aforesaid ... £1' Whether this was a spy, traitor or a fraudster is unknown, but the English believed that Owain was in north Wales at this time, and had men specially posted at Cymer Abbey, Strata Florida and Bala.

There is a note of payment on 27 June 1413, by an exchequer clerk after the accession of Henry V: 'To John Weele, esquire. In money paid to his own hands, for the expenses of the wife of Owen Glendourdi, the wife of Edmund Mortimer, and others, their sons and daughters, in his custody in the city of London at the King's charge, by his command ... £30'. There is a record in the Chester Archives of John Weele on 10 May 1408, whereby he was made captain of Oswestry, and notably Glyndŵr's former supporter John Kynaston is named:

Defeasance of a Bond in £100 by Robert Sutton to Richard de Riddeley, to observe the Award of John Weele captain of the township of Oswostre, Richard de Cholmundelegh, Thomas de Brereton, Gruffyn le Wareyn, John de Kynaston, Randle de Brereton, Thomas de Lauton and John de Golborne, concerning the Lordships, lands and tenements in debate between them as by right of their two wives, in the townships of Malepas, Egge and Wiggelond.

It seems that Weele had been put in charge of Glyndŵr's family in the Tower of London.

However, sometime before 1 December 1413, Catrin Mortimer, her three daughters, her son Lionel Mortimer (an heir to the crown), Glyndŵr's wife Marged and a sister of Catrin all had 'died' in the Tower of London. There is a small monument to Catrin Glyndŵr, placed by the Catrin Glyndŵr Memorial Society, in the memorial garden of St Swithin's Church in the City of London (the medieval church was demolished in 1962). The only record of their death is in the Exchequer documents of 1413: 'To William del Chambre, valet of the said Earl (Arundel). In money paid to his own hands, for expenses and other charges incurred for the burial and exequies of the wife of Edward *(this should be Edmund)* Mortimer and her daughters, buried within St Swithin's Church London ... £1.'

On 10 March 1414, the Earl of Arundel and Sir Edward Charleton were at Bala to supervise the official surrender of the remaining core of Glyndŵr's army. No less than 600 men were forced to give up their arms, kneel and agree that they deserved to die, before being fined and pardoned. Also in this year, there were strong rumours that the Lollard leader, Sir John Oldcastle, was communicating with Owain. Because of this, reinforcements were sent to the major castles across Wales. Oldcastle was praised in the Gesta Henrici Quinti for 'slaughtering and pillaging the Welsh' when fighting with Prince Henry for a decade of the Glyndŵr War. Bandits, the remnants of Glyndŵr's army, were still active in Snowdonia.

THE SOUTHAMPTON PLOT 1415

In 1415 Gruffydd Yonge and Philip Hanmer were in France, again trying to get French help, so it may be that Glyndŵr was still alive. He certainly had strong contacts with Sir John Oldcastle via his border in-laws. In this year the Southampton Plot occurred, intending to kill Henry V and replace him with Edmund Mortimer, the Earl of March, the true heir to Richard II. Henry Percy was to raise the north, and Sir John Oldcastle was to raise the west, which makes the rumours of him trying to speak with Glyndŵr all the more believable. Henry's first cousin Richard, Earl of Cambridge, Sir Thomas Grey of Heton and the King's treasurer, Lord Scrope of Masham, were condemned as the ringleaders, with Grey immediately being hung, drawn and quartered. Scrope and Cambridge were beheaded after a trial by their peers. Cambridge had married into the Mortimer family, and was the brother of the Duke of York, himself previously involved with plotting against Henry IV. Henry Scrope was the nephew of the executed Archbishop of York. The plot had been disclosed by the Earl of March, who waited some days before informing the King. His only brother had already died mysteriously in the King's custody, and Mortimer obviously wanted to save himself from a similar fate.

David Howel was charged with conspiracy to begin a rising in North Wales in conjunction with the Southampton Plot. The Earl of Cambridge indicted him, giving evidence that the Earl of March was to be taken to North Wales, the royal castles seized, and the young Mortimer placed on the throne. Somehow Howel escaped imprisonment, but was indicted of treason by John Eliot in front of the King's justices. Howel complained to Parliament and the charges were dropped. Perhaps the authorities were afraid of another rising if Howel was killed. Before he left for France and Agincourt, Henry V gave orders for some rebuilding on monasteries he had despoiled in Wales, for example at the Abbey of Llanfaes near Beaumaris. There was even a provision that two of the monks had to be Welsh.

MORE PARDONS OFFERED 1415-1421

Gruffydd Yonge and the Hanmers were in Paris from February 1415, attempting to get French intervention, and even in 1418 Gruffydd was still trying. Gruffydd, in the Council of Constance in France, stated that Wales was a nation, and should have a vote in ending the papal schism. Unable to return to Wales, he later went to Scotland, becoming Bishop of Ross and Bishop of Hippo in Africa.

Before going to France, Henry instructed Gilbert Talbot from Porchester that he had authority to pardon any rebels who wished to submit, and Talbot went to Wales on 5 July. He was instructed to receive Glyndŵr and other rebels into the King's obedience, so Owain was believed to be alive at that date, although it was unlikely that he would trust any offer from the English crown that had killed all but one of his extended family. On 5 July 1415 Lord Gilbert Talbot was appointed to negotiate with Glyndŵr for peace and grant a pardon. On 24 February 1416 a second commission was given to Talbot to negotiate with Glyndŵr's surviving son Maredudd, and to receive Glyndŵr's allegiance and that of any other rebel who sought pardon. There is no mention of Owain in the pardon offered to Maredudd on 30 April 1417, so some presume that Owain had died by then. Maredudd ab Owain was in Snowdonia when he finally accepted a pardon on 8 April 1421, suggesting that Owain was dead. Despite the enormous rewards offered, neither Owain nor his son was ever betrayed. Maredudd may have served with the King in Normandy, and in 1421 received letters patent granting him pardon for all offences, 'as on the testimony of the Holy Writ, the son shall not bear the iniquity of the father'.

GLYNDŴR'S LAST DAYS

He *(Owain)* was not destined however, to find an opportunity of carrying out his glorious ideas, and the last years of his life were spent as a fugitive, largely among the hills around Dolgelley.

He passed away like a mist on his own mountains, with his mission unfulfilled. No man knows when he died, no man knows where he was laid to rest. There is no monument to him, save the memory of him enshrined in his people's hearts. May it live there for ever; a greater soul, a nobler

spirit, never dwelt among these mountains. He gave all he had for them and his people – life, fame, case, wealth and possessions, and counted not the cost. Nevertheless, though he failed to outward appearance, he did not actually fail. Some of his dreams were realized under the Tudors, who, in many ways, were directly inspired by him; others have been realized in our own days; others await realization. It is a true enough instinct of the Welsh people to hark back to him as their embodiment of national hero-worship; and Dolgelley's greatest claim to fame is that Glyndŵr regarded it with affection. Glyndŵr is sometimes called a 'rebel'. So he was; but he rebelled not against a lawful king; he alone was true to the memory of the murdered king, Richard II. He rebelled against tyranny, oppression, economic exploitation, and against that outlook, common enough even to-day, which would make his land and the welfare of his people of little account. He rebelled against the extinction of the church of his people, and, herein, he was supported by the best of his day in that church. He rebelled against that deprivation of the means of learning, which, until our own day, was the settled policy adopted towards Wales. Requiescat in pace. Memoria ejus floreat in aeternum.With his passing, the hand of oppression fell, heavily, again on Wales, and the name of Dolgelley does not emerge for another 50 years or so.
(T.P. Ellis 1923.)

A brief fifteenth-century memorandum associated with the lordships of Oswestry and Chirk gives the 'day of St Matthew, apostle, 1415' as the day of Glyndŵr's death. Peniarth MS 135 agrees: '1415 – Owain went into hiding on St. Matthew's Day in Harvest (21 September), and thereafter his hiding place was unknown. Very many said that he died; the seers maintain he did not.' An agreement between the men of Powys, Gwynedd, and Deheubarth in 'the sixth year after the revolt of Owain ap Gruffydd, the year of Christ, 1421' (Peniarth MS 86) indicates that 1415 was regarded as the end of the rebellion, if not the year of Glyndŵr's death. Adam of Usk also concluded that Owain died in this year:

> AD 1415 Died Owen Glendower, after that during four years he had lain hidden from the face of the king and the realm; and in the night season he was buried by his followers. But his burial having been discovered by his adversaries, he was laid in the grave a second time; and where his body was bestowed may no man know.

There is a tradition that Glyndŵr died and was buried at his estate in Sycharth or on the Herefordshire estates of his daughters' husbands, Kentchurch or Monnington Straddel. At Kentchurch Court there is a medieval tower known as Glyndŵr's Tower, within which a secret passage leads to a room called 'Glyndŵr's Bedroom' (it is also associated with Sion Cent, Jack of Kent). Owain's daughter, Alys, had illegally married Sir John Scudamore, Sheriff of Herefordshire, possibly as early as 1404. In 'The Mystery of Jack of Kent and the Fate of Owain Glyndŵr', Alex Gibon argues that the poet-priest Sion Cent (Jack of Kent), the family chaplain of the Scudamore family, was Owain Glyndŵr. He claims that Owain spent his last years living with Alys, passing himself off as an aging Franciscan friar. Another daughter, Margaret (Marged) had married Roger Monnington. There is a mound at the deserted village of Monnington Straddel, near Monnington Court Farm, Vowchurch, which was believed to be Owain's burial place. According to the MSS of the Harleian

Collection, Glyndŵr's body, which was entire and of 'goodly stature', was discovered at Monnington in that Shire during the restoration of the church in 1680.

He may have been sheltered by Gwenllian, possibly an illegitimate daughter, who married Philip ap Rhys of Cenarth in Gwrtheyrnion. Philip ap Rhys seems never to have surrendered. Some say Owain died in a cave in Pumlumon (Plynlimon), where it all started, mourning the death of his wife and all but one of his six sons. There is a claim for Corwen Churchyard, Valle Crucis and also for Trefgarne or Wolfscastle in Pembroke, where he had lands. Monnington-on-Wye in 1415 is also given as his burial-place, as are the deep oak woods of Glamorgan and a mountain ridge in Snowdonia. Lawton's Hope Hill between Leominster and Hereford, Rhuthun, Harewood Forest (eight miles from Hereford heading to Ross-on-Wye) and Haywood Forest (three miles from Hereford) are all candidates for Owain's place of death. An Italian, Tito Livio, was commissioned in 1436 to write an eulogistic life of Henry V, and wrote 'Owen, for fear and in despair to obtain the king's pardon, fled into desert places without company; where in caves he continued and finished his miserable life.' The bards raided Arthurian legend to put him sleeping with his men in a cave to be awakened again in Wales' hour of greatest need. Owen M. Edwards reconts the legend:

One early morning the abbot of Valle Crucis was walking along the hillside above the abbey, and praying. Owen Glendower appeared and said, 'Sir abbot, you have risen too early.' 'No,' answered the abbot; 'it is you who have risen too early – by a hundred years.' And Glendower knew that he was not the Owen that prophecy had spoken of, and he disappeared.

As to the date of Owain's death, T.J. Llewelyn Prichard wrote *The Heroines of Welsh History* in 1854, in which he quotes the Rev. Thomas Thomas, vicar of Aberporth writing The Memoirs of Owain Glyndŵr: 'Our hero terminated his hopes and fears on 20th of September 1415, on the eve of St Matthew, in the 61st year of his age, at the house of one of his daughters; but whether of his daughter Scudamore or of his daughter Monnington is uncertain.' Prichard also mentions Glyndŵr's 'Life' in the *Cambrian Plutarch* by John Humphreys Parry, but it is difficult to source either book. Marie Trevelyan of Llanilltud Fawr wrote *The Land of Arthur* in 1895, dedicated to Llewelyn ap Gruffydd, and states that Glyndŵr was born on 28 May 1354 and 'on September 20th, 1415, this celebrated 15th century leader of the Welsh people, and last hero of Welsh independence, died in Herefordshire'. A 'penny booklet' recently acquired by the author is *Hanes Owain Glyndŵr, Tywysog Cymru* by Thomas Pennant o'r Downing, printed by H. Humphries at Caernarfon around 1900, which gives the same death date of 20 September 1415. For most Welsh people, he never died, and lives on representing not nationalism, but freedom.

THE REPERCUSSIONS

By 1415 there was almost peace in Wales. Plant Owain were dead, imprisoned, or impoverished through massive fines. The cost in loss of life, physical destruction and ruined lives was enormous. Wales, already a poor country, was further impoverished by pillage, economic blockade and communal fines. Not just castles and abbeys were ruined, but productive land was now wasteland with no tenants to work it. As late as 1492 a royal official in lowland Glamorgan said that he was unable to deliver promised revenues to the King because of the devastation caused by the war. Over sixteen years, the small country had seen its monasteries ruined, farms destroyed, towns burnt and people killed. With a population of only around 150,000 in 1400, the effects were terrible. Wales was still regarded as enemy territory by the English, and yet more penal laws were enacted to keep the Welsh in submission and impoverished. The scenario was similar to the economic vengeance wreaked upon Germany after World War I. Welshmen, instead of working the lands, escaped being accused of being rebels by enlisting for the French and Scottish wars. The Welsh did not have the privileges of citizenship, serve on juries or hold responsible jobs. Lands across Wales were confiscated and given to English absentee landlords, and the rate of settling English in bastides was increased.

The cost of castle garrisons was immense to a country which was also at war with France. In 1411, at Carmarthen, Harlech and Caernarfon alone there were 300 men-at-arms and 600 archers stationed. Soldiers had been stationed all over Wales in this military occupation, not just along the coasts but in the heartlands. From the proceedings of the Privy Council we can see that even in 1415 there were 40 men-at-arms and 80 archers at Strata Florida. Cymer and Bala and had 300 men-at-arms and 60 archers each. It was not known even if Glyndŵr was dead, and there were fears of another war while Henry was in France.

Not only had the Percies and the crown been virtually bankrupted by keeping soldiers in Wales on a war footing for sixteen years, plus the cost of six royal expeditions, but the incomes from Wales had been lost for that period. In 1399, the lordship of Brecon had been raising £1500, but by 1403 no rents or taxes were taken. Even when the revolt had fallen away, in 1409, only £364 could be raised in revenues. In September 1413, coming to the throne, Henry V demanded £1,200 in payments, partly as a welcome gift and partly in compensation for the wars. The devastated counties of Wales were sucked dry in the next twenty years to try and refill the royal coffers. Massive taxes were raised to pay for the invasions of the two Henrys, but Welshmen were not allowed to help each other to harvest their fields, causing major food shortages. If merchants of any towns were robbed in Wales, and the property was not returned within a week, they could retaliate upon any Welshman that they could seize. A Welshman's word against an Englishman was not accepted in a court of law.

Many prominent Welsh and Marches families were ruined. Lord Grey, as we have seen, was broken financially. In 1411, John Hanmer pleaded poverty as a reason why he could not pay the fines imposed on him. Henry Dwn accepted a pardon, and somehow avoided paying it. For many years after his surrender and despite official proscriptions, he was said to have sheltered rebels. He also levied fines on 200 individuals that had not supported him and even plotted the murder of the King's justice. Nevertheless, his grandson fought with Henry V in 1415 at Agincourt.

As late as 1430, John Scudamore tried to have Owain's outlawry reversed so he could claim Cynllaith from John Beaufort, Earl of Somerset. Instead, he was dismissed from his posts as he had married a Welsh woman, Glyndŵr's daughter. Many of Owain's supporters went into exile, being unable to trust the English and angry at the loss of their lands. Henry Gwyn (White Henry) was heir to the Lordship of Llansteffan, but left Wales forever and was to die in the service of the King of France at Agincourt.

As late as 1415 Welsh rebels were present in the county of Meirionnydd. There is evidence to suggest, for example in the poetry of the bard Llawdden, that some Welshmen continued to fight on, even after Maredudd accepted a pardon in 1421 under the leadership of Owain's son-in-law Phylip ap Rhys. In 1420, the sheriffs of Caernarfonshire and Meirionnydd appealed for rebels to surrender and be pardoned. In 1422 Robert ap Doe was hung in Welshpool for being a Glyndŵr rebel. The 1430s and 1440s still witnessed ambushes and murders of government officials across Wales. It is likely that the area around Dinas Mawddwy never settled, leading in the next century to the 'Gwylliad Cochion Mawddwy' (red-haired bandits of Mawddwy), who terrorised the area and killed Sheriff of Meirionnydd, Baron Lewis Owen.

Keith Dockray (*Warrior King: The Life of Henry V*) notes the importance of the Glyndŵr War to the reigns of Henry IVand V, and the acceptance of the House of Lancaster:

> Perhaps Wales, galvanised into real nationalistic fervour by the charismatic and dynamic Owen Glendower, provided the most potent challenge to the new Lancastrian dynasty and it was here, too, that Henry of Monmouth spent much of his teenage years. The Welsh revolt broke out in 1400, and, from the autumn of that year, the Prince of Wales was nominally incharge of both the country's administration and the task of regaining control of his own newly granted principality. Early in 1403 he was appointed the king's lieutenant in Wales, and clearly, from then until the fall of Harlech Castle in February 1409 (which finally ended Welsh resistance) he played an active role in the long process of defeating Owen Glendower's challenge to English rule: indeed, the Lancastrian reconqusest of Wales firmly established his military reputation.

Regarding this success of the Lancastrian Kings, the end of the Wars of the Roses only occurred when Henry Tudor, Duke of Richmond, secured the Lancastrian succession in 1485 by defeating the Yorkist Richard III at Bosworth Field. For this succession of the Tudurs of Penmynydd, Anglesey, to the English crown, we have to return to Iolo Goch and the Tudur support for Glyndŵr. One account gives Glyndŵr's kinsman Gwilym ap Tudur from Anglesey, who vanished from records in 1406, accepting an offer of pardon from Henry V, rather than being killed in the war. Iolo Goch also intriguingly gives us a different version of what happened to the Tudurs of Penmynydd. He states that Gronw ap Tudur was not killed at the start of the war, and Ednyfed also died before the war. Thus in one version of events, we have all four Tudur brothers (Gronw, Ednyfed, Gwilym and Rhys) dying, and in another only Rhys dying. Perhaps there was another Gronwy/Gronw ap Tudur from Penmynydd, but it is unlikely.

Iolo Goch wrote a poem, *Praise of Tudur Fychan's Sons*, and also an *Elegy for Tudur Fychan's Sons*. Tudur Fychan's second wife Margaret was the sister of Glyndŵr's mother, so the Tudurs were kinsmen of Owain. The four sons mentioned were all the children of Tudur Fychan's first wife, so they were not blood relatives. In the latter poem, Rhys and Gwilym are dressed as black-robed monks because of the deaths of Gronwy and Edynfed. Gronwy was Constable of Beaumaris Castle, and was drowned in Kent on 22 March 1382, being buried at the Franciscan Llanfaes Friary. His tomb was probably moved to Penmynydd Church. At the time of Gronwy's death, as the older brother he lived at Penmynydd, Edyfed at Trecastell, Rhys at Erddreiniog and Gwilym at Clorach. (Iolo Goch gives us these homes for the brothers.) Gronwy was succeeded as Forester of Snowdon by Rhys.

There is no mention of the half-brother Maredudd in the poems. He was the son by Tudur Fychan's second wife Margaret, so he was a blood cousin to Glyndŵr. The Tudurs had controlled Anglesey and much of north-west Wales in the fourteenth century. The family seemed destined for passing out of history until this fifth Tudur brother, Maredudd, went to London and established a new destiny for the family.

Maredudd ap Tudur (d. 1406) married Margaret ferch Dafydd Fychan, Lord of Anglesey, and their son was Owain ap Maredudd, which he Anglicised to Owen Tudor. He entered the service of Queen Catherine of Valois as keeper of the Queen's household soon after the death of her husband Henry V in 1422. At some time, living in Wallingford Castle, she married Owen Tudor, and they had at least six children. After Catherine's death, Owen was imprisoned, then later led the Lancastrian army at the Battle of Mortimer's Cross (1461). He was beheaded after being defeated.

Of the children of Owen Tudor and the dowager Queen, Edmund Tudor (1430-1256) became Earl of Richmond, married Lady Margaret Beaufort and fathered Henry Tudor. Henry was born shortly after his father died in Carmarthen Prison, imprisoned by the Yorkist. Edmund's brother was Jasper, Duke of Bedford (1431-1495), who became the most noted warrior of the Wars of the Roses. Owing to Jasper's efforts, Henry VII began the line of Tudor kings and queens. On his march through Wales to Bosworth Field, Henry Tudor was acclaimed by the bards as the 'mab darogan', the expected son of prophecy to free the Welsh, just as Owain Glydwr had been eighty-five years previously.

Gwilym ap Gruffydd (d. 1431), married a daughter of Gronwy ap Tudur, and came to live in Penmynydd from 1400, having been Sheriff of Anglesey in 1396-7. His wife's uncles, Rhys, Gwilym, and Maredudd ap Tudur, supported Glyndŵr, and he was forced by his family to throw in his lot with the Owain about 1402. Both his father and uncle died fighting for Glyndŵr. His brother, Robin of Cochwillan, also rebelled but abandoned Owain before 1408, when he appears as a crown official in Caernarvonshire. Gwilym also made his peace with the King before November 1407, when he was restored to his forfeited possessions and was granted, in addition, the lands of twenty-seven Anglesey adherents of Glyndŵr, who had probably died in rebellion. By 1410, he had been granted the forfeited lands of his wife's uncles, Rhys and Gwilym ap Tudur, both of whom stayed loyal to Owain. Through various circumstances, he came to own the patrimony of the Tudurs of Penmynydd, a major reason for Owain Tudur leaving Anglesey to seek his fortune in London. On such chance events, dynasties hang in the balance.

THE VERDICT

So why is Glyndŵr not lauded in British history? In *The Welsh Border Country* by P. Thoresby Jones (1938) we read:

> Certain criticisms of Owen Glyndŵr in this volume may give offence. They proceed, however, from a genuine belief that Owen Glyndŵr, far from meriting the title of Welsh patriot, did the Welsh people long-lasting damage, first by using Welsh soldiers wholesale as arrow-fodder, secondly by arousing in the English an exaggerated panic which resulted in the enactment of savage penal laws against the Welsh.

One would think from this that Glyndŵr led an army of conscripts (as was the English army) rather than volunteers. It is utterly certain that had he been English or French, his name would be known across Europe.

The noted English historian, G.M.Trevelyan, called Owain 'this wonderful man, an attractive and unique figure in a period of debased and selfish politics'. The French historian, Henri Martin, calls Glyndŵr a man of courage and genius. Most English encyclopaedias do not mention him - one of the truly great, principled and forward-thinking men in British history. Welsh schools have not taught the history of Glyndŵr and nationhood in any depth whatsoever for over a hundred years, but his name still inspires Welshmen all over the world. J.E. Lloyd puts Glyndŵr into his proper perspective in the Welsh national psyche:

> Throughout Wales, his name is the symbol for the vigorous resistance of the Welsh spirit to tyranny and alien rule and the assertion of a national character which finds its fitting expression in the Welsh language ... for the Welshmen of all subsequent ages, Glyndŵr has been a national hero, the first, indeed, in the country's history to command the willing support alike of north and south, east and west, Gwynedd and Powys, Deheubarth and Morgannwg. He may with propriety be called the father of modern Welsh nationalism.

When Maredudd ab Owain eventually accepted the King's pardon upon 8 April 1421, it had been twenty years and six months since Owain Glyndŵr had proclaimed himself Prince of Wales. These two decades of fighting against overwhelming odds, of reclaiming Cymru from the Normans, are neglected in all British history books. Glyndŵr had no funeral elegy from the bards - he was probably a broken man - but in Welsh mythology his disappearance from history, rather than his capture and execution, gave the poets and gives the nation a hope for the future - Glyndŵr is THE Welsh hero par excellence. This is a story of culture, humanity, nobility, treachery, courage, bitter defeat, glorious resurgence and a mysterious finale. Can anyone think of a better story for a Hollywood epic? It was not until 1948 that a Parliamentary Act, declaring Glyndŵr to be a proscribed traitor, was repealed.

> He came too soon for success, while the power of the House of Lancaster was increasing. Of all figures in the history of Wales, that of Owen Glendower is the most striking and the most popular.

The place of his grave is unknown, his lineage and the date of his death a matter of conjecture; there is much mystery about even his most brilliant years. But his majestic figure, his wisdom, and his ideals remained in the memory of his country. His ghost wandered, it was said, around Valle Crucis. His spirit, more than that of any hero of the past, seems to follow his people on their onward march. This is not on account of his political ideals, but because he was the champion of the peasant and of education.

(Owen M. Edwards.)

Appendix:
Adam of Usk

Adam of Usk, Adda o Frynbuga, was born between 1352 and 1360, and died in 1430. Born in Usk, he had the patronage of Edmund Mortimer, 3rd Earl of March, who became Lord of Usk through marriage. Edmund presented Adam with a studentship in laws at Oxford. There Adam became a doctor, and when he was lecturer in canon law, there was strife in 1388-89 between 'northerners' and students from Wales and the South. In the first year, the northerners were driven away from the university, Adam being blamed, as being a ringleader of the Welsh. In the second year, there was a battle lasting three days, with northerners losing some men. Adam and others were tried by jury and barely acquitted. From 1390-97 Adam practised as an advocate in the court of the Archbishop of Canterbury, sat in Parliament from 1397-99 and then joined Thomas Arundel, the Archbishop, when he returned from exile with Bolingbroke to seize the throne.

Edward Charleton had become Lord of Usk through marriage to Eleanor, the widow of Roger Mortimer, 4th Earl of March, and came to know Adam. Adam was at Bristol with Bolingbroke, and claimed to have negotiated peace between Charleton and Henry Bolingbroke, who in July 1399, was about to proceed from Bristol to ravage Eleanor's lands. According to Bradney she had refused Bolingbroke's advances and the people of Usk had fled to 'Montstarri'. Henry was persuaded to spare the town of Usk and to take Charleton among his followers, on his march to Chester against Richard II. Charleton was afterwards in great favour with Henry IV and his son. As a lawyer Adam was in demand, and influential, and obtained the confirmation of Sir James Berkeley as Lord of Raglan in 1400, and took up the Lancastrian cause. Adam was a member of the commission appointed to find legal grounds for the deposition of King Richard II and met with Richard during the King's captivity in the Tower. Adam was rewarded with various church livings, but there was a dispute over Llandygwyndd in Ceredigion with a Walter Jakes. Adam and two servants were charged with highway robbery against Jakes in 1400 and in 1402 he went to Rome, being pardoned in 1403. In Rome Adam met Pope Bonicface IX and Pope Innocent VII, who nominated him to English bishoprics including Hereford and St David's, but Adam could not take up the appointments. He practised as a lawyer for the Pope in Rome, and was even nominated as Bishop of Llandaf Cathedral by the French pope in Avignon.

In 1405 the Pope fled to Viterbo and Adam followed him after hiding from the Roman mob. He practised law in France and Flanders, having no papal patronage, and in Bruges met with Northumberland and Bardolf, who were planning the overthrow of Henry IV. Adam returned to Wales, landing at Barmouth in 1408 and being held by Glyndŵr. He escaped to join Edward Charleton, who was now Lord of Powys, and hid at Welshpool for two years. Adam received Henry's pardon in 1411 on the grounds that he had not voluntarily joined Glyndŵr's men. Thomas Arundel, Archbishop of Canterbury, returned his livings to him, and Adam's epitaph is on a brass plaque in Usk Priory Church. *Chronicon Adæ de Usk* is his legacy. One of the tales it recounts from his time at the papal court is the papal coronation. Adam tells us that when the newly elected Pope passed the image of Pope Joan (Agnes) he turned away in repugnance. After entering the Lateran, the Pope was carried, sitting on the 'sedes stercoraria' so that the papal legates could check that his testicles fell through the hole in the chair and that he was indeed a male.

Gruffydd ab Owain

Glyndŵr's son was captured at Usk, badly wounded, in 1405. The next record is in Rymer's Foedera, noted by J.Y.W Lloyd: 'In October 1410 the following Welsh prisoners were received at Windsor Castle: Howel ab Leun ab Howel, Walter ab Levan Fychan, Madoc Bach, Jenkyn Bachen, Davydd ab Cadwgan and Thomas Dayler. In this year, likewise, the king issued his letters to Richard Grey of Codnor, Constable of Nottingham Castle, to deliver to the Constable of the Tower of London, Grufydd ab Owain Glyndourdy, and Owain ab Gruffydd ab Richard, his prisoners. Gruffydd died soon after.'

Select Bibliography

Adam of Usk *Chronicon - The Chronicle of Adam of Usk* gives an eyewitness account of the fall of Richard II and the Glyndŵr revolt. The excerpts are from *Chronicon Adae de Usk (A.D. 1377-1421)*, ed. Edward Maunde Thompson (London, 1904).

Allday, D. Helen *Insurrection in Wales*, Terence Dalton, Lavenham 1981

Barber, Chris *In Search of Owain Glyndŵr*, 1998.

The Rev. A.T. Bannister *The History of Ewias Harold*, 1902

Barnard's *History of England*, Alex Hogg, London, 1783. This work demonstrates how history used to be taught before *The Constitutional History of England* (1897) of Bishop William Stubbs began to date English history from the 'civilization' of the Teutonic invasions to satisfy a Germanic court. Stubbs and his followers, such as AJP Taylor, have ever since ignored what Taylor called 'the lesser breeds' of Wales, Scotland and Ireland in the history of the British Isles. Early Welsh Christianity gives Wales the longest unbroken Christian heritage in the world, and the history of the British has been ignored in favour of that of German and French invaders.

Bradley, A.G. *Owen Glyndŵr and the Last Struggle for Welsh Independence*, 1902.

Bradney Sir J.B. *A History of Monmouthshire*, 1904-1933.

Brough, G.J. *Glyn Dwr's War: The Campaigns of the Last Prince of Wales*, Glyndŵr Publishing, 2002.

The Rev. J.S. Davies (ed.) *An English Chronicle of the Reigns of Richard II, Henry IV, Henry V and Henry VI, written before the Year 1471*, 1855-56

Davies, R.R. *The Revolt of Owain Glyn Dwr*, Oxford University Press, 1995.

Dodd, Gwilym (ed.) *The Reign of Richard II*, Tempus, Stroud, 2000.

Edwards, Owen, M *A Short History of Wales*, 1922.

Ellis, Tom *Memoirs of Owain Glyndŵr* (supplement in Owen, Nicholas *A History of the Isle of Anglesey*), 1775.

Ellis, T.P. *The Story of Two Parishes - Dolgelley and Llanelltyd*, 1923.

Flood F.S. *Prince Henry of Monmouth - His Letters and Despatches During the War in Wales 1402-1405*, Transactions of the Royal Historical Society vol IV, 1889.

Froissart, Jean. *Chronicles*, Harmondsworth, 1983.

A. E. Goodman *Owain Glyndŵr before 1400*, Welsh History Review, 1970-71.

Goodman, Anthony *The Loyal Conspiracy: The Lords Appellant under Richard II*, Routledge and Kegan Paul, London, 1971.

Griffiths R.A *A Tale of Two Towns: Llandeilo Fawr and Dinefwr in the Middle Ages*, published in *Sir Gar: Studies in Carmarthenshire History by Carmarthenshire Antiquarian Society*, 1991, ed. Heather James.

Hardyng, John *Chronicle*, ed. H. Ellis, 1812.

Haydon, F.S, ed. *Eulogium Historiarum*, vol iii, London, 1858-63.

Henken, Elissa R. *National Redeemer: Owain Glyndŵr in Welsh Tradition*, Cornell University Press, 1996.

Hodges, Geoffrey *Owain Glyn Dwr and the War of Independence in the Welsh Borders*, Logaston Press, 1995.

Iolo Goch: *Poems*, ed. and trans. D. Johnston, 1993.

Lloyd, J.E. *Owen Glendower (Owain Glyndŵr)*, Oxford, 1931.

Lloyd, J.Y.W. '*The History of the Princes, the Lords Marcher, Ancient Nobility of Powys Fadog - The Ancient Lords of Arwystli, Cadewen and Meirionydd*' London 1881.

Massingham H.J. *The Southern Marches*, 1952.

T. Matthews (ed) *Welsh Records in Paris*, 1910.

Nicholas, Thomas *Annals and Antiquities of the Countiers and County Families of Wales*.

Owen, William *Hanes Owain Glandwr*, (sic) 1855.

Peniarth MS 135 (the equivalent to Hengwrt MS. 104) was written around 1556-1564 by the poet Gruffydd Hiraethog. Its original text was ascribed to the early fifteenth century by Professor Ifor Williams, so it probably dates from shortly after the Glyndŵr War of Independence.

Pennant, Thomas *Hanes Owain Glyndŵr*, 1884.

The Retrospective Review *History of Owen Glendowr*, 1826 (this is a valuable source for the avarice of the Grey family and anti-Welsh laws).

Skidmore, Ian *Owain Glyndŵr: Prince of Wales*, Christopher Davies, Swansea, 1978.

Thomas, Thomas *Memoir of Owain Glyndŵr*, Haverfordwest, 1822.

Walsingham, Thomas *Historia Anglicana*, ed H.T. Riley, London, 1863-64.

Walsingham, Thomas *Annals of Richard II and Henry IV*, ed. H.T. Riley, London, 1866.

Williams, Glanmor *Owain Glyndŵr*, University of Wales Press, 1993.

Williams, Taliesin (ab Iolo Morganwg) *A Selection of Ancient Welsh Manuscripts ... for the purpose of forming a continuation of the Myfyrian Archaiology*, Liverpool, 1888.

List of Illustrations

in the war. Courtesy of Terry Breverton.

10. Llyn Padarn in Snowdonia, where Glyndŵr may have imprisoned Lord Grey in Dolbadarn Castle in 1402. Dolbadarn overlooks Llyn Padarn and was built by Llywelyn the Great to guard the strategic Llanberis Pass through Snowdonia. Courtesy of Terry Breverton.

11. This Holy Well at St Mary's Church, Pilleth, was covered over in medieval times, and was said to cure eye ailments. Glyndŵr drank here when he prayed before the Battle of Pilleth, on St Alban's Day, 1402. Courtesy of Terry Breverton.

12. Pilleth Church, on the hill of Bryn Glas, which was set alight before the battle where Edmund Mortimer's royalist army was defeated on 22 June 1402. Courtesy of Terry Breverton.

13. The Wellingtonia fir trees on the hill to the left of the church were planted in the nineteenth century by a local landowner, Sir Richard Green-Price, to mark a mass grave. The bones were reburied in the church. Courtesy of Terry Breverton.

14. The mighty Carreg Cennen Castle, on a crag 300 ft above the Cennen River. It was surrendered by Sir John Scudamore in July 1403, after his wife was refused safe conduct. Courtesy of Terry Breverton.

15. This remarkable stainless steel statue of Llywelyn ap Gruffydd Fychan stands outside Llandovery Castle (Castell Llanymddyfri), at the place where he was slowly hung, drawn and quartered on 19 October 1401 for refusing to betray Glyndŵr. Courtesy of Rhobat ap Steffan.

16. Gatehouse of Caernarfon Castle, built by Edward I as headquarters for the Justiciar of North Wales, and one of the most impressive castles in Europe. Glyndŵr almost captured it in the sieges of 1403-1404. Courtesy of Terry Breverton.

17. The gatehouse of St Quintin's Castle, Llanbleddian, which overlooked Cowbridge and was destroyed by Glyndŵr's forces in 1403. Courtesy of Terry Breverton.

18. Fortified Norman Church of the Holy Cross, within Cowbridge's thirteenth century town walls. The market town was probably sacked when Llanbleddian Castle fell and Glyndŵr won at Stalling Down (Cowbridge Common). Courtesy of Terry Breverton.

19. The view across the battle site of Stalling Down, 1403, from the remains of Llanquian Castle towards Stalling Down. Courtesy of Terry Breverton.

20. Gatehouse of the Bishop's Palace outside Llandaf Cathedral, Cardiff. This castellated palace was burnt and ruined by Glyndŵr, but the nearby cathedral was spared. Courtesy of Terry Breverton.

21. Cardiff Castle – the great Norman motte inside the later walls, on the site of the Roman fort alongside the River Taff. The town of Cardiff was burnt by Glyndŵr at least twice, and the castle taken at least once. Courtesy of Terry Breverton.

22. 'Barber-surgeon' at Cardiff Castle – all armies needed these injury specialists among their camp-followers. Without immediate and prolonged attention, Prince Henry would have died after the Battle of Shrewsbury. Courtesy of Terry Breverton.

23. The great gatehouse at Castell Cydweli, which was rebuilt by the Lord Rhys around 1190, and repeatedly besieged by Henry Dwn and Glyndŵr's southern forces. Courtesy of Sian Ifan/Llysgenedhaeth Glyndŵr.

Index

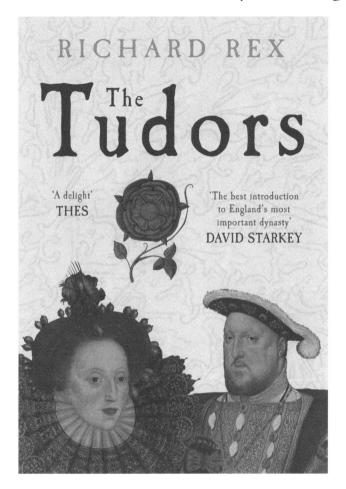

Available from July 2009 from Amberley Publishing

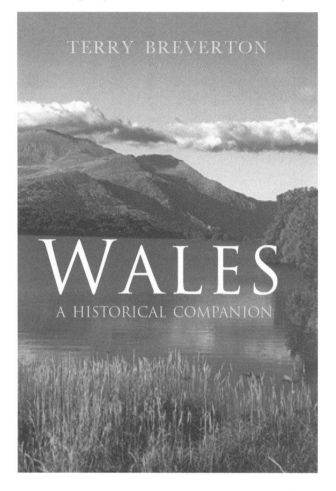

A comprehensive and authoritative companion to the history of Wales.

This comprehensive and authoritative companion to Wales, its people and its millennia of
history can be enjoyed by armchair travellers and tourists alike. The respected historian Terry
Breverton presents the characters, events, buildings and institutions that have shaped Wales
over the ages, from its earliest origins to the present day.

£17.99 Paperback
34 colour illustrations
320 pages
978-1-84868-326-6

Available from all good bookshops or to order direct
please call **01285-760-030**